I0878980

Richard Scheib

A VIEWING GUIDE TO THE PANDEMIC

Depictions of Plague and Pandemic on Film and TV

HEADPRESS

A HEADPRESS BOOK
First published by Headpress in 2025, Oxford, UK
headoffice@headpress.com

A VIEWING GUIDE TO THE PANDEMIC
Depictions of Plague and Pandemic on Film and TV

Book layout and cover design : MARK CRITCHELL mark.critchell@gmail.com
With thanks to Gareth Wilson and Jennifer Wallis

10 9 8 7 6 5 4 3 2 1

A CIP catalogue record for this book is available from the British Library

ISBN 978-1-915316-39-4 paperback
ISBN 978-1-915316-40-0 ebook
ISBN NO-ISBN hardback

Exclusive NO-ISBN special editions and other items of interest are available at HEADPRESS.COM

HEADPRESS. We publish the books you love.

For M,
the best companion ever for any pandemic,
And for Louise,
for continuing to keep the author alive

CONTENTS

CONTENTS

COVID AND ME: DISPATCHES FROM DEATH'S MAILBOX

"I have some bad news, honey," M says to me on her usual call from work during her lunch hour.

"Okkkay?" I say dubiously, thinking that maybe she has received notice that she has been laid off.

"My workmate's just tested positive. She had to be sent home."

There is a dreadful sinking feeling as I am processing this. I am mindful of all the rigorous questions I had asked M — "Are you sure you are staying masked at work? ... How many people are around when you take your mask off to eat lunch?" — to the point she would give me the eyeroll and start moving her fingers in the air as though playing strings to indicate I was harping.

"Have you been wearing a mask around your workmate?" I ask.

"Mostly." And then in a quieter, more apologetic tone. "Although I can't say I have *all* of the time."

It is at this point a cold dread settles in — as though all the bones down your back had been replaced by an icicle. Although by the time she got home, that icicle had started to thaw. I spend the next few hours doing my research, seeking the advice of a medical friend, reading Centers for Disease Control (CDC) guidelines on quarantine, and having a plan of action worked out. Of course, in the ensuing five days what seems a rational plan to survive isolation turns out to be a nightmare where it seems at times that we might end up killing each other before the virus ever gets around to doing so.

The irony of this is that the phone call came at the very moment I was working on the final draft of a book about depictions of plague and pandemic on film and TV to deliver to my publisher — the very volume you are reading. I had survived two plus years by playing it careful, getting my vaccine and booster shots, masking up at all opportunities, even continuing to do so when venues had started to relax their mandates. Maybe this was just whoever is in charge of our fates sitting back laughing, saying "Did you really think you were going to deliver a work about a pandemic without going through it in person?"

A VIEWING GUIDE TO THE PANDEMIC

Depictions of Plague and Pandemic on Film and TV

When Covid-19 was first declared a worldwide pandemic in March 2020, we were there and ready. Both M and I have respiratory disorders — I suffer chronic COPD; she has asthma and severe allergies. As we were watching things play out on the news, particularly as the virus started to strike around the world, I remember turning to her and saying "We are in the high-risk category. We are going to have to start being careful about this."

It still didn't hit me until I was travelling home on the train. This was just before the WHO had declared an emergency and nobody was masked up yet. It was a crowded train, and I was standing holding a vertical steel pole. I had a dry throat and started inadvertently coughing, as sometimes happens with my meds. I looked up and suddenly was aware that, on this crowded train, there was a circle of people all backing away from me, putting their elbows up to cover their faces.

The two of us masked up. We pored over the guidelines from the health department. Perhaps over-diligently. We established the front door of our house as a cordon where everything that came through had to be sanitized. We gradually relaxed to allow a couple of friends and neighbours in after sufficient time had passed without them showing up symptomatic. We would spray down all the grocery bags as we brought them in. I figured I was maybe overdoing it around the point that M gave me a withering look when we were unpacking the groceries and I asked what was the best way to sanitize the cucumbers.

We successfully shut the pandemic out. I work at home via the internet, so isolation involved no big lifestyle change for me. We have a fantastic enjoyment of one another's company and are at ease with the other's ways of doing things. We both sat in our isolation bubble, played with the cat and watched a whole bunch of TV and bad movies. Just like we did on most non-pandemic evenings.

The world outside did its thing. It was sweet and peaceful for a time. No cars on the roads, no roar of planes coming in overhead towards the airport. You could hear the birds sing in the silence of empty streets (something that became a delight to our cat, Bolphunga the Unrelenting, who used the opportunity to master his hunting skills).

The most anybody we knew had come down infected during this time was when our neighbour's ex went on a drinking bender and decided to get away with it by calling into work and saying he had tested positive — only to send the workplace into a panic, hurriedly organizing everybody to be tested.

And then restrictions were lifted and the peace and quiet evaporated. Everything went back to normal as though it was no different than people returning to work after a holiday weekend. Nothing had changed and the Great Pause was a mere blip of inconvenience in the course of things.

Over the next eighteen or so months, things see-sawed as the provincial government changed its mind every second week as to whether things could be relaxed, whether masking mandates needed to be put in place in public venues, and what exemptions there were.

One thing I did during the pandemic to cope with social isolation was contacting people. I went through my list of social media contacts on Facebook and messaged people, asking if they wanted to have a video chat on Skype or Zoom. Not everybody wanted to talk but of those that did, it proved to be an enormous amount of fun. I spoke to people I hadn't seen for over twenty or thirty years, in some cases since I went to school. I made contact with people that I had had extensive correspondence with but had never met in the flesh. I had conversations all around the world — from the USA and UK, from Spain to Mexico, India to South Africa, Budapest to Belgium, Australia and New Zealand.

Another great irony that occurred during our Covid experience was that only a couple of weeks before quarantine was officially declared, M and I started watching the British TV series *Survivors* (covered in Chapter 3) about life among those who survive a deadly pandemic. I had seen it many years earlier, but I hooked M on it with the elevator pitch of "It's like *The Walking Dead* but without zombies."

During these video conversations, the show was mentioned, and some friends were asking. "*Survivors*? I want to watch that. Can you send me a copy? I think I need to start learning some tips on what to do."

I run a film review website (www.moriareviews.com). Other people were asking me for similar recommendations about pandemic films. At the same time, I started noticing a whole bunch of search queries on the website for phrases like "pandemic", "epidemic", and titles of various related films.

This gave birth to an idea — I would write a viewing guide on films and the way they depict plague and pandemic. I immediately started searching out films and shows. And of course by the time the book started taking shape, there had been a whole bunch of other films made depicting various aspects of the Covid pandemic.

And that's the way things went for the better part of two years: us in a cozy isolation bubble dutifully masking up whenever we went out; me working on my book and cramming all my spare time with pandemic films and TV shows.

I did have the surreal experience at one point of going for what must have been my second or third vaccination shot. This took place in a converted school gymnasium that was filled with ordered rows of seats with coloured flags to indicate which vaccine you were having, and so forth. I remember sitting waiting for my shot. I had brought my e-reader and while I was waiting I was reading *The Hot Zone* (covered in Chapter 5) to do my research for the book.

The person to deliver my shot — an off-duty fireman — came up and we began conversing. "What are you reading?"

"It's a book about the outbreak of Ebola. It's an incredibly gore-drenched story," I enthused.

He glanced away at the dozens of other people lined up waiting to get their shots and gave me a strange quizzical look with one eyebrow raised as though to say, "You are surely kidding?"

Certainly, the rest of the world did enter into cozy bubbles at assorted points. M had to go into hospital for surgery, during which she was laid off work. Two days after she came out and was meant to be on bedrest, we learned that our house was being sold. For Christmas 2020, the province had told us that we could have a maximum of four people in our isolation bubble for Christmas dinner. The same law also permitted the realtor to hold an open house meaning that, while we could only have two friends for Christmas dinner, we had to put up with an unknown number of total strangers walking through the house to peruse it. The owner, rubbing his hands with glee, said, "The housing market is hot, hot, hot," and, while relishing making a $2.3 million sale, dismissed any concern we had that people might be contaminating the house as they came into it.

Other friends I know became infected. Thankfully nobody I know has died. On the other hand, a few have wandered off into anti-vaxxer conspiracy land.

By mid-2022, even we had started relaxing our standards. We would still put on masks at the supermarket and on public transport. But maybe we'd not worry about doing so as much in the hallways or when going down to the laundry of the apartment building. Somewhere along the line, we stopped disinfecting our groceries as we brought them in. We felt reasonably safe in our triple vaccination.

Around us, everybody has relaxed their standards. In the supermarket, maybe one in ten people are still masked and the common feeling is "Covid's over." The idea of herd immunity as an official response was ridiculed at the start of the pandemic but it now seems an official unspoken government response. The number of ongoing deaths are dismissed as usually being "just the unvaccinated," even though the city is reporting over 200 hospital admissions and nearly thirty deaths in the last week alone.

There is a false sense of safety in the air. As I think about it, it comes down to calculated risk. Everyone makes a calculated risk about the way they deal with the infection. Everyone from the anti-vaxxer believing it is all a government ploy to implant microchips, to the twenty-year-olds playing skate hockey in the parking lot of the building, to the people going unmasked to the supermarket, to M and I not putting on a mask to go do the laundry. The calculated risk is "I'm healthy, it won't affect me ... I'm vaccinated, I'm safe ... A couple of moments of exposure won't be enough to get me ... There is good airflow in the room, I'll be fine."

That icicle down the back that came when I received the phone call had melted to room temperature by the time M came home. It became an organized flurry of "we need to isolate. We should wear masks at all times". The main problem is that between the start of Covid and now we had moved from a half-house — where it would have been easy to isolate in another room — to a much smaller one-bedroom apartment.

We juggled logistics. The CDC and local health department recommendations are that the infected person is isolated in a separate room but that isn't practical in a single bedroom house. It is not as though I can go and stay with a friend — who wants someone turning up on their doorstep who might be potentially infected? "You sleep in the bedroom at night, I can sleep on the couch," we decided. There came the inevitable questions — is it safe to go into a bedroom where someone infected might have been sleeping in order to get my clothes in the wardrobe? Is it good enough if we just open the window and keep the fan on full blast?

We hammer out a common agreement. Masks on when in common areas. We sit on separate couches, which aren't six feet apart, but we are both masked, have fans on and the patio door open. That is good enough for TV watching. I feel like a bad person when M elects to banish herself outdoors to eat her meals alone, but it is summer, so evenings are not unpleasant.

We can sanitize doorknobs, light switches, the fridge door, and microwave. Then comes the tricky question of the bathroom. We came up with an agreement to sanitize the toilet seat and bathroom sink each time after use. But then the bottle of peroxide has been handled by a potentially infected hand, leading to the convoluted conundrum of how you sanitize the spray bottle of sanitizer. (The solution: placing spray into a piece of toilet paper and wiping it down). It is these logistical conundrums that become a source of dispute in the next week. We are having to think on our feet and invent solutions as we go along.

I suggest we both wear gloves indoors. All we have to hand is a pair of woollen winter mittens and a pair of glow-in-the-dark Halloween gloves. At least that way potential contamination stays on the glove rather than transfers to hands. However, this breaks down into matters like preparing and eating food.

M keeps forgetting to put on her gloves. I give her my Stern Glare™ and this ends up in a dispute.

"Stop harping and going on about things."

"Well, when it is both of our lives on the line, aren't I allowed to be just a little nagging?"

But even my own insistence on following protocol starts doing things to my head. Every action I take needs to be thought out: go get food from fridge, put glove on to open fridge door, with hand in glove pick up plate and take foil off, use gloved hand to hold plate and ungloved hand to hold fork and knife. It is such an automatic process normally that you forget halfway through.

Or else — going to the toilet. Sanitize the seat before use. Use foot with slipper on to lift lid. Take glove off to hold one's bits and pieces while peeing. Use elbow or raise foot to depress the flush button. Use bare hand to turn on tap in sink. Wash hands. Use sweater-covered elbow to turn tap off lest you infect clean hands. Dry hands. Put glove back on to open bathroom door.

This is problematic enough but when you start forgetting whether you did something with glove on or off, everything falls down. Did I switch the computer on while wearing a glove? Can't remember — best disinfect the whole keyboard again. Have I used gloves or bare hands to touch the TV remote? And then there is the moment where after having agreed to use separate towels, M and I both thought we'd placed our towel in a different place, and it turned out we were using the same one.

Or even just the question — I am going to sleep in the lounge. I've been airing the room out for an hour with the fan on full blast since M and I were watching a show. How long should I keep airing the room out before it is clear of potential contamination? Should I go to sleep wearing a mask just in case? That proves an uncomfortable task while wearing a medical mask. Can I safely go to sleep wearing just a cloth rather than a medical mask? Or is it safe to even remove the mask altogether if I keep the patio door open and fan on?

By the end of five days of isolation from the time of M's potential exposure, neither of us were symptomatic, and multiple home tests proved negative. We sighed a breath of relief, took our masks off and gave one another a kiss.

All of which would be a perfect normal light-hearted ending to the story. Our brush with Covid. It drove us crazy for a few days, but it proved to be a negative result in the end. We can look back and laugh at the ridiculous mental contortions it took us through. Chalk it up to learning the lesson that we should always be vigilant.

Only that wasn't quite the end. Our quarantine came to an end on the Sunday. M went back to work on Monday, I delivered my manuscript a couple of days later. All seemed well. But then on Thursday, M reported "I have a terrible headache. It feels like someone is attacking my head with an axe."

So I say "We still have several home test kits. Take one when you get home."

And when she does. "It came out negative. I guess I am maybe just coming down with a cold."

And by Friday, it is "I have a sore throat too."

"Take another test."

"I did. It's negative." As was the one after that.

By Saturday, it's "I appreciate your worrying. But I took two tests, and they were negative. Plus, I don't have symptoms like loss of taste. I am sneezing and you are not meant to do that when you are infected."

And so I relax, and we go and cuddle up and have a mid-afternoon nap. I sleep in a little longer. When I get up, M informs me: "I took another test. I think it might be positive." And surely enough the tiny creeping red line grows thicker by the end of a tension-laden thirty minutes.

We rushed to put back into place the quarantine procedures from last week. Last time, we had the underlying feeling of "Well it might only be a possible infection. She was masked up most of the time. So there's a reasonable chance she didn't get infected." There was a certain feeling of safety that M wasn't showing symptoms and we had the margin of not knowing whether she was infected or not. More calculated risks. But this time there is no uncertainty.

I am spending the evening of Saturday night kicking myself and regretting not quarantining earlier. She has been symptomatic for two days. During that time, we have kissed, gone to sleep in the same bed, she has handed me a plate of food, we've held hands, I reached over her shoulder to the keyboard to sort out a computer problem. And so on.

I also have severe COPD meaning that I have thirty percent of the lung capacity of the average person. We are triple vaccinated but a full case of Covid can be a potential death sentence for me. M has similar respiratory problems, although not quite as severe.

As I write this, I can hear her through the closed door of the bedroom hacking her lungs out. It's the most terrible sound in the world because I can't go in to offer any help or give gentle hugs, or any of the things I want to and that I know she appreciates when unwell.

I hope she will be fine. I will be devastated if anything gets worse with her because I think both of us have reached a point in life where life without the other is unbearable. We have video messenger conversations between the bedroom and lounge that are filled with the gallows humour we share in an effort to keep our spirits up.

These things intermingle with my own fears — those two days of us saying "relax, it was just a cold" weigh in on me like a grim ticking clock. I have had a headache all day. I am afraid of what will happen next.

POSTSCRIPT

That was written in a heat of fearful alarmism and at a point where severe headaches were affecting my concentration.

On that weekend, I had reached a dreadful point where I was sorely contemplating putting my personal effects in order. It became a sobering point of clarity.

On Sunday I contacted my medical friend again, who suggested that I get onto a course of Paxlovid — a drug designed for high-risk patients. I spent most of Monday morning on the phone. Surprisingly, in contrast to the usual run of delays where getting an appointment can take up to two weeks due to doctor shortages, I was able to get official approval and a prescription by mid-afternoon.

I sit finishing writing this a week later on the last day of my course of the Paxlovid. The results have been frankly miraculous. Within less than a day of taking it, the headaches had disappeared. All other symptoms had tapered off to an occasionally runny nose and a sniffle. That and a persistent hacking cough that rattles the chest from time to time. In all honesty, I feel like I have had colds that were far worse than this.

All of which has M giving me evil glares for managing to shortcut the suffering she went through. But she's feeling much better — up and walking around, nothing to report apart from over-exhausting herself by trying to do too much.

My good friend Elaine (who sadly passed before this book came out, although not due to Covid) used to have a running joke. After I was down with a cold or a dose of the flu at one point, she called to check in on me. "Are you still at Death's Door?"

"No," I replied, "I've safely retreated down Death's Driveway and am now at Death's Mailbox." Thereafter this became an ongoing joke in determining state of health. We developed a scale of judging ailments that ran between Death's Mailbox, ranging all the way to Death's Sidewalk, Death's Traffic Lights and Death's Corner Shops.

And so from the safety of Death's Mailbox, I can report all is well. We're on the mend. We survived Covid.

But it is also worth remembering that with a worldwide death toll of more than six million, many others have not. In injecting a little humour into my own story, I don't wish to in any way make light of the tragedy that others went through, the losses that those close to them feel, nor the often disastrous mismanagements, the hysteria and misinformation that has led to so many unnecessary deaths. There's a future story to be written there.

Kind Regards and Stay Well,
Richard Scheib, April 2022

DISCLAIMER

A disclaimer before you read this volume. I am a film critic, not a virologist or an epidemiologist. I have no medical training. I have made a point of researching background on everything here but sometimes things slip through. Any mistakes or errors are my own. If you come across these, please write and let me know at moria.reviews@gmail.com, and these will be included in any future reprintings.

This is as exhaustive a list of films depicting plague and pandemic as I have been able to make. There have been a handful of works that have been missed because I have been unable to find viewing copies. And others that I simply may not be aware of. Feel free to let me know about these.

Aside from that, there is probably also a reasonable body of TV series that may have a single episode or episodes that feature a pandemic or plague outbreak. Time and the amount of research involved has simply precluded one from doing an exhaustive search of *every* TV series in an effort to find these. Again, any omissions in this regard, please forward to me.

PART ONE

THE ESSENTIALS OF THE PANDEMIC AND OUTBREAK FILM

Panic in the Streets (1950) with a bad boy Jack Palance on the run.

CHAPTER 1
EARLIEST TREATMENTS

EARLIEST TREATMENTS

The first screen depiction of a plague on film is the German-made *The Plague of Florence (Pest in Florenz)* (1919), which is discussed in Chapter 4. The first film to depict the world in the aftermath of a pandemic was the silent US-made *The Last Man on Earth* (1924), which is discussed in Chapter 11.

The period between 1950 and 1995 was when treatments of pandemic on film and TV coalesced into a distinctive genre. The genre had three separate strands, each of which is dealt with in this and the next two chapters:

i. The Pandemic and Outbreak Film concerning the spread of contagion and the efforts by authorities and scientists to contain it and find a vaccine;

ii. The Biowarfare Thriller, a series of thrillers and action films that centre around the release, or more commonly the threat of release, or else the efforts to retrieve, biowarfare agents;

iii. The World After a Pandemic — works that depict a post-apocalyptic world that has been devastated by pandemic.

THE BEGINNINGS OF THE PANDEMIC AND OUTBREAK FILM

Panic in the Streets (1950) has the distinction of being the first film made specifically about a viral epidemic — I suppose in that one section of the film does show an infected ship heading out into international waters, that this technically also makes it the first film made about a pandemic. While *Plague in Florence* was more of a morality play and *The Last Man on Earth* a war of the sexes comedy, *Panic in the Streets* is the first film of what I call the pandemic and outbreak film where we see a contagion spread throughout a population and/or around the world.

Panic in the Streets is set in New Orleans, and stars Richard Widmark as a public health officer who investigates a man found dead on the docks after fleeing from a card game run by the criminal underworld. In quick course, Widmark discovers that the man was suffering from pneumonic plague (one of the three forms that the Black Death takes). He then mobilizes the police to conduct a search for the man's identity and to find and vaccinate everybody who may have come in contact with the body.

The film comes from Elia Kazan, one of the great directors of this era. Immediately after this, Kazan went on to make films like *A Streetcar Named Desire* (1951), which brought Marlon Brando to prominence, *On the Waterfront* (1954), *East of Eden* (1955), *Baby Doll* (1956), and *Splendor in the Grass* (1961), among others. These are films that saw Kazan being nominated for four Academy Awards, winning twice during his lifetime. (*Panic in the Streets* also won that year's Academy Award for Best Screenplay Story.)

Panic in the Streets was made at the height of film noir — an era of moody, morally ambiguous stories, usually detective thrillers, shot in B&W. We usually think of film noir in terms of its cliché images — of gumshoes in fedoras and trench coats amid visual stylistics that make high contrast of light and darkness such as the shadows of twirling fans on a ceiling, slatted venetian blinds on the wall and the like. *Panic in the Streets* is not quite a full work of film noir but shows the genre's clear influence, particularly in the opening scene where the infected man flees from a card game through the dockyards, a scene filled with some great B&W photography of shadows illuminated along the sides of buildings.

Where Elia Kazan impresses the most is simply in that he went outside the studio and shot in the real world as opposed to the controlled conditions of studio sets like most other films of this era. There are scenes taking place in employment lines, backstreet rooming houses or rundown cafes that strike you with their verisimilitude (and look great in B&W). It looks like a strikingly grounded film. The film arrives at a tense chase climax with the police pursuing criminal kingpin Jack Palance (in his first film role — billed as Walter Jack Palance — where he looks menacingly tall and at his bad boy best).

Whereas subsequent pandemic films created images of figures in contamination suits arriving to place areas in quarantine, *Panic in the Streets* is more akin to a police procedural of the era — one with Richard Widmark moving through the city in search of the dead man's identity. The climax of the film, pursuing Jack Palance through the docklands and under the wharfs belongs far more to the regular crime film of the day — one where Palance would probably be a standard wanted murderer fleeing from police pursuit — than anything that holds allegiance to what would later

Panic in the Streets (1950).

solidify into the tropes of the pandemic and outbreak thriller.

Watching the film in the midst of a real world pandemic, you are also struck by the lack of basic precautionary procedures that people use in dealing with a deadly infection. Certainly, we do see a scene where all the police officers who were in the vicinity of the body are lined up and given an immunization shot. However, nobody wears any kind of masking or breathing protection, which would be needed for an airborne infection like the pneumonic plague. We also see Richard Widmark and others handling infected bodies with their bare hands without any rubber gloves or protective gear in sight.

At one point, Widmark returns home and does the correct thing, where he removes his clothing to put it in the laundry because it could be contaminated, and tells wife Barbara Bel Geddes to keep her distance — and then ignores this, simply balling his clothing up and tossing it on top of a wardrobe and allowing her to bring him a cup of coffee and sit in a chair only a couple of feet away from him.

A mere two months after *Panic in the Streets* came out, there was *The Killer That Stalked New York* (1950). Evelyn Keyes plays a woman whose no-good husband has persuaded her to smuggle a cache of diamonds back into the US from Cuba. With a Treasury agent hot on her heels, she finds her husband has been untruthful, not to mention is having an affair with her sister. In her travels, she has also been infected with smallpox. She becomes a Typhoid Mary figure, transmitting infection wherever she goes. The authorities mount a massive public hunt to find her.

This is a work steeped in film noir even more so than *Panic in the Streets*. The very title seems like one that leaps out from a lurid crime paperback of the era. There is the rather hilarious depiction of Evelyn Keyes as a classic noir *femme fatale*. As the voiceover narration states: "Death didn't sneak into town riding the rods or huddled in a boxcar. It came in on a streamliner, first class, extra fare ... And when it finally stepped out onto the platform, it was something to whistle at. It wore lipstick, nylons and a beautifully tailored coat ... Its name was Sheila Bennet. A pretty face with a frame to match ..." Much of the drama is centred around Evelyn Keyes' Sheila who is on the receiving end of her husband's underhand dealings and is then hunted as a fugitive by public health authorities.

The Killer That Stalked New York comes very much informed by the smallpox epidemic that struck New York in 1947 (the film is even backdated three years earlier to specifically occur then). In that instance, a businessman returning from a trip to Mexico carried the virus with him. The mayor's office and Commissioner of Health mounted a massive campaign, vaccinating six million people within the space of a month. The epidemic ended up only infecting twelve people, killing two — in fact, more people died due to complications from the vaccine than from the smallpox itself.

The film often resembles one of the newsreels of the day — short films that would screen in theatres before the main feature dealing with some news issue of topical interest. We get montages of the people of New York City lined up to receive

Charles Korvin and the infected Evelyn Keyes in *The Killer That Stalked New York* (1950).

their vaccination shots. Doctors shake their heads as they speak of patients: "A simple thing like vaccination could have saved his life." The end credits are dedicated "to the men and women of public health — the first line of defense between mankind and disease."

In a complete reversal of how the authorities are depicted in most pandemic films, where they are usually seen as obstructive and concerned about loss of profits/tourism, the mayor immediately devotes all resources to combatting the outbreak. "I need a vaccine. Lots of it. And you drug manufacturers are going to supply it," he states with declarative intent. When they protest that it has to be broken down into single doses and that this takes time, he responds: "Medical regulations — break them. Send it over in beer bottles, but get it here." And when they protest a lack of needles, he demands: "Get me a sewing machine company. They make needles, we'll sterilize them."

Another early depiction of a pandemic came in the long-running British science fiction TV series *Doctor Who* (1963–89, 2005–) with the story *The Silurians* (1970), which aired in seven weekly half-hour episodes. This concerns the discovery of the Silurians, a race of humanoid dinosaur people who have remained in suspension in their underground habitat since the Palaeozoic era but are woken in the present day by a nuclear cyclotron that has been built nearby. Believing the Earth to be their natural home, they release a virus intended to wipe out humanity.

The last three episodes feature the virus spreading and in quick course making its way across international borders, which makes this the first screen depiction of a pandemic. Unlike present-day outbreaks, the Doctor (Jon Pertwee) quickly whips up an antidote in the laboratory and the Silurians are fooled into retreating back to their habitat.

The BBC TV series *Doomwatch* (1970–72) came from two *Doctor Who* writers, Gerry Davis and Kit Pedler, whose greatest claim to fame is having created the Cybermen. *Doomwatch* concerned a government organization set up to investigate unethical scientific research or unforeseen mishaps. During the series run, the team investigates everything from poisons and pesticide usage, genetic engineering, intelligent rats, drug trials, stolen atomic materials, and germ warfare. Many of the episodes are now lost but several concern us here. *The Web of Fear* (1971) has a team dealing with a mutated virus carried by spiders that breaks out at a health clinic, while *The Inquest* (1971) deals with a fatal outbreak of rabies.

The next major depiction of a viral outbreak came with *The Andromeda Strain* (1971). This was based on a novel by Michael Crichton. Crichton graduated from Harvard Medical School in 1964, became a doctor and then published the novel version of *The Andromeda Strain* (1969), which duly became a bestseller. The book was then adapted into a film by Robert Wise, the director of *The Day the Earth*

Wildfire scientists investigate the town of Piedmont in *The Andromeda Strain* (2008).

Stood Still (1951), *West Side Story* (1961), *The Haunting* (1963), and *The Sound of Music* (1965), among other classic works.

Subsequently, Michael Crichton went on to write a string of other novels in assorted fields, covering everything from dinosaurs to Victorian train robberies, sexual harassment lawsuits to Japanese business culture, airline crashes to the claim that global warming is a conspiracy manufactured by ecological activists. Crichton made his debut as a director with the original *Westworld* (1973) and went on to make several other films. His greatest success was writing the novel that became the basis of *Jurassic Park* (1993). As a result, he enjoyed a renewed popularity throughout the 1990s and 2000s with other film adaptations of his books that include *Rising Sun* (1993), *Disclosure* (1994), *Congo* (1995), *Sphere* (1998), *The 13th Warrior* (1999), and *Timeline* (2003).

The Andromeda Strain film, which follows the book in close detail, concerns Wildfire, a top secret underground facility in the Nevada desert. Without any notice, a selected group of five scientists and medical experts are brought to the facility. A NASA probe has crashed back down to Earth, bringing with it an extraterrestrial virus that has wiped out the entire population of a tiny Arizona town with the exception of the town drunk and a baby. The film follows the team of scientists as they work around the clock to identify the virus and find a cure.

Crichton's medical background is key to the book and film's success. All of Crichton's books come with a great deal of research placed into them and are frequently illustrated with graphs and charts. In the film, great effort is made to obtain a similar authenticity and realism, with Robert Wise adopting a documentary-like approach moving back and forth between government offices and labs, using much in the way of official jargon, even displaying some of Crichton's graphs. The scenes with the scientists working to isolate the virus, especially navigating the interior of the capsule with an electron microscope and the eeriness that comes in the discovery of the lifeform present, make for gripping drama.

Unlike most other works about pandemics discussed throughout this book, *The Andromeda Strain* never deals with any widespread outbreak of the epidemic beyond the town. Rather the focus is on the scientists in the underground facility labouring to find a cure for the virus. However, in the scenes where we do visit the town, the film did create one of the key visual images of the pandemic and outbreak genre: that of scientists moving through an infected area in contamination suits to take samples and locate survivors.

Amid the surge of interest in Michael Crichton properties through the late 1990s and 2000s following *Jurassic Park*, there was a remake of the book/film with *The Andromeda Strain* (2008), a TV miniseries that originally aired on the US A&E network in four one-hour time slots.

The miniseries repeats the essence of the book and film but blows everything up with a ridiculous number of plot additions including a conspiracy by the military to eliminate witnesses and journalists. Events are expanded well beyond the small town with the virus being carried to other population centres, infecting all the wildlife and foliage along the way as it heads towards California — we even get an attack of killer birds at one point. Furthermore, the infection does not only kill people, it also causes some of them to go crazy.

In Michael Crichton's conception, Andromeda was simply a virus that had been picked up by an orbiting satellite. In the miniseries however, we get a stack of explanations: time travel, wormholes, possible nanotech design, the virus being encoded with messages sent from the future, and the need for ecological intervention in order to find an antidote. Oh, and the virus also appears to be intelligent and able to transmit information to its distributed parts. If nothing else, you have to admire the conceptual audacity of the miniseries' writer Robert Schenkkan in continually piling wild ideas on top of the original. In all other regards, the results are absurd.

The idea of the extraterrestrial virus actually appeared earlier in the low-budget SF film *Spacemaster X-7* (1958), concerning a Mars rocket ship that returns to Earth with samples of 'ganglionic brain tissue'. This emits spores that infect a housewife (Lyn Thomas) who is at the centre of a child custody dispute and is travelling back to Honolulu, unwittingly acting as a Typhoid Mary and spreading the alien fungi along the way.

After some not very convincing scenes of what look like oatmeal-coated plastic spread out over a lab, the alien organism is largely forgotten about. The film then turns into a standard 1950s detective drama centred around the hunt for the housewife. To this extent, it adopts the didactic narration, hard-boiled characterizations and documentary-like style of the hit contemporary TV series *Dragnet* (1951–59). The film is not particularly good but does have the novelty of featuring Moe Howard of the Three Stooges fame in a brief scene as a cab driver.

THE COALESCING OF THE PANDEMIC AND OUTBREAK THRILLER

The 1970s was the era when the pandemic and outbreak film began to come together as a genre. *The Cassandra Crossing* (1976) was made as part of the era's fad for disaster movies. The disaster movie was a short-lived trend that had been created by the big box-office success of films like *Airport* (1970) and its sequels, *The Poseidon Adventure* (1972), and *The Towering Inferno* (1974). The disaster movie was predicated around taking some man-made edifice — a cruise liner, a plane, a skyscraper — and showing it struck by tidal waves, fires or volcanoes, and collapsing or crashing amid much catastrophic spectacle, while a cast of name stars underwent assorted melodramas as they tried to escape.

The plot of *The Cassandra Crossing* concerns terrorists who break into the World Health Organization laboratories in Geneva, during which a beaker of pneumonic plague is broken. One of the infected terrorists makes an escape and boards a train from Geneva to Stockholm. As those aboard start to become affected, no European nation wants the train to stop within their borders, leaving it being shunted from country to country. Plans are made to divert the train across the title crossing, an old rickety bridge in Poland, where it is hoped (without those aboard being informed) that the bridge will collapse in the process.

The typical line-up of disaster movie characters include Richard Harris as a doctor who conveniently happens to be aboard, his ex Sophia Loren, Ava Gardner as the wife of an arms manufacturer, a psychotic gun-waving Martin Sheen as her drug dealer toy boy, and O.J. Simpson as an undercover FBI agent!

In the hands of director George Pan Cosmatos, who subsequently went on to make *Rambo: First Blood Part II* (1985), the film offers a melodramatic treatment of pandemic themes, largely focused on the petty dramas of the passengers aboard the train. The dramatic scenes involving a climb along the train roof are let down by shoddy rear projection effects. Nevertheless, the film comes with

A VIEWING GUIDE TO THE PANDEMIC

Depictions of Plague and Pandemic on Film and TV

Soldiers in contamination suits stop the train in *The Cassandra Crossing* (1976).

memorable images of soldiers in contamination suits welding the doors of the train shut to prevent passengers from escaping.

Canadian director David Cronenberg gained a cult reputation with films like *Shivers/They Came from Within* (1975), *The Brood* (1979), *Scanners* (1981), *Videodrome* (1983), *The Fly* (1986), *Dead Ringers* (1988), and *Crash* (1996), among others. His first full-length film *Crimes of the Future* (1970) is discussed in Chapter 11. Throughout his career, Cronenberg has developed a unique body of work where he becomes fascinated with bodily transformation and flesh as a metaphor. In Cronenberg's films, the horror that runs through most mad scientist films is reversed and the person affected by the transformation instead greets the process as a psychologically transformative one.

Cronenberg's third full-length film was ***Rabid*** (1977), which stars porn actress Marilyn Chambers in a regular acting role as a woman who has a motorcycle accident, after which she is given an experimental skin graft. The side effect of the graft is a small needle-like growth that emerges from under her armpit and periodically needs to consume blood. As she attacks or seduces various people to feed the growth, they become infected with a plague that causes them to become rabid and go berserk.

As with much of Cronenberg's work of this period, the central idea of *Rabid* comes with a good deal in the way of sexual metaphor — you can read much symbolism into the image of the small phallic parasite under Marilyn Chambers' armpit, while the whole film acts as a wildly exaggerated metaphor for sexually transmitted disease and the 1970s swinging lifestyle. Mostly, *Rabid* plays out as a scientific vampire film.

The latter section of the film comes with a series of graphic images of victims going berserk—a scene where a doctor slices off his nurse's finger and starts trying to suck the stump in the midst of an operating theatre; the image of a department store Santa being gunned down; a woman biting the ear of a fellow passenger on the subway—forcing Montreal to be placed under martial law.

The film underwent a remake with *Rabid* (2019), directed by Canadian twin sisters Jan and Sylvia Soska, with Laura Vandervoort inheriting the Marilyn Chambers role. This changes the original in many ways, including updating it to the era of transhumanism and stem cell medicine, and is not uninteresting in its own right. The scenes with the rabid infectees remain, although are not as prominent a plot element.

Plague (1978) (aka *M3: The Gemini Strain*) was an obscure and rather dull entry from Canada. A biochemist (Brenda Donohue), tired of waiting for official approval for her experiments, develops a strain of mutated M3 bacteria. However, the new strain proves

Marilyn Chambers in *Rabid* (1977).

deadly and kills her, before escaping into the outside world through the lab's faulty ventilation system. One woman is infected but proves asymptomatic and escapes custody, becoming a Typhoid Mary as she carries the contagion across the country.

One has seen enough viral outbreak and pandemic thrillers that much of what happens here quickly slips into cliché — the virus's accidental release from the lab; the imposition of martial law by authorities; the Typhoid Mary character who travels through the countryside unwittingly spreading contagion; the scientists working around the clock to find a cure.

What strikes one about this film's depiction is how shoddy the research facility's safety protocols are, clearly a case of the film not having done its homework — the door to the test lab is an ordinary door without any airlock or negative pressure seal; the scientists handle dangerous materials with their bare hands; people shut off power — thus safety procedures — without even looking to see if the lab is occupied; while the bacteria is able to spread to the outside world via a ventilation system that simply ejects waste contaminants into the air outside.

The Hamburg Syndrome (Die Hamburger Krankheit) (1979) was an offering from West Germany. The story follows Helmut Griem as a professor who is in Hamburg about to deliver a lecture at a medical conference just as one of his colleagues collapses and he is asked to attend. A mysterious plague is affecting people all across the city. He is quarantined but joins others as they decide to break out from the facility. Stealing a van, they head across the country as the plague is causing society all around to collapse into chaos and anarchy.

The tropes of the plague and pandemic film were starting to fall into place by this point. In comparison to these, *The Hamburg Syndrome* often feels like a film that has a vague sense of where it is going and spends a good deal of its time milling around searching for it. Despite having a doctor as hero, the film never seems to have any medical interest in depicting the plague — to avoid any technicalities in this regard, the plague is said to be mysterious and unknown in origin.

Mostly the film seems to champion an oddball line-up of characters and follows them as they break out through the military cordon and travel across the country, gathering assorted others along the way. There is something of Jean-Luc Godard's *Le Weekend* (1967) in watching their journey across a countryside that is becoming increasingly more surreal as society is in the process of collapsing into chaos around them. The film feels like it wants to aim for some grand social satire/ commentary in these scenes but never really goes anywhere.

PLAGUE AS AN ALLEGORY FOR NAZISM

The Plague (1992) is adapted from one of the novels of renowned French writer Albert Camus, best known for works such as *The Stranger* (1942), *The Myth of*

Sisyphus (1942), and *The Fall* (1956). Camus was a major figure in twentieth-century French literature and a key name in the development of the absurdist tradition, which concerns itself with the futility of the search for meaning in an essentially meaningless universe.

Camus wrote *The Plague (La Peste)* in 1948. It takes place in the city of Oran as it is affected by plague and the authorities institute martial law. Camus wrote the book as a metaphor for the Nazi Occupation of France during WWII. It circles around images of totalitarian oppression and concerns itself with a cross-section of humanity and their varied reactions to 'the absurd' — in this case the meaninglessness of certain death.

The film version, made by Argentinean director Luis Puenzo, is an international production that transfers the locale to an unnamed South American republic. The story is focused on William Hurt as a doctor dealing with the outbreak, along with various others caught in its midst as the city comes under quarantine, including Sandrine Bonnaire as a French TV reporter and Raul Julia as a taxi driver.

There are occasional moments where the film does strike with some effect — the sermon in the church where the priest says the plague is there to deliver people to Paradise and William Hurt challenges him to come down to the hospital and change blankets; the altar boy who keeps failing to hit the high notes as he succumbs during singing practice. Mostly, though, the film seems to miss Camus's metaphors and simply becomes a dull work, lacking in any of the drama of the outbreak film.

A much more fascinating work to tie pandemic to allegories for Nazism was the Czechoslovakian-made *Skeleton on Horseback* (1937) (aka *The White Plague*) (*Bílá Nemoc*), which is adapted from a 1937 play by Karel Čapek, the Czech writer who also wrote the play *R.U.R.* (1920), the work that introduced the term 'robot' to the English language.

The story takes place in an unnamed European country led by the fascistic Marshal (Zdenek Stepánek) who is threatening to go to war with their smaller neighbour. At the same time, there is the plague Morbius Chengi, or the White Disease, which affects people with white spots in a condition similar to leprosy. Dr Galen (played by the film's director Hugo Haas) has developed a cure, but he refuses to release it until all nations of the world swear to forsake war.

This is less a film about a pandemic than an anti-war parable. The film was made eighteen years after the end of WWI. The 'War To End All Wars' had resulted in the death of 9-11 million military and 6-13 million civilians, who became referred to as The Lost Generation. The 1920s was a decade of numbed retreat from the devastation and there had been a massive anti-war movement worldwide, made up of disaffected former soldiers and leading intellectuals of the day.

Skeleton on Horseback is a not uninteresting reflection of the anti-war movement and prefigures the brimming tensions that would become WWII. It has the failing of many early films of the sound era in that seeing people speaking on a screen was considered a novelty for movie-going audiences and so characters on screen did nothing except talk – much of the film is static speechifying. Nevertheless, the writing does make sharp and potent allegories between militancy and peace at all costs.

The analogies between the Marshal and Adolf Hitler are clear. Like Hitler, the Marshal stages smaller scaled but similar rallies preaching to his followers. By 1937, when the film was made, Hitler had begun a massive rearmament campaign in Germany and had started to threaten his neighbours, including Czechoslovakia, just like his fictional counterpart in the film.

Three months after the film came out, Hitler began his campaign of conquest by annexing Austria. In September of 1938, Hitler marched in to occupy the Sudetenland (the German-speaking provinces of Czechoslovakia). Indeed, it was the rest of Europe's desperate desire to maintain peace and appease Hitler and prevent another war that led to Neville Chamberlain's famous "peace for our time" speech. Six months later, Germany ignored this and moved in to conquer the whole of Czechoslovakia, just as the film predicts. Six months after that, Europe was enmeshed in world war once again.

CHAPTER 2

BIOWARFARE AGENTS AND THREATS

Biowarfare, or what used to be called germ warfare and these days also gets referred to as bioterrorism, concerns itself with the militarized use of plagues and viruses (although this definition also includes chemicals and defoliants). The terms biowarfare, germ warfare, and bioterrorism have subtle distinctions, but these do not concern us in this volume — all three refer to the use of deadly bio-agents as weapons.

This has had real world application. The UK maintained the Porton Down facility since 1916, originally set up during WWI to find a means of combatting German use of mustard gas and other chemicals. From WWII onwards, this expanded beyond defensive purposes into active research. The USA maintained a biological warfare division in the aftermath of WWII, receiving greater funding for research in the 1960s until President Richard Nixon signed an order to ban the use of chemical and biological weapons in 1969.

Since 1972, the international Biological Weapons Convention has prohibited biological warfare, allowing only research for defensive purposes against any attack. This has been signed by most countries with the exception of Egypt, Israel, Syria, and several African nations. Despite being a signatory, it was reported that the Soviet Union was still conducting research up until 1991. The most well-known country to have contravened the convention was Iraq under Saddam Hussein during the 1980s and nineties, most notably with the release of mustard gas and Sarin and VX nerve agents on the Iranian village of Halabja in 1988, which killed between 3,000–5,000 people.

The idea of biowarfare has been frequently employed in the fictional sphere, primarily in various thrillers and action films. In almost all of these cases, the biowarfare agents are what Alfred Hitchcock used to call a McGuffin, a term he coined to explain an object around which the plot and action in a film occurs. A McGuffin can be anything from a suitcase of money, a buried treasure, a scientific formula to a Maltese Falcon, the One Ring, a nuclear weapon, or a bioweapon. That is to say, McGuffins are a prized object sought by all the parties with reasons that can range from the object's wealth, its weapons potential or its curative or magical possibilities. Rarely are any of these works about seeing the McGuffin employed but rather the drama of the story centres around the race to find, or efforts to retrieve, a stolen McGuffin.

Almost all the works discussed in this chapter are McGuffin films. In only a few of the works are there instances in which the release of bio-agents occurs, making them identical to a whole bunch of other films about theft and hijacking of nuclear weapons — both are bodies of works in which the weapon in question only appears as a potential, rather than actual, employed threat.

FIRST DEPICTIONS

The very first film to deal with the use of bioweapons was the British-made Counterblast (1948). Mervyn Johns plays a Nazi war criminal wanted for his experimentation on human prisoners (clearly modelled on real-life Josef Mengele). In England, he impersonates a doctor who is brought in from Australia to run a bio-research facility near Cambridge. There he seeks to perfect a vaccine against a deadly virus he has created that will wipe out all but selected ethnic populations.

This was what was referred to as a 'quota quickie' — a series of British films made between the 1930s and 1950s, usually produced cheaply and in B&W, to fulfill a government mandate that twenty percent of British films should be locally made.

While most quota quickies are forgettable, this is a rather well-made thriller in the vein of the films being made by Alfred Hitchcock around this time — see works like *Secret Agent* (1936), *Sabotage* (1936), *Suspicion* (1941), *Saboteur* (1948), and *Notorious* (1946).

Director Paul L. Stein is no Hitchcock, but generates some worthwhile tension. There is a fine scene with Mervyn Johns struggling to get a trunk that contains a body out of a hotel and onto a train. In other scenes, there is great suspense as people start to expose holes in Mervyn Johns' cover story, or where he meets a woman who knows the doctor he is impersonating. It is rare to see a film in which the villain is the protagonist and where the sympathy of the story is focused on helping him evade detection. In the role, Mervyn Johns, a popular actor of the era used to more milquetoast roles, gives a nicely cold and clipped but understated performance.

The first Hollywood film to deal with the threat of bioweapons was the US-made The Whip Hand (1951) from William Cameron Menzies, a former production designer during the silent era, later turned director where he was known for works like *Things to Come* (1936) and *Invaders from Mars* (1953), among others. *The*

Whip Hand also has the distinction of being one of the very first films to deal with the so-called Reds Under the Bed hysteria of the 1950s — the belief that the USA was under threat of infiltration by Communists and their agents.

Elliot Reid plays a journalist on a fishing trip with his girlfriend. After receiving a minor cut, he stops off at the nearby town to get it seen to by a doctor. However, the locals seem eager to be rid of him by the next morning, which stokes his curiosity. He eventually discovers that a former Nazi bacteriologist who defected to the Soviets is conducting germ warfare experiments in the town as part of a planned Communist fifth column attack on the USA.

Though the politics exist in the realm of the wildly alarmist fears of the day about the threat posed by Soviet fifth column forces, the film draws on film noir stylistics to create a world of shadowy paranoia and perpetual suspicion and distrust. The central image is of a small archetypal American town being overtaken by an ideological menace that has the semblance of everyday life but is secretly intending to subvert the nation. Here and in *Counterblast* the threat of germ warfare is merely a suggested threat, never one we actually see.

The first full biowarfare thriller was the US-made The Satan Bug (1965), adapted from a 1962 novel by Scottish author Alistair MacLean, best known for popular adventure and war novels such as *The Guns of Navarone* (1957), *Ice Station Zebra* (1963), *When Eight Bells Toll* (1966), and *Where Eagles Dare* (1967), many of which have undergone film adaptations. The film was made by John Sturges, then an acclaimed director of Westerns such as *Bad Day at Black Rock* (1955), *Gunfight at the OK Corral* (1957), and *The Magnificent Seven* (1960).

In the film, George Maharis is recruited back to his former job as the security head of Station 3, a top secret germ warfare laboratory in the Mojave desert. Someone has broken into Station 3 and stolen a flask that contains the Satan Bug, a strain of botulinus so potent it could destroy all life on Earth if released. During the course of his investigation, Maharis discovers that a mad millionaire (Richard Basehart) has been posing as one of the scientists and is threatening to release the Satan Bug in Los Angeles unless Station 3 is dismantled.

As is the case with most of the biowarfare thrillers discussed here, they are almost never about seeing the viral agents released or being spread. John Sturges does give us one such scene with George Maharis and two agents trying to survive after a flask of botulinus is thrown into a barn, but that is it. Sturges creates a number of tensely effective scenes — in particular a climactic mid-air fight for the flask between George Maharis and Richard Basehart in a careening helicopter. This serves as a tense and effective, no-nonsense introduction to the genre.

Rage (1972) was a directorial effort from actor George C. Scott who was best known for playing the title role in *Patton* (1970), which had won him an Academy Award for Best Actor. As well as directing, Scott also plays the lead role as a

Wyoming rancher who goes out camping with his son (Nicolas Beauvy), only to wake in the morning to find his son delirious and convulsing. It is discovered they were in an area where the MX3 chemical aerosol was accidentally released by the military. After his son dies in hospital, Scott arms himself with guns and dynamite and creates a one-man vigilante campaign, demanding that the military tell the truth about what happened.

The film was based on a real-life incident in 1968 where samples of VX nerve agents from a US Army testing ground in Dugway, Utah were accidentally released and killed 6,000 sheep, although no people. (In an interesting trivia note, the same incident also inspired Stephen King with the novel *The Stand* (1978), which is discussed in Chapter 3).

George C. Scott was never an actor afraid of speaking his mind or getting political and this is him clearly angry about the culture of military cover-up during the era of the Vietnam War. *Rage* is notable for being one of the few screen treatments in this chapter where we see a biowarfare agent actually released.

ACTION MOVIE AND THRILLER TREATMENTS

A number of these biowarfare thrillers end up falling into the action movie genre. Shaker Run (1985) is a routine effort that has Cliff Robertson and Leif Garrett as two stunt show drivers on a tour of New Zealand. Lisa Harrow is a scientist who has discovered a deadly bio-agent and fears the military will use it as a weapon. She hires Robertson and Garrett to drive her to a rendezvous where she can safely deliver the bio-agent into the hands of the CIA. This involves a cross-country chase where they are pursued by New Zealand authorities.

Doomsday Man (1998) was a thriller in which Esai Morales plays a retired epidemiologist who is brought in to stop his brother James Marshall, a scientist with the US Army's Bacteriological Weapons Research Department, who has gone rogue. Upset after his wife's death due to the deadly bio-agent Keller, Marshall has stolen several vials of the virus. A cross-country hunt ensues as Marshall heads to California, threatening to release the vial.

Like most of the entries in the chapter, this is a thriller that concerns the potential threat of release but where the actuality is never allowed to happen. Crucially, for a film that purports to be a cross-country thriller, most of it gives the appearance of being shot along the same stretch of placid, rural backwater road.

One effort that did release its bio-agent was *The Patriot* (1998), a vehicle for Steven Seagal. Seagal was a martial artist who developed a career as an action star from the late 1980s onwards. In the film, Seagal is improbably cast as a former CIA virologist now working as a family doctor in small town Montana. In no time, Seagal is pitted against Gailard Sartain as a militia group leader who has appropriated samples of the deadly virus NAM-37 and releases it in the town. After realizing he and his daughter have a natural immunity, Seagal flees into the hills on horseback pursued by militiamen, while trying to isolate the source of the immunity to create an antidote.

This is a film with a bizarre identity crisis. On one level, it wants to be a biowarfare thriller, on another level it is the typical action film that Steven Seagal built his career on, on another a Western, and on yet another one of the pro-environmentalist, Native American-sympathetic films that Seagal was making during this period — see also the absurd *On Deadly Ground* (1994). None too surprisingly, it ends up being none of these.

The director was Australian cinematographer Dean Semler, best known for his stunning work on films such as *Mad Max 2* (1981), *Dead Calm* (1989), *Dances With Wolves* (1990), and *Waterworld* (1995), among others. Semler has clearly set out to make a modern Western and loves all the epic poses — the images of the wide-open Montana plains, galloping horses, and the like. The Western poses also allow Seagal to get right into Native American spirituality. The ending where native medicine triumphs over Western medical knowhow and the sky rains with flowers seems preposterously heavy-handed in this regard.

Equally, the film seems to go out of its way to paint Seagal as a decent man — he cares for his daughter, looks after animals, is a doctor who excuses the poor from paying their bills, and has quit the army's biological warfare division over the uses to which his work was being put. This sits at odds with the customary brutal and sadistic action poses of a Steven Seagal film, like the ending where he breaks a wine glass and plunges the stem into the militia leader's neck.

Deadly Outbreak (1995) was another action vehicle with Jeff Speakman headlining, a karate champion who gained a minor name as an action star throughout the 1990s and early 2000s. In the film, Speakman plays a security officer attached to the US embassy in Israel who is assigned to accompany a group of scientists on a tour of a biological weapons research facility. In actuality, the scientists have been replaced by terrorist impostors (led by Ron Silver) who take over the facility at gunpoint with the intention of obtaining biological weapons.

Many action films of the 1990s took their lead from the hit *Die Hard* (1988) in which Bruce Willis plays a lone hero who defends a skyscraper as it is taken over by criminal forces. Other films recycled this, with similar plots that had their respective heroes defending everything from battleships to trains and nuclear power plants. Here we get Speakman as a lone action hero defending a bioweapons facility from hostile takeover. Speakman displays some snappy martial arts moves and atrocious puns but there is little else to the film.

Spill (aka *Virus)* (1996) is a Canadian-made action film starring former NFL quarterback turned actor Brian Bosworth. Bosworth plays the head of the Secret Service detail for the US President, who is conducting a security assessment of the locale at a geothermal springs where the President is due to give a speech. At the same time, a tanker containing a bio-agent stolen from a biowarfare research laboratory goes off the road in the area due to the driver drinking at the wheel. Bosworth and others are infected and struggle to get back to deliver a warning before the bio-agent is carried downstream to where the President is due to speak.

This seems to be a viral outbreak thriller made without much awareness of virology. The tanker crashes in the park and people are infected. Those affected are quarantined but Bosworth leads them to make an escape in an effort to get the message out as to what is happening. From the point that the group breaks out of quarantine, the film forgets all about their being infected — there is no concern that they may be carrying a transmissible agent otherwise that would surely make their break for freedom entirely reckless.

In a convenient plotting sleight of hand, an antidote is found when Bosworth realizes that his cold acts as a natural antidote (improbably, all four of the escapees seem to have colds at the same time). Added to this is a conspiracy plot where persons close to the President are the ones who were seeking to deliberately release the bio-agent.

In a similar vein is <u>Contagion</u> (aka <u>Epidemic</u> and <u>The Last Breath</u>) (2002), an intriguing sound thriller in which two criminals shoot the US President (Bruce Boxleitner) with a dart containing a lethal bio-agent. Alas, this is one film where I have been unable to find a viewing copy.

In the completely ridiculous stakes was <u>Chill Factor</u> (1999), another action film. This concerns a chemical weapon nicknamed Elvis that killed an entire military unit after being released on an island ten years earlier. The colonel (Peter Firth) responsible was sentenced to jail but is now free and seeking revenge. Skeet Ulrich is a convenience store clerk who is handed the last existing supplies of Elvis by a dying friend. If the temperature rises above 50 degrees Fahrenheit, the weapon will destroy everything in a five-mile radius. And so Skeet is forced to conscript the services of his friend Cuba Gooding Jr, the driver of an ice cream truck. The two of them set out with the weapon in the back of the ice cream truck as they seek to deliver Elvis to the safety of a military base, with Firth's colonel and a team of mercenaries in furious pursuit.

<u>WW3</u> (aka <u>The Winds of Terror</u>) (2001) was a TV movie thriller that aired on Fox Television. It features Timothy Hutton as an FBI agent investigating a viral outbreak aboard a cruise liner. In the course of this, Hutton discovers that the infection is caused by a variant of the Marburg Virus (the earliest known variant of Ebola) that was engineered in US biowarfare labs in the 1960s. As infection strikes at a baseball game in Chicago and rapidly spreads across the city, Hutton uncovers a

terrorist plot to unleash the virus on four corners of the American continent where it will spread to obliterate twenty-five percent of the population within seven days.

WW3 came out in July of 2001 — two months before the September 11 attack on the World Trade Center masterminded by Osama bin Laden. What is fascinating to see is how the film names bin Laden as one of the potential threats who might unleash such a viral attack. One has to remember that July 2001 was a time when few people outside of intelligence circles had any real idea who Osama bin Laden was. This makes *WW3* not only extraordinarily predictive but an amazingly astute perception of the world political stage.

Eventually though, *WW3* is not imaginative enough to actually conceive what the new world order and political fears of the 2000s would look like in the aftermath of the 9/11 attacks and falls back on old Cold War thinking and clichés of East-West rivalry where the villains are disaffected post-Soviets as opposed to militant jihadi Islamists.

While the virus here does get to be released, *WW3* is unconcerned with depicting much of this, possibly for budgetary reasons. It is more focused far more on the apprehending of the terrorist before he unleashes the virus on Washington, D.C., along with side dramas about Timothy Hutton reuniting with his ex-wife.

Another uncannily predictive film was the Canadian *Anthrax* (2001), which was made just before the anthrax mail scare of September-October of 2001 in the US (discussed at the end of this chapter), but ended up being delayed in release as a result.

The film takes place in a small Alberta town where Ed Begley Jr maintains a research facility attempting to find cures for anthrax. This has become a source of opposition for the locals who believe that he is infecting and killing their cattle. Under the encouragement of US journalist David Keith, several locals break into the facility and chain themselves to the doors. However, things go wrong when an elderly man (Jan Rubes) breaks a vial in the lab, spreading contamination. David Keith in fact proves to be an agent of the US government who steals samples of the anthrax and then goes rogue and threatens to unleash them. This is an average, largely unremarkable entry in the genre that passes its time without ever doing much to generate tension.

Anthrax also features in *Fire and Brimstone* (1972), a now missing episode of the TV series *Doomwatch* (discussed more in Chapter 1). In this episode, one of the Doomwatch team (Simon Oates) has a breakdown and holds the government to ransom, threatening to unleash vials of anthrax.

Anthrax also turns up in *Bad Blood* (2006), an episode of the British TV series *Foyle's War* (2002-15). The series features Michael Kitchen as Christopher Foyle, a police chief in a small rural community during WWII and the immediate years after. This is one of those works that holds a genteel nostalgia for a romanticized, more simple village life that Britain regularly turns out — and does it well with the soft-spoken, deft-witted Kitchen at his empathetic best, ably aided by his Dr Watson, a pixyish Honeysuckle Weeks.

In this episode, the investigation into a Quaker conscientious objector, who appears to be guilty of murdering a man, has a parallel plot where it is uncovered that the army has been conducting covert experiments in weaponizing anthrax in the area. The infection spread to a nearby farm and killed one woman, as well as infecting Honeysuckle Weeks (although an antidote is handily provided by the end of the story).

Pandemic (2009) is one of three works with the same title covered in this book. (The other two are discussed in Chapter 6). This version was a B-budget film from Jason Connery, the son of actor Sean Connery. Jason had some credits as an actor before making his debut as a director here and going on to helm a handful of other low-budget films.

The film is set in a small New Mexico town and stars Alesha Clarke as a veterinarian dealing with a mysterious illness that is killing cattle. When humans become affected too, she and the local doctor call the CDC. The town is quickly placed under military quarantine, but a conspiracy theorist (Pete Holden) suggests that the military have actually been testing a deadly bioweapon in the town's water supply.

Connery does a fair job establishing the locale of a US desert town. When the military arrive and establish a cordon around the town, it feels as though the film is heading into similar territory as the latter scenes in *Outbreak* (1995). However, from about the halfway point when Pete Holden starts expounding conspiracy theories, the film discards any further depiction of the epidemic and becomes a military conspiracy thriller and goes full-on *The X Files* (1993–2002, 2016–18) with Alesha Clarke and Pete Holden on the run from shadowy pursuing figures as they seek to obtain the truth about what is going on.

The Tuxedo (2002) features Jackie Chan as a chauffeur who is given the titular tuxedo by a dying spy friend (Jason Isaacs). In putting it on, Jackie finds that the suit is a highly sophisticated piece of technology that reacts with his body to turn him into a dazzling fighting machine and provide gadgets and utmost cool for all occasions. The film features a McGuffin plot where the villain is a bottled water manufacturer who is attempting to infect all drinking water with a virus that fatally dehydrates the human body.

The film is only concerned with putting Chan through the comic possibilities involving the suit in action, although being a US-made film, these scenes are a pale shadow of the extraordinary stunt work and fight scenes where Chan made his name back in Hong Kong in the late seventies and early eighties.

Essentials of the

PANDEMIC AND OUTBREAK FILM

BIOWARFARE MCGUFFIN PLOTS IN ONGOING ACTION SERIES

On Her Majesty's Secret Service (1969) was the sixth of the James Bond films produced by Albert R. Broccoli and Harry Saltzman based on the best-selling books by Ian Fleming. *On Her Majesty's Secret Service* has some controversy in the canon of Bond films — it is the film that came out following Sean Connery's departure from the role after his initial five film run. He was replaced by the Australian George Lazenby, a male model who had no acting experience prior to this. Lazenby has been surrounded by much debate since, with people debating the pros and cons of his performance. Defenders of the film, of which I include myself as one, point out that it gives Bond a more complex emotional side than usual and has the best action scenes of any of the Bond films of this era.

None of this concerns us here, but what does is the plot, where Bond travels to a sanatorium in the Swiss Alps in pursuit of the villain Blofeld (Telly Savalas). There, Bond discovers that Blofeld is operating a clinic that supposedly treats allergies. After sleeping with one of the women who are said to be cured of their allergies, Bond discovers a plot where they are being brainwashed and used to distribute biowarfare agents to the rest of the world.

Moonraker (1979) was the eleventh James Bond film, the fourth after Roger Moore inherited the role of Bond. This saw the Bond series trying to compete with the massive success of *Star Wars* (1977) a couple of years earlier and offering a much more science fiction-type plot that took Bond into space. This was also the point where the Roger Moore films gained a campy, massively over-budgeted excess and no longer seemed to be taking proceedings seriously.

The plot begins with the theft of the titular Moonraker space shuttle. Bond is dispatched on a globe-trotting journey to investigate. This brings him up against the villain Hugo Drax (Michael Lonsdale) who is building a space station peopled with his master race. From there, Drax is preparing to eliminate the world's population via toxins developed from an Amazonian plant so that he can repopulate it with his chosen few.

No Time to Die (2021) was the twenty-fifth Bond film and came out just short of the series' fiftieth anniversary. It was the fifth to star Daniel Craig as Bond and was Craig's highly publicized final outing in the role.

The plot features a retired Bond being dragged back into action to trace Heracles, a nanotech-designed bioweapon that can be programmed to exclude some people's DNA. We do see this unleashed against the patrons of a nightclub in one scene, but this is another McGuffin and only a minor aspect of the plot.

Very briefly worthy of mention is *Billion Dollar Brain* (1967), one of the numerous imitators of the James Bond series during the 1960s. This was the third of three films adapted from the works of author Len Deighton featuring Michael

Caine as Cockney spy Harry Palmer and produced by James Bond series producer Harry Saltzman.

The previous two entries, *The Ipcress File* (1965) and *Funeral in Berlin* (1966), were strong realistically grounded entries. However, *Billion Dollar Brain* suffers sprawling budgetary excess, along with a convoluted plot that involves the titular computer and a mad US general trying to overthrow the Soviet Union. The film opens with Michael Caine receiving a phone call from the computer and being assigned to deliver a flask of eggs to Helsinki. These are later revealed to contain a deadly virus, although this only forms a minor part of the plot.

In a similar vein to the James Bond series comes the *Mission: Impossible* films. The series began with *Mission: Impossible* (1996), a big screen remake of the popular TV series *Mission: Impossible* (1966-73). The TV series featured a team of experts, each with skills in different fields, that would go into action in spy capers on a weekly basis. The films, of which there have been six to date with two others awaiting release at the time of writing, have been reconceived as vehicles for Tom Cruise as Agent Ethan Hunt, featuring him engaged in a series of spectacular stunts, while the team of experts have been relegated to being his support crew.

Two of the *Mission: Impossible* films deal with biowarfare threats. *Mission: Impossible II* (2000) features a villain (Dougray Scott) who has stolen the antidote to the lethal bioweapon Bellerophon and is planning to auction it off. *Mission: Impossible III* (2006) has Ethan's wife (Michelle Monaghan) abducted by arms dealer, Owen Davian (Philip Seymour Hoffman), who demands that Ethan mount an operation to steal a deadly bio-agent known as The Rabbit's Foot. In both of these films, the respective bioweapons act as McGuffins in the most literal sense — they are no more than devices to connect the action set-pieces throughout and we in fact never actually see them, let alone their effect.

Fast & Furious Presents Hobbs & Shaw (2019) was a spinoff from the *Fast and the Furious* films, the ninth film in all and an offshoot from the main series featuring Luke Hobbs (Dwayne Johnson) and Deckard Shaw (Jason Statham) who had appeared as law enforcement nemeses in the previous entries.

The first few *Fast and the Furious* films were realistically grounded entries about busting a gang of high-end carjackers and similar kinds of heist plots, which built up an ongoing family of characters. With subsequent entries, the stakes kept rising to the point where the entire world is routinely threatened. Hobbs and Shaw were introduced in earlier entries as bad guys where Statham was seeking to kill Vin Diesel, before — in an abrupt about-face — both are cast as the heroes here.

This film's nominal plot involves the two, in between slinging one-liner insults at the other, being paired to find a woman who appears to have stolen the programmable Snowflake Virus. The woman turns out to be Shaw's sister (Vanessa Kirby) who has been infected with the virus. This involves a chase from London to

Moscow and Samoa, pursued by Idris Elba's cyborg villain, in an effort to find a way to defuse the virus before it is activated with deadly effect.

Later in this chapter, I deal with ridiculous and comic biowarfare threats. In contrast to these, *Hobbs & Shaw* is a film that is not even making an effort to take itself seriously. It serves up spectacular effects — figures fighting halfway down the side of a glass building; high-speed vehicular chases through London streets in luxury cars; and the beyond ridiculous image of four tow trucks hooked in a chain up into the air trying to bring down a helicopter at the same time as they are engaged in a chase along the side of a cliff road.

This is a film where its muscular over-buffed heroes have almost become superheroes who can walk through any fight or action scene without a scratch. Their only dialogue is absurdly over-the-top insults where you feel like the scriptwriters are competing to show how clever the lines they can come up with are, as opposed to anything any human being would actually say. Between the physics-defying spectacularity of the action set-pieces and the flip one-liners, this is a film that has about the same level of realism as a Road Runner cartoon.

There have been assorted bioterrorism plots in various TV series — too many to conduct a full list. The *Hawaii Five-O* revival series has the distinction of two such plots with the episodes *Touch of Death* (2012) and *La Po'ino* (2015).

An unusual variant was *The New Avengers* episode *The Midas Touch* (1976) where Steed, Purdy and Gambit come up against a gold-obsessed former bacteriologist (David Swift) who has created Midas, a young man infected with a host of deadly diseases. Midas is immune but can kill with his touch — at one point, we see him dipping his hands into the punch bowl at a party (while in costume as the Red Death!). Steed and Gambit arrive at the scene shortly after to find everybody dead. The scientist's scheme is to sell Midas's services as an assassination tool — someone who can kill with a mere kiss or touch of the hand.

The X Files (1993–2002, followed by a later two-season revival between 2016–18) was a TV series that proved massively popular and gained a cult following during its heyday. The series featured David Duchovny and Gillian Anderson as FBI agents Fox Mulder and Dana Scully, who operate the FBI's X Files division that investigates unexplained phenomena. The series' run involved them looking into everything from Bigfoot to vampires, werewolves, faith healers, genetic engineering mishaps, Golems, and Frankenstein monsters. What formed the backbone of the series mythology was an increasingly improbable and contorted conspiracy involving UFOs and secret cabals that reached deep within the US government, colluding to aid alien forces while acting to keep the existence of aliens a secret.

The X Files (1998) was the first of two theatrically released films spun off from the TV series. This rehashes the major story arcs of the first three seasons in a condensed feature-length plot. This has Mulder and Scully investigating more UFO phenomena and coming up against the shadowy conspirators once again. During the course of this, it is discovered the conspirators are planning to release a deadly virus developed from a prehistoric oil found in Texas. At one point, Scully is infected after being stung by bees that have been genetically engineered to deliver the virus whereupon she is snatched away to a secret base in Antarctica.

Cowboy Bebop: The Movie (2001) is a film spinoff from *Cowboy Bebop* (1998), a Japanese anime TV series centred around a group of interstellar bounty hunters. The film's plot sees the group pursuing a former soldier who was used as a subject in a series of military experiments and infected with a nanotech virus. Suffering hallucinations, he now seeks to infect the rest of the populace with the same virus.

In the realms of the bizarre was Lara Croft, Tomb Raider: The Cradle of Life (2003), sequel to the Angelina Jolie-starring *Lara Croft, Tomb Raider* (2001). This was based on the hugely popular series of *Tomb Raider* video games from Eidos Interactive that premiered in 1996 and has extended to some twenty games to date. In the films, Jolie plays Lara Croft as a British aristocrat who spends her time in a series of globe-trotting adventures uncovering archaeological artefacts.

In *The Cradle of Life*, Jolie is pitted against a villainous Ciaran Hinds who is preparing to hold an auction of the contents of Pandora's Box — no less than the artefact from Greek mythology. According to the Greek myth, Pandora was the first woman, whom Zeus gave a box and told her never to open it. Eventually overcome by curiosity, she opened the box only to unleash all the woes of humankind — pain, sorrow, illness, greed etc. In the film, we are told that this is the "Sunday School version" and that the box actually held a virus that offers the possibility to end all human life. As with most of the above examples, this improbable piece of confabulation acts as yet another McGuffin.

L: Change the World (2008) was a spinoff from the Japanese films *Death Note* (2006) and *Death Note: The Last Name* (2006), both of which were based on a popular manga series concerning Light Yagami, a youth who obtains a notebook that allows him to write a person's name in it, which summons a Death God that then kills the person.

In the films, L (played by Kenichi Matsuyama) was Light's detective nemesis. Matsuyama gave a supremely weird performance in the role, socially withdrawn and eating strange combinations of confectionery and desserts every time we see him in between dazzling bursts of elucidation. *L: Change the World* was an eminently forgettable film given over to Matsuyama, which pits L in a McGuffin plot where he is seeking a scientist who has developed an antidote to a deadly virus.

BIOWARFARE FILMS OF THE COVID ERA

Art of Deception (2019) was a low-budget action film starring Richard Ryan (also the film's director) who has had his identity erased so that he can work on developing a viral program on behalf of the CIA. He then discovers that the agency's duplicitous deputy director has released a virus, and is planning to distribute an antidote that contains a microchip that will control human behaviour. After his wife is abducted, Ryan goes on the run to save her.

This is an action film that suffers in the budgetary department, in particular when it comes to the action scenes and the lack of a proper fight choreographer. The greatest amusement is seeing how the idea that the government is secretly placing microchips in people via a vaccination program went from the realm of fiction to a conspiracy theory believed by many anti-vaxxers opposed to Covid vaccines in 2021.

The Canadian-made *Hall* (2020) did not premiere until August of 2020, when it was assumed to be another Covid film. This takes place in a hotel where Carolina Bartczak has checked in with her husband and daughter. As gradually becomes apparent, she is seeking to escape a physically abusive marriage and sneak out with the children while her husband is asleep. Also present at the hotel is Julian Richings who, for reasons never explained, unleashes a viral bio-agent into the hotel's air conditioning system, causing people to start collapsing in the hallway.

Certainly, this was the only one among the Covid era films to still be using plot devices involving bioterrorism threats, while one scene where the infected get back up and begin staggering suggests that it is drawing on the zombie film. As a premise, the film seems limited — it essentially revolves around one woman having to walk down a hallway filled with convulsing infectees. It feels like a short film premise that has been extruded to make up an eighty-minute runtime.

The Swedish-made *Black Crab* (2022) takes place in a near future setting after Sweden has been invaded by an unspecified enemy. Noomi Rapace is recruited by the military on the promise of being reunited with her daughter. She is asked to go on a top secret mission that will alter the fate of the war. She and a team of soldiers must skate across the ice of a frozen-over archipelago to deliver a package. During the course of the journey, they open the package to discover that they are delivering two vials of a biological weapon.

This is a strong and effective work that evokes something of WWII commando films like *The Guns of Navarone* (1961) and *Where Eagles Dare* (1969). Much of the film's effect occurs during the tension-fraught night journey across the ice with the team having to deal with everything from sub-zero temperatures and thin ice to being open targets for the enemy.

Less effective is the ending where the team arrives at their destination to find their military already established in a base. Given the number of helicopters, you keep wondering why their own side didn't just fly the canisters to their destination, instead making winning the war dependent on a dangerous mission where people were not expected to survive. Also the sacrificial ending to destroy the weapon makes little sense — your only thought is that surely the military cannot have made only two vials of the bio-agent, and that even with those destroyed the manufacturing process would still be in place.

BIZARRE AND COMEDY TAKES

The most bizarre of these McGuffin plots is surely the one that comes in *Inferno* (2016). This was the second of two film sequels to *The Da Vinci Code* (2006), which was based on the massively successful best-selling 2003 novel by Dan Brown. *The Da Vinci Code* concerned an international hunt to find a series of clues hidden in classic artworks and architecture that lead to a secret bloodline descended from Jesus Christ. Brown produced several other books, which were duly adapted to film as sequels with *Angels & Demons* (2009) and *Inferno*. All three films feature Tom Hanks as Brown's hero Robert Langdon, a Harvard professor and expert in symbology, who becomes involved in solving a series of international mysteries, all of which are based around deciphering cryptic clues. All three films were directed by Ron Howard of *Apollo 13* (1995) and *A Beautiful Mind* (2001) fame.

In *Inferno,* Hanks' Langdon wakes up in a hospital in Florence with amnesia, unable to remember anything that has happened in the last forty-eight hours. In his clothing, he finds a biological containment tube that projects a classical illustration of *Dante's Inferno* with clues embedded in the painting. This has been left by a late billionaire bio-geneticist who has created a deadly virus that is intended to purge ninety-five percent of the world's population. The plot requires Langdon, pursued by the WHO and a secret cabal, to follow a trail of clues hidden in classical artworks across Europe to find the whereabouts of the virus.

This is essentially *The Da Vinci Code* rehashed with a biowarfare McGuffin. For reasons that only make sense to the plot, the mad billionaire is obsessed with the Renaissance poet Dante Alighieri and has secreted various cryptic clues in classic artworks around Europe leading to the location of his virus. You wonder why, for instance, the billionaire didn't just release the virus rather than leaving a trail for people who have the power to stop it?

For equally improbable reasons — one that makes no real sense when it is viewed in terms of reverse logic — Tom Hanks being given amnesia and pursued by law enforcement all happens to be part of the scheme to get him to solve the puzzle. You realize by the end of the film that all that Hanks needed to do to not endanger the world was sit back and do nothing.

Things get even more bizarre with Carnosaur (1993), a low-budget dinosaur film from producer Roger Corman (who is discussed with *The Masque of the Red Death* [1964] in Chapter 4). *Carnosaur* was intended to jump on the bandwagon of Steven Spielberg's *Jurassic Park* (1993) — and actually ended up being released before *Jurassic Park*.

Most of the film is concerned with scientist Diane Ladd, who has genetically engineered dinosaurs from chickens. The dinosaurs are represented by some pitifully cheap-looking effects. At the same time, Ladd has distributed regular household eggs that contain a virus that causes women to become pregnant and give birth to dinosaurs — all as part of a mad science scheme to eliminate humanity and allow dinosaurs to repopulate the Earth. The film spawned two sequels, although neither feature any bio-engineered viruses.

After the bizarre biowarfare offerings, there come those that are outrightly comical. The Japanese Memories (Memorizu) (1995) was an anime film that was an anthology consisting of three episodes, all of which were adapted from manga stories by Katsuhiro Otomo, the creator/director of the cult anime hit *Akira* (1988).

The second of the three episodes was *Stink Bomb*. This concerns Nobuo, a lowly technician at a research laboratory who turns up to work with a cold and is recommended to take some experimental cold pills, only to swallow a military toxin by accident.

The toxin then reacts with his cold and kills everybody in the lab. As Nobuo walks out into the countryside, he radiates a huge stink cloud that kills everybody in the surrounding area. The armed forces array all their might to destroy Nobuo. There is the rather funny image of squadrons of helicopters, navy vessels and tanks lining up to wipe out a nerdish technician riding along on a motor scooter, only for the stink cloud he radiates to interfere with their equipment and bring them all crashing down.

Casino Royale (1967) is a madcap James Bond film. It is based on Ian Fleming's first Bond novel but due to copyright complications ended up outside the regular Sean Connery series and was made as a comedy. It is a sprawling mess with five different directors, although it does have occasional amusements. One of the funnier sections comes towards the end where Woody Allen turns up as Bond's nephew Jimmy, revealed as the villain of the show suffering from an inferiority complex and planning to release a virus that will kill every man in the world over the height of 4'6". The 2006 version of *Casino Royale*, starring Daniel Craig, is more faithful to Fleming's novel.

TRUE-LIFE BIOWARFARE INCIDENTS

Finally, we come to a discussion of works based on real-life bioterrorism threats. *The Hot Zone: Anthrax* (2021) was a TV miniseries produced in six one-hour time slots. It was a follow-up to *The Hot Zone* (2019), the TV miniseries based on the true-life Ebola outbreak in Reston, Virginia. The first season is discussed in Chapter 5.

This series was based on the anthrax mail scare that occurred between September and October of 2001, only a week after the USA was reeling from the aftermath of 9/11. Letters containing anthrax spores were sent to various politicians and media outlets. Five people ended up dying, most of these being mail workers who were infected because the anthrax had leaked through the envelope. A massive FBI manhunt was conducted to find the party responsible. As the series recounts, the George W. Bush White House and FBI hierarchy were eager to blame this on al-Qaeda, but evidence pointed to the anthrax coming from the Ames strain held in US biocontainment laboratories. The FBI accused biological weapons expert Stephen Hatfill, who strenuously denied his involvement and was eventually exonerated after suing the government. The miniseries identifies the principal suspect as Bruce Ivins, a leading anthrax expert who was working at USAMRIID (United States Army Medical Research Institute of Infectious Diseases).

This is a radically different series in tone to *The Hot Zone*. In the first series, the Ebola story is told with much detail given over to the laboratory and contamination procedures, and the series is at its most vivid with the scenes entering the monkey house. While there are scenes that take place at the USAMRIID laboratories, the bulk of the show is centred around an FBI investigation. Here the tone of the series is more akin to *American Crime Story* (2016–), a series that uses each season to conduct methodical dramatized replications of the details of various true crime incidents (the O.J. Simpson trial, the murder of Gianni Versace, the Monica Lewinsky scandal).

The series zeroes in on Bruce Ivins (played by Tony Goldwyn) as suspect, a USAMRIID biochemist who suffered mental health issues, and as much time is spent on him and his backstory as is given over to the FBI investigation. It should also be stated that the series comes out with a far clearer certainty about Ivins' guilt than was the case in reality — Ivins was never charged or arrested in real life, and speculation ended when he committed suicide in 2008. A number of people have questioned Ivins' guilt; or even whether the facilities at USAMRIID would have been able to produce the anthrax spores used in the letters. In defence of Ivins as a likely suspect, those questioning his guilt have failed to produce any other likely suspect among the few who had access to Ames and the knowhow to produce the spores.

The miniseries also concentrates events, giving the impression that the drama takes place within a few weeks after 9/11, whereas events such as Ivins' suicide took place seven years after the principal drama. While the miniseries does give equal time to Ivins and depicts his disturbed state of mental health, what it fails to do is give any clear motivation as to why he sent the letters.

The Salisbury Poisonings (2020) was a miniseries for the BBC in three one-hour episodes. The miniseries was based on an incident in March 2018 where two Russian nationals, both former intelligence operatives, fell unconscious in the British town of Salisbury and were rushed to hospital. It was determined that they had been poisoned with the Russian-developed nerve agent Novichok. An investigating police officer was also infected but all three recovered. Three months later, two British locals were infected in the neighbouring town of Amesbury after a man brought a bottle of perfume home for his girlfriend after finding it in a trash bin. It is believed that the bottle is the one that carried the agent from the Salisbury attack. The woman died, while the man survived. The persons responsible were later identified as Russian GRU agents.

The miniseries is a solid, fact-driven replication of the poisonings as it follows Anne-Marie Duff who plays the district public health official who instituted quarantine areas and mounted a massive search for the source of infection. The miniseries develops a creepy fascination when it comes to scenes of authorities searching the area for what could be no more than a single molecule of contaminant.

CHAPTER 3

THE WORLD IN THE AFTERMATH OF A PANDEMIC

The very first depiction of the world in the aftermath of a pandemic took place in the silent film *The Last Man on Earth* (1924), a comedy about a plague that kills all men, leaving one man in a world now run by women. (This is discussed in Chapter 11 among other pandemics that wipe out one or other gender.)

Next up were the unrelated *The Last Man on Earth* (1964) and *The Omega Man* (1971), both based on Richard Matheson's novel *I Am Legend* (1954) and set in a post-apocalyptic world with a single man left fighting plague-created vampires and mutants. (These are discussed in Chapter 9 about vampirism as a plague).

STORIES OF SURVIVALISM

The first and one of the best depictions of the post-pandemic apocalypse is the one that appears in the British TV series Survivors (1975–77) made for the BBC. This came from Terry Nation, best known as the creator of the Daleks in TV's *Doctor Who* (1963–89, 2005–) and of the cult series *Blake's 7* (1978–81).

The series takes place following a pandemic, which is shown rapidly spreading around the world in a montage during the opening credits. The first episode opens with the unnamed pandemic eliminating almost the entire human population with the exception of a few thousand people in the UK (although we do meet survivors from Norway in later seasons).

Over the course of three seasons, the series charts the stories of a diverse group of people from various walks of life as they come together, set up a refuge (which burns down and forces them to relocate between seasons), and try to improvise the rudiments of survival and farming, while dealing with the constant threat of marauders, militia groups, and tentative cooperation with other communities.

Survivors offered a depiction of the end of civilization in the tradition of British author John Wyndham, who wrote the classic novel *The Day of the Triffids* (1951),

Survivors reduced to a subsistence lifestyle following the collapse of civilisation in *Survivors* (1975–77).

which takes place in the aftermath of a comet that blinds most people, leaving them prey to killer plants. *The Day of the Triffids* has a surprising influence over a number of entries listed in this book. Wyndham's book has a cozy British domesticity and depicts the public across all class divisions pitching in together (a view no doubt informed by the Blitz of WWII). *Survivors* falls very much under this same Wyndham-esque influence.

During its thirty-eight episode run, *Survivors* featured some strong well written stories centred around the morality and ethics of the small community as they dealt with rule-breakers, outsiders, and the necessities of survival, as well as a subsequent smallpox outbreak. The second season shows the group trying to create a life by subsistence farming, while the third season deals with efforts to unite the disparate communities, restore telephone communications, rail transport, and create a nominal government. The final episode of the series ends with a debate on whether it is a good idea to turn the electrical grid back on again.

The series was far less effectively remade as Survivors (2008–10) in two seasons for a total of twelve episodes. Almost all fans of the original ended up disliking this. The remake certainly adds a much-needed diversity — the original is noted as taking place with only white people surviving. On the other hand, this series started to fall apart after it abandoned the original's central premise of a small group of people trying to create the basics of survival and community, and delved into government conspiracies and the revelation of a genetically engineered virus.

Virus (1980) was a Japanese-made entry in which the deadly MM88 virus is released after a US military plane collides with a mountainside. What is referred to as the Italian Flu then spreads around the world with massive fatalities. The only survivors are stationed at various Antarctic bases, who remain unaffected because the virus does not thrive in the cold, and the crew of the British nuclear submarine Nereid. As they struggle to cooperate and survive, a Japanese seismologist predicts that a large earthquake will strike Washington, D.C. in several weeks time. This will be registered as an attack by the US defense computers that will trigger the ARS (Automatic Reaction System) automated response and initiate a nuclear war, including a missile aimed at the Antarctic base. Two men are chosen to go on a suicide mission to the ruins of Washington, D.C. in order to turn the system off.

Virus was made by the Kadokawa publishing company and produced on one of the biggest budgets of any film made in Japan up to that point. Kadokawa had previously made the big-budget disaster movie *The Submergence of Japan* (1974), only to see it bought up by a US distributor and re-edited with new footage shot with American actors and released as *Tidal Wave* (1975). Seeking to second-guess this, Kadokawa brought in a number of American stars and shot the film in a mix of English and Japanese in the belief that it would play in both markets. Unfortunately, these efforts fared equally dismally, and the US distributor cut the film from 150 to 108 minutes, dropping nearly all the Japanese scenes and retaining those featuring the American actors.

Virus is an interestingly ambitious film. It takes place in multiple international locations and features an amazing cast. The plot covers the elimination of the entire planet by a deadly virus, squabbling among the handful survivors in the Antarctic, a desperate suicide mission across a ruined America, and an end where the world is destroyed in a nuclear holocaust. It is the most grandly scaled of all the works discussed in this book but still manages to be a ploddingly dull film.

Director Kinji Fukasaku had been raised in the Technicolor era making samurai films, although he did subsequently go on to make the cult film *Battle Royale* (2000). In large part due to the way that Fukasaku was used to making films, *Virus* is a stolid spectacle, never anything that seems to move into intimate conflict between any of the people. The most interesting part of the film is in the later scenes where the survivors decide they must cope with the disparity between 800 men and eight women by creating a new order where the women have multiple sexual partners, but again this seems something driven more by the script than it ever plays out as a drama between characters.

One of the best films set in the aftermath of a pandemic was <u>*Carriers*</u> (2009), an English language film directed and written by Spanish brothers Alex and David Pastor who would later go on to make *The Last Days* (2013) discussed in Chapter 11.

The film concerns two brothers (Chris Pine and Lou Taylor Pucci) and their respective girlfriends (Piper Perabo and Emily VanCamp), who are on a cross-

Piper Perabo, Chris Pine, Lou Taylor Pucci, and Emily Van Camp on a road trip across an infected countryside in *Carriers* (2009).

country road trip from Colorado to Turtle Beach in the midst of a pandemic that kills everybody it infects. At the outset, the film could easily be a familiar one about a group of twenty-somethings on a road trip. Instead it becomes a film constantly pushing itself into uncomfortable moral choices — whether to take an infected father and daughter, whether to help when the daughter starts to cough up blood, and whether to abandon the father and daughter. The tension the film generates is emotionally gruelling and it must be considered one of the best works on the topic.

The epic work on the subject of the world after a pandemic was the Stephen King novel *The Stand* (1978). The book begins with almost everyone in the world killed off following the accidental release of a virus at a military base. Nicknamed Captain Trips, this spreads with rapid effect, wiping almost everyone out. The story follows a large ensemble of survivors as they make their way across the ruins of the US and ultimately connect. Some are drawn by their dreams to Mother Abigail Freemont, a 106-year-old woman living on a farm in Nebraska. Led by visions from God, she guides them to set up a new home in Boulder. Others dream of joining a demonic envoy known as Randall Flagg, gathering the crazies, rejects, and criminals, and building a base in the ruins of Las Vegas. The book plays out on a huge canvas that draws these characters together for a final showdown between good and evil.

A film adaptation of *The Stand* had been planned for many years, including at one point by George Romero, director of *Night of the Living Dead* (1968) (discussed in Chapter 8), but the book's 1000+ page size defeated any easy film treatment and it eventually ended being filmed twice for television, poorly.

The first adaptation was The Stand (1994), a TV miniseries that originally aired on the CBS network in four two-hour episodes. This came with a script from Stephen King himself and was directed by Mick Garris, one of the most recurrent and one of the worst of the King adaptors with other film and TV works such as *Sleepwalkers* (1992), *The Shining* (1997), *Riding the Bullet* (2004), *Desperation* (2006), and *Bag of Bones* (2011).

I loved Stephen King's novel when I read it and upon subsequent re-readings and would say it is my all-time favourite King novel. On the other hand, I hated the 1994 miniseries even though it comes with a script by King. On the book's page, King has a mastery of building grand sweeping fates, showing the forces of good and evil pitted against one another like pieces on a chessboard. It is a story filled with eerie presentiments and an epic sense of fate and predestination coming into play.

The book, and in particular the 1994 miniseries, take place in a world that seems to have some unsavoury divides — those with mental health issues, criminal pasts or who are just weird and socially ill-adept are on the side of evil (and gather in Las Vegas, which is considered the sin capital of the USA). In contrast, all the folk on the side of good (in the 1994 miniseries at least) are filled with homespun decency, come dressed in plaid, look as though they have just come from church and are guided by a woman who is God-fearing, down to earth and full of flinty wisdom (albeit with a harshly ascetic fundamentalist spin).

On screen, in the clod hands of Mick Garris, to whom subtlety and understatement seem alien concepts, all of this translates to thuddingly heavy-handed Biblical imagery. Mother Abigail talks like a nineteenth-century preacher — she is seen sitting on her porch singing *What a Friend We Have in Jesus*, she drives Flagg back with her prayers and refers to the survivors as 'Children of Israel', while offering plentiful warnings about God's will and her own sinful pride.

In the 1994 miniseries, all this heavy-handed Biblical imagery is unsubtly tied to imagery of the American flag. You cannot help but think in Mick Garris's interpretation that King's Baptist vision of the aftermath of the end of the world has somehow gotten tied up in Manifest Destiny. The American flag features in the background of many shots. There is the supremely embarrassing scene where the town council is formed in Boulder (in a hall where the backdrop is a pioneer mural) and the first order of business is Gary Sinise asking everyone to stand up for a rendition of the American National Anthem.

Furthermore, the story only takes place on the American continent — there is zero mention as to whether any other parts of the world were affected or whether the survivors in these regions had their own equivalents of Flagg and Mother Abigail (the 2020–21 miniseries does have an epilogue that briefly deals with this). Indeed, the book and miniseries does not even encompass the whole American continent — there are no survivors from South America or Canada coming to join the group, even though the end of the world would surely mean any concept of borders are now meaningless. Like *Survivors*, it is an apocalypse that seems to mostly spare white people — there are a number of Black faces but no Asian or Latino people among the survivors.

The main issue I have with the 1994 version is Mick Garris as a director, who reduces King, no matter what the scene is, to a series of crudely lunging in-your-face jump shocks. There is the occasional moment where Garris stumbles onto something more — the image of Adam Storke strumming *Eve of Destruction* (1965) on a guitar at the end of a line of abandoned cars while Des Moines burns in the background — but mostly he feels like an amateur director who takes every opportunity to go "boo" to his audience.

The other thing that kills the miniseries is some ridiculous casting, including Jamey Sheridan as Randall Flagg who is outfitted in the denims and big hair of an eighties rocker, where his scenes come with the amiable bonhomie of said rocker greeting the boys at the neighbourhood bar rather than evil incarnate.

Even more ridiculous is Laura San Giacomo as Nadine Cross, who becomes Flagg's bride. The scene at the start of the fourth episode never fails to crack me up — San Giacomo heading off to her wedding night with Flagg, driving through the Utah desert on a pink motor scooter with matching pink scarf flying in the breeze. It is an image that seems absurdly banal in what is supposed to be a serious work about the end of the world and the ultimate showdown between good and evil.

Things improve none with *The Stand* (2020–21), another miniseries treatment that aired on the US CBS network in nine episodes of around forty-five minutes each. This came from a variety of different directors and writers, including one episode written by King.

I would have loved to have seen *The Stand* as a full TV series that let the story play across a large canvas as we see characters gradually coming together towards an epic showdown — Captain Trips and the aftermath could have made a whole first season, introducing the survivors and their backstories, building up as they start to come together and we see the purpose uniting them, while the second season could be set around the reconstruction of life in Boulder, followed by maybe a third dealing with the showdown between sides in Las Vegas.

The most frustrating thing about the 2020–21 series is that it opens in the middle of the book — with the survivors already arrived and set up in Boulder. The entire first half of the book then plays out in flashback. It makes for one of the most confusing adaptations of a book I have ever encountered. It is as if they were thinking "Who cares about the lead-in in a story? Let's cut to the chase." It is as if George Lucas had decided all the scenes on Tatooine in *Star Wars* (1977) were too slow and decided to start the film on the Death Star and then throw in a handful of flashbacks to tell everyone how the group got there.

Missing or diminished is the epic arc of the book depicting the outbreak of the pandemic and the immediate aftermath as the survivors come together and we then see them being drawn by prescient dreams into two camps of good and evil, something that takes up nearly the first half of the book (some fifty chapters). On the other hand, minor aspects of the book, like Harold Lauder building a bomb, which King only devotes three chapters to, is dragged out for six of the eight episodes. After watching the series, I am unable to discern any purpose that was served by messing around with the narrative order of the book, but it is a choice that ruins the story's grand sense of fates playing out on a massive canvas.

This version does some things occasionally better than the 1994 version, including making the survivors a much more diverse group. Amber Heard makes for a much better Nadine, while Alexander Skarsgård's sardonic, dryer-than-dry delivery is absolutely perfect for the role of Randall Flagg.

There were three TV series set around post-pandemic futures, all on themes of young people being the only ones who survive. The Tribe (1999–2003) is a New Zealand-made series for young adults, set in a world that has collapsed into anarchy after a virus has wiped out all adults. The series, in its surprisingly long run (five seasons of 260 half-hour episodes), focused on the various groups that form in the aftermath and their fighting for resources, attempts to obtain supplies, and create an antidote. Later seasons became improbably stretched out around plots involving brainwashing, virtual reality, and artificial intelligence.

In Jeremiah (2002–04), Luke Perry plays the titular loner wandering the post-apocalyptic wasteland after a deadly viral outbreak nicknamed The Big Death has wiped out all adults. In between encountering wasteland marauders, he joins a group who set up in a former NORAD base and are attempting to rebuild society. This takes an often darker and more morally complex outlook than *The Tribe*.

A similar premise occurs in the Danish-made TV series The Rain (2018–20). This takes place after a rainfall carries a deadly virus that devastates the world. The series follows two siblings who have been left in a bunker by their father. They emerge six years later as supplies start to run low, and make a journey across the landscape where civilization lies in ruins, all the while seeking to evade the deadly rainfall, gathering other teen survivors in the search for their father.

Quarantine (1989) is a Canadian-made film from director Charles Wilkinson who has since become an activist documentary-maker. The film is set some time in the future in a dystopian society where those at risk of spreading contagion are banished outside the city. Beatrice Boepple plays a woman who fails in an attempt to assassinate the senator responsible for the banishments. On the run, she seeks refuge with Garwin Sanford, a programmer who is designing the city's new security system.

The dystopia here never goes much beyond a few halls and apartments overlorded by a cruel and power-hungry senator (Jerry Wasserman) and his security enforcers dressed in black and wearing jackboots. We learn nothing more about the contagion, other than that the regime is using it to banish people and that it may not even exist.

As with most dystopian tales, there are two lovers pitted against the system. Here Beatrice Boepple is simply a girl on the run who hides in Garwin Sanford's office and helps him before they form an attraction. This feels less like the great love story you might get in a work like *Nineteen Eighty-Four* (1949) than the complications that might occur in a standard thriller.

The Last Ship (2014–18) was a TV series from Platinum Dunes, the production company of Michael Bay, director of the *Transformers* films and *Pearl Harbor* (2001). Platinum Dunes also produced *Songbird* (2020), one of the first films of the Covid pandemic (discussed in Chapter 14). *The Last Ship* aired for five seasons, a total of fifty-six one-hour episodes, on the US TNT network.

The series takes place aboard the US Navy destroyer Nathan James, which has been in the Arctic as the deadly Red Flu pandemic strikes, wiping out most of the world's population. Aboard the ship is a microbiologist (Rhona Mitra) who is on the trail of a cure for the virus. The ship is made into a mobile laboratory as the crew cross the world, seeking supplies and clues to a vaccine, all as society collapses around them. Various plotlines involve Russian takeovers of the ship, capture by the Chinese, contact with surviving outposts and other vessels, armed factions led by people with an immunity to the virus, a scientist whose rival attempt to develop a vaccine has resulted in a mind control drug, and in later developments their efforts to help restore and defend the US government and distribute the vaccine around the world.

The series started with a passable survival scenario, with the crew on the quest to find a cure and those with immunity. However, this became diluted after a cure was found at the end of Season 2, leaving subsequent seasons less interestingly focused on the geo-political scenario. This was divided into simplistic black and whites — one side represented by servicemen who seemed to have stepped out of a US Navy recruiting commercial and everywhere else (Russia, China, the Middle East, Britain, and South America) cast as one-dimensional villains. The American-centric focus (a constant in Michael Bay films) and prominent emphasis on military hardware and the armed forces in heroically-posed action amid much flag-waving became a turnoff.

There were a number of survival shelter dramas made during the 2010s, with the likes of *10 Cloverfield Lane* (2016) and the devastatingly raw nuclear apocalypse film *The Divide* (2011). Two of these fall into pandemic themes, both centred around people barricaded in homes and survival shelters against infections outside.

It Comes At Night (2017) is the more traditional of the two, with husband and wife Joel Edgerton and Carmen Ejogo and their son sheltered in their home in the woods from the plague that ravages the world outside. They keep the house boarded up and cautiously venture out in ventilator masks. A man (Christopher Abbott) tries to break into the house, but Joel makes him a prisoner. Joel cautiously decides to trust the other man and combine their mutual supplies.

As survival shelter dramas go, the characters here are well drawn and everyone gives reasonable performances. The best sections come during the latter third of the show where the film develops reasonable tension in the standoff between those in the shelter over possible infection.

Hidden (2015) comes from the Duffer Brothers, Matt and Ross, who subsequently went on to create the hit TV series *Stranger Things* (2016–). This has a very similar plot to *It Comes At Night* and features Alexander Skarsgård and Andrea Riseborough as a husband and wife who huddle in an underground shelter along with their daughter. Above ground, a viral pandemic has wiped out much of civilization and they are fearful of The Breathers, creatures that roam the surface.

The film creates an intensely paranoid feel — the shelter is a contained area where the lighting level has been reduced to no more than lamplight. The Duffer Brothers rack up a great deal of tension as things start to go wrong — the attempt to kill a rat starts a fire, leading to ash spreading up through the air vent; the family trying to be silent but their position being given away by the pull-string of the daughter's talking doll when it is hooked on a nail.

However, the real effect that *Hidden* has comes in its subversion of the underground shelter drama. The first half features shadowy creatures with glowing eyes bursting in and attacking the party and we are led to assume they are mutants of some type. In a gimmicky twist, it is revealed that the Breathers are actually soldiers in night camouflage gear and infrared goggles, and that the family are a group of infectees hiding inside the quarantine zone.

ACTION AND B-MOVIE TREATMENTS

The British-made Doomsday (2008) comes from director Neil Marshall, who made films like *Dog Soldiers* (2002) and the standout underground horror *The Descent* (2005). The film is set in the year 2035, following the outbreak of the Reaper Virus. The British government has responded by creating a vast wall that locks off all of Scotland, abandoning the infected on the other side. Rhona Mitra plays a soldier who is given the assignment of leading a unit over the wall to investigate evidence of signs of life there in the hope this means there might be a cure and returning with it. In quick course, most of her team are eliminated and their vehicles and equipment destroyed, and she is left to survive on foot in the anarchic wasteland surrounded by gangs of crazies.

Neil Marshall blatantly borrows from *Escape from New York* (1981), the classic film where Kurt Russell is sent into the ruins of Manhattan, which has been turned into a walled-off maximum security prison, with orders to retrieve the President and make it back out past the crazies that inhabit the ruins.

The other big source of inspiration Marshall draws from is *Mad Max 2* (released as *The Road Warrior* in the USA) (1981), the classic and highly influential post-apocalyptic action film, which has influenced a number of other films discussed here. From *Mad Max 2*, Marshall lifts images of the wasteland of mohawked and leather-clad crazies and in particular the furious road chase sequence that climaxes the film. Out of this, Marshall creates a full-paced action film, which throws everything from steam-trains, medieval jousting and high-speed road races into the mix with satisfyingly visceral effect.

The Terror Within (1989) is a negligible entry from B-budget producer Roger Corman, who directed *The Masque of the Red Death* (1964) discussed in Chapter 4. It is set after the world has been devastated by a plague and is centered around a group of survivors sheltered at an underground laboratory in the Mojave desert. The survivors bring a pregnant woman back from the surface only for her to give birth to a mutant creature a matter of hours later. Thereafter the film turns into a copy of *Alien* (1979), with the mutant monster hunting the survivors through the darkened corridors of the survival shelter.

Cyborg (1989) is an action film from Cannon Films. Jean-Claude Van Damme stars as a martial artist entrusted with escorting a cyborg woman, who has vital medical data, to Atlanta to save a plague-ravaged world. Their journey takes them across the post-apocalyptic landscape, while pursued by a gang of wasteland crazies. Director Albert Pyun, who spent much of the 1990s creating a series of almost interchangeable kickboxing cyborg films, certainly creates wall-to-wall action without let-up, but with little in the way of plot.

Cold Harvest (1998) is a B-budget action film set following the collapse of civilization due to a meteorite that has caused environmental catastrophe and unleashed a plague. Former kickboxing champion turned B-movie action star Gary Daniels is a bounty hunter tasked with rescuing six people who have immunity after their convoy is hijacked by a warlord.

Both *Cyborg* and *Cold Harvest* are post-apocalyptic action films that hold strong allegiance to the tropes set down by *Mad Max 2*. In these, the pandemics depicted are no more than plot devices to drive the action scenes in the story.

Adrenalin: Fear the Rush (1996) is another action film from director Albert Pyun, who made the aforementioned *Cyborg*. The film is set in 2007 after a plague has ravaged Europe, requiring the infected to be placed in quarantine zones. Christopher Lambert and Natasha Henstridge are law enforcement officials hunting an escaped infectee who has developed superstrength. Almost the whole of the film is centred around their pursuit of the infectee through the sewers while he plays cat-and-mouse games with them. Beyond that, the pandemic scenario and the world of the future is minimally sketched.

The Lost Future (2010) was a film made for the Syfy Channel. It is set after the collapse of civilization where the remnants of humanity live as primitive tribes, while fighting off others that have been reduced to mutant savages by an airborne infection. The film follows three people as they discover the truth about their situation, and fight a warlord for supplies of a yellow powder that provides immunity against the infection.

Several other science-fiction films depict future worlds ravaged by plague and pandemic as in The Last Chase (1980) and Exam (2009). Although, in these, the pandemic is no more than a backdrop to the drama that occurs.

There are also several future-set films where the search for a vaccine to a pandemic forms a McGuffin that drives the action. Examples include City Limits (1985), Johnny Mnemonic (1995), Barb Wire (1996), The Sector (2016), Flashburn (2017), and Supergrid (2018). In all cases, the films are about something other than the pandemic itself — at most, we might see the depiction of one or two infected persons or mention of such in the background.

OTHER TREATMENTS

More exotic epidemics occur in Conquest of the Planet of the Apes (1972), a prequel to *Planet of the Apes* (1968) and the fourth in the original *Planet of the Apes* film series. This goes back in time to show how the world evolved into the one where apes ruled and humans were reduced to unspeaking animals. Here we see how everything began in the aftermath of a plague that has wiped out all cats and dogs, resulting in humanity adopting apes as pets and domestic servants, before Roddy McDowall's Caesar leads the apes in a revolution.

War of the Planet of the Apes (2017) is the third in the *Planet of the Apes* reboot series of the 2010s. It depicts a world where humanity and talking apes maintain a tension in the aftermath of the collapse of civilization — only for humanity to be rent by a plague that is causing people to become mute, the implication being that this leads to the ape-ruled future we see in the original 1968 film.

The Canadian-made Riot Girls (2019) from director Jovanka Vuckovic takes place in a town after a disease has killed all adults. Rather than something along the lines of the abovementioned *The Tribe*, *Jericho*, and *The Rain*, the plague here only features as a negligible introductory aspect to the story and is never mentioned again. The film otherwise focuses on the war that divides the surviving teens between the tyrannical rule of the school football team and a community of oddball all-inclusive outsiders.

12 Monkeys (1995) comes from Terry Gilliam, a former member of the Monty Python troupe, who has maintained a strong career as a film director since then with *Time Bandits* (1981), *Brazil* (1985), *The Adventures of Baron Munchausen* (1989), *The Fisher King* (1991), *Fear and Loathing in Las Vegas* (1998), *The Imaginarium of Doctor Parnassus* (2009), among others.

12 Monkeys is a feature-length remake of the classic experimental French short film *La Jetée* (1962). The story features Bruce Willis as a man in a future where a plague has wiped out most of humanity and forced the survivors to relocate underground. (No pandemic features in *La Jetée*, where the world has been devastated by nuclear war.) Willis is sent back in time to find the cause of the plague and stop it. In between various time jumps, he comes to believe that a bug-eyed and demented Brad Pitt, leading the revolutionary Army of the 12 Monkeys, may have released a bio-agent stolen from his virologist father (Christopher Plummer).

Beyond the scenes set in the future, most of the film is a work of time paradox, where, with considerable plotting dexterity, Willis' efforts to stop the plague end up being the cause of it. The film was later expanded as a TV series, *12 Monkeys* (2015–18), which involved much more in the way of time travel over the course of the show's four seasons.

A similar plot also appears in Diverge (2016), which is set following the collapse of civilization due to a pandemic. Ivan Sandomire and wife Erin Cunningham struggle through the desert wasteland that used to be New York. Ivan is approached by physicist Jamie Jackson, who sends him back in time to before the plague. There Ivan was a biochemist pursuing research into a blue flower that could offer an antidote, only for his research to be sidelined by his superior.

This is essentially *12 Monkeys* made on a low budget. There is the same plot — a survivor sent back from a plague-ravaged future to prevent the plague from occurring. Rather than Bruce Willis' crazed survivor in *12 Monkeys*, this has an eminently more sensible plan of sending back a biochemist with the capacity to synthesize an antidote. Where *Diverge* diverges from *12 Monkeys* is that it drops the time paradox and heads into some quite different directions in the latter half.

One oddity among these was *Domain* (2016). Set seven years after the deadly Saharan Flu has swept the USA, it follows the selection of 500 people who have been placed in single occupancy bunkers all across the country. They are connected in pods of seven by a group video chat link called Domain. Amid one of these groups, Phoenix and Denver have formed a romantic attachment despite never having met. The others vote to cut off the link from the offensively needling Orlando. When Orlando's feed is switched back on eight months later, it is discovered he is missing, while video recordings indicate that a contamination-suited figure entered his bunker. As the survivors debate what this means, others among the group start to disappear.

Domain is a frustrating film. It comes with a mid-film twist that you can fairly much predict from the outset, where it is revealed that there is no plague and not even any survival shelters — the group are actually placed in a warehouse in units that are right next to each other. As a further twist reveals, they are all in fact convicted prisoners and this is a novel penal rehabilitation technique to force them to renounce their former selves and develop new online personas within their pod. It is a bizarre scheme, where the entire premise of the film is improbably dependent on the prisoners developing a selective form of amnesia and none of them ever discussing their pasts with one another.

One of the more unique works was The Lathe of Heaven (1980), a TV movie for the US PBS network based on the 1971 novel by celebrated SF/fantasy author Ursula K. Le Guin. As in the novel, the film deals with a young man, George Orr (Bruce Davison), who sees dream specialist Dr William Haber (Kevin Conway). Orr is insistent that his dreams have the ability to change reality when he wakes up.

After Dr Haber discovers that Orr is speaking the truth, he starts using the ability to change the world for a better place — asking Orr to clear up pollution, to dream of a world of racial equality (only to wake up to find everybody now has grey skin), and to stop nations warring with one another (whereupon he wakes to find all nations are united against the threat of an alien invasion). One of these changes involves Haber asking Orr to dream about a less overpopulated world only to wake up and find a plague has wiped out three-quarters of the world population.

The film (and book) have an undeniable conceptual fascination in seeing what happens every time the protagonist wakes. This aspect was minimized in the disappointing remake Lathe of Heaven (2002) with Lukas Haas as Orr and James Caan as Haber, although we do still get the scenes where Orr wakes from the dream and a plague has wiped out a large percentage of the world population.

UP TO THE ARRIVAL OF COVID

With the arrival of the Covid-19, we started to see a body of films set in the aftermath of a Covid pandemic — works that predict the pandemic stretching well into the future, devastating much of the world's population, or else resulting in the imposition of totalitarian quarantine conditions. These post-Covid films are dealt with in Chapter 14.

Some of the works covered in Chapter 14 — *Anthropocene* (2020) and *Station Eleven* (2021–22) — straddle both eras in that they were conceived or started shooting before Covid but pivoted in mid-production to adopt pandemic themes or publicity campaigns.

The last ever pre-Covid films about the world in the aftermath of a pandemic are discussed in this section. The first of these was *The Directive* (2019). This came out twelve months before the official declaration of the Covid pandemic but found a new level of interest subsequently.

The film takes place in the aftermath of an unspecified pandemic, which appears to have been released by the Amherst Corporation, and has wiped out ninety-nine percent of the world population. Kyle Abraham is a lone survivor, getting by on a supply of Red Cross rations and trying to amuse himself amid the boredom. Kyle then comes into the possession of an artificially intelligent Amherst robot that he nicknames Sam. Sam reminds Kyle that his provisions are running low and persuades him to set out on a trek to the nearest quarantine zone.

The Directive has been made on a micro-budget — the post-apocalyptic ruins consist of Kyle Abraham wandering around backcountry Utah, where his shelter is a long-abandoned shack, and the quarantine zone consists of no more than a couple of tents and a vinyl safety fence.

Kyle is the sole person present through almost the whole film, apart from one or two others who appear in a couple of scenes. Much of the film involves montages of scenes where we watch Kyle bored and amusing himself by play-acting in the ruins — doing action poses with an empty gun, pretending to drive abandoned vehicles, throwing a ball at a wall, even sitting on his back and spitting a ball out of his mouth and catching it again. In one scene that goes on for several minutes, we watch him drink an entire case of beer. As post-apocalyptic heroes go, Kyle comes across as a jerk — his dialogue with the robot consists of throwing a barrage of insults and threats at it; while at one point, he comes across another man and robs him of his food supplies.

His companion through much of the film is Sam, which looks like a clunky toy robot left over from the 1980s. In a patiently logical voice, it persuades Abraham to head to the quarantine zone. This does come with a nasty sting in the story — the only point at which the film raises any interest.

When Everything's Gone (2020) was released during the Covid pandemic but was shot well before. (The film's website shows that it was crowdfunding as long ago as 2016. According to the film's writer and co-director Alex Alessi, the film was completed in 2018.) Alessi plays a man who emerges after having spent some time living in the woods, during which time a pandemic has wiped out most of the world. He wanders through empty houses, until he comes to one where Alex

Emmanuel and his daughter (Catherine Blades) and ailing wife are still alive. He is welcomed in, and he and the daughter duly develop an attraction. After the wife dies, the three others set out on a journey through the woods in search of the refuge called Eden.

This is another micro-budgeted film. The pandemic is offered as an explanation for the collapse of society but is barely mentioned — we are given no details about it, while there is only a single dead infectee shown throughout. Indeed, there is no depiction of the aftermath of societal collapse either — no destroyed cities or people searching the ruins for supplies as you usually get in these films.

Most of the film takes place in a single suburban house (where the collapse of society doesn't seem to have affected the power supply) and a stretch of river in the woods. It is a slow, sometimes evocative, film where the focus is on the characters, but not much happens.

One of the best works set in the aftermath of a pandemic was To the Lake (Epidemiya) (2019–), a Russian-made TV series that aired on Netflix in eight episodes. A second season appeared in 2022.

The series starts in Moscow as the city is overrun by an outbreak that turns the infectee's eyes red and then blinds them before bringing death, all within the space of three days. The series follows two neighbours, Aleksand Robak, who has settled down with a pregnant stripper nearly half his age, and has a wayward daughter, and Kirill Karo, who has moved in with his marriage counsellor and her autistic son who has a crush on the wayward daughter. Also along for the journey is Kirill's ex-wife and their shared son, and Kirill's aging father, as well as a doctor they pick up en route.

As Moscow is quarantined, the two families decide to break through the cordon. In a vehicle convoy, they head to an island in the middle of a frozen lake where the grandfather has refurbished a ship that ran aground there as his getaway refuge. The bulk of the series concerns the flight from the city and journey through wintry countryside as society around them is collapsing into anarchy. There are assorted brushes with others along the way, in particular militia groups who are rounding up and exterminating the potentially infected. The series ends on a cliffhanger as the Chinese military arrives.

This becomes a harsh survival story as we follow the characters on a perilous and often hair-raising journey. (It may well say something about social conditions in Russia that Moscow has descended into looting and pillaging by soldiers *before* quarantine has even been established.) You can only think that if either of the aforementioned versions of *The Stand* had put a fraction of the tension into telling the first half of their story, they would have ended up being classics.

PART TWO

REAL WORLD PANDEMICS

CHAPTER 4
THE BLACK DEATH

The Black Death is the name given to a pandemic that swept most of Europe and Central Asia during the fourteenth-century. The pandemic goes by several other names including The Pestilence and The Great Death. (The most common, The Black Death, was not actually coined until the eighteenth-century). It is commonly referred to as the bubonic plague, although this is not strictly accurate as bubonic is only one of the three forms that the plague takes.

As I write, new archaeological evidence has traced the sources of the Black Death to Kyrgyzstan in 1338–39. The first identified case was in Kaffa in Crimea in 1347 where Mongol hordes besieged the city, catapulting infected bodies over the walls. A Genoese trading ship fled the city and arrived in Sicily with all dead. From there, the plague spread throughout Europe all the way across to England and as far afield as Scandinavia, North Africa, and Asia. It is estimated that some 25–200 million people were killed between 1347 and 1351. The death of a substantial percentage of the labouring class led to the demolition of serfdom and considerable changes in social mobility.

The common misapprehension is that the Black Death was limited to Europe in the Middle Ages. The first outbreak was the Plague of Justinian, which affected Persia and the Byzantine Empire in the years 541–549, killing between 15–100 million people. Outbreaks occurred across various parts of Europe throughout much of the sixth, seventh, and eighth centuries. Indeed, the WHO still reports some 1,000–2,000 cases of the plague today, including about seven on average in the USA each year, although this is now easily treatable with antibiotics.

The Black Death comes from the bacteria *Yersinia Pestis*, which is spread by rats and fleas. In the Middle Ages, rats would have snuck aboard shipping and been carried between ports. The fleas then allowed the plague to become airborne and spread rapidly.

Bubonic plague is the most common of the forms of the Black Death, which comes from the bite of an infected rat or flea. Along with fever, chills and body aches, the infectee develops buboes — swollen lymph nodes in the groin, neck and armpits, which can become engorged to the size of a fruit. Following infection, death will occur within seven days.

The other forms of the Black Death are the pneumonic plague, an airborne variant that comes from inhaling drops from the lungs of an infected person. This is believed to be the most common form of transmission of the Black Death historically once the plague travelled inland. It is also the most fatal of the variants with symptoms akin to acute pneumonia. The least common is septicemic plague, which is carried via blood infection. Symptoms include the infectee bleeding from their orifices and their skin turning black.

The Black Death has appeared as a background element of assorted films set during the Middle Ages — *The Seventh Seal* (1957), *The Devils* (1971), and *Flesh+Blood* (1985). We are not concerned with charting minor appearances here; rather, this chapter deals with films in which the Black Death forms a significant theme in films.

GERMAN EXPRESSIONISM AND EDGAR ALLAN POE

The Black Death briefly appears in *Faust* (1926), a classic work from German director F.W. Murnau, who also made *Nosferatu* (1922) (discussed in Chapter 9) and *Sunrise: A Song of Two Humans* (1927), which is regarded as one of the greatest of all silent films.

Faust is a retelling of the classic story that has been laid down by writers such as Christopher Marlowe and Johann Wolfgang von Goethe, concerning the aging scholar who makes a deal with the Devil for youth so he can pursue the love of a woman. This has been filmed a number of times.

F.W. Murnau made *Faust* at the height of the German Expressionist movement of the 1920s. This was inspired by the classic German silent film *The Cabinet of Dr Caligari* (1920), which utilised a unique design scheme consisting of angular sets and heavily shadowed B&W lighting—before a twist ending that revealed all of this was taking place inside the mind of a madman. The films that followed *The Cabinet of Dr Caligari* broke away from the camera being a documentary-like depiction of the real world and created a stylized subjective world of exaggerated shadows and distorted sets.

The films during the era of German Expressionism often sat astride a medieval view of the world. *Faust* is not a film about the plague per se, but it forms one aspect in the background of the story. In the opening scenes, F.W. Murnau grants us an astonishing vision of the Devil and four horsemen of the apocalypse racing across the earth and then of the Devil standing over a town and casting the shadow of his cloak to infect the town with the plague.

F.W. Murnau also made *Nosferatu*, the first screen adaptation of Bram Stoker's enormously influential novel *Dracula* (1897). This is discussed more aptly in Chapter 9 dealing with vampirism as a plague, along with its remake *Nosferatu the Vampyre* (1979). *Nosferatu* does feature the key image where Murnau associates the vampire Orlok (his stand-in for Dracula) with the Black Death — Max Schreck's performance as Orlok resembles a rat, and Murnau has him accompanied by an army of rats as he moves in to infect the town of Bremen.

The Masque of the Red Death (1842) is a classic short story by Edgar Allan Poe. The story is set in the medieval period as a plague known as the Red Death ravages the land. Prince Prospero holds a masked ball for the nobles in his castle. One of the costumed guests turns up as the Red Death, wearing a funeral shroud splattered in blood and the face of Death. The Red Death is eventually unmasked to reveal the costume is empty. With the realization that this is the real Red Death, all the attendants at the ball fall dead.

There have been several film versions of the story. The first of these — in fact, the first depiction of any plague to appear on screen — was The Plague of Florence (Pest in Florenz) (1919) made in Germany by director Otto Rippert. This comes with a script from Fritz Lang, still a couple of years before he became the leading director of German silent cinema, making classic works such as *Dr Mabuse, The Gambler* (1922), *Siegfried* (1924), and *Metropolis* (1927), among others.

The film takes place in medieval Florence. The cardinal, a member of the city's ruling council, is angered when the path of his litter during a parade is cut off by that of the beautiful Julia, a courtesan just arrived from Venice. The council have banned revelry in the city and so the cardinal sends a monk to enquire about Julia's religious beliefs. When she replies that she worships love, they decide she is a threat. Julia responds by holding a festival and inviting all in the city. The ruling council tries to arrest her, but the locals rise in protest, forcing them to back down. As Julia encourages all to relish love and sensuality, the ruling council responds by calling up the plague.

As an adaptation of *The Masque of the Red Death*, this is an oddity. There is no Prince Prospero; instead the equivalent role is taken up by Marga Kierska as Julia the Venetian courtesan. For Poe, Prospero was a symbol of aristocratic privilege who holds a masque for the nobles, whereas Julia is far more democratic and holds a party and invites all, rich and beggars alike. There is a Red Death of sorts who is played by a woman (Juliette Brandt) who wears a hood and bloodied robes, but this figure only turns up after the one-hour point, while it is actually a monk who carries the plague inside the city.

Initially, you are engaged with Julia, who seems a sympathetic character in her crusade against the members of ruling council and clergy who staunchly disapprove of any kind of fun. After she is released, Julia inspires the people to stand up and celebrate 'love and sensuality' and we see them engaged in a PG-rated orgy in the grounds of her palace. The city's morality police then go away and appear to be able to pray up the plague to attack the city. In the latter sections, we have a monk (Erner Hübsch) who sacrifices himself to carry the plague into the city and kill Julia.

This is the bizarreness of a film that starts out in one direction — championing freedom and love and extending the middle finger to the stern moralists before doing an about-face and becoming a sermon about Christian morality and condemning the revelry. The end of the film, implying that the condemning priests have God on their side as they allow a monk to carry the plague to strike down the woman who stood up to them, arrives at very different sympathies than those it starts out upholding.

This is another of the epic-sized architectural fantasies made in Germany during this era — something that Fritz Lang specialized in when he became a director. It is filled with glorious images — during the party scenes, we see Marga Kierska being rowed around a massive fountain while lounging on a decorated raft, while elsewhere we get visions of the monk going down to Hell and walking through a literal river of bodies.

The best of the adaptations of the Edgar Allan Poe story was The Masque of the Red Death (1964), directed by Roger Corman, better known since the 1950s as prolific producer of low-budget films with over 500 films to his name (several of which are discussed in other chapters). Corman directed a string of eight Edgar Allan Poe films between 1960 and 1964 beginning with *The House of Usher* (1960), all but one of which starred Vincent Price.

In *The Masque of the Red Death*, Vincent Price plays the coldly autocratic Prince Prospero as well as the unmasked face of the Red Death. The Poe story runs to only three pages long and is essentially a set-up for the bleak ending where the Red Death attends Prospero's ball in person and everybody dies. As with most Poe screen adaptations, this has to be embellished considerably to pad out the running time of a feature film. Also added to the mix are elements from the Poe story *Hop-Frog* (1849), while in this version Prospero and his sister are also Satanists.

The script comes from Charles Beaumont, a writer on many episodes of the original *Twilight Zone* (1959–63). The early sections of the story are padded out with a series of scenes showing Prospero's treatment of the peasants. Here Beaumont's script becomes an amazing study of cruelty and sadism. In one scene, a husband and wife come begging for asylum from the Red Death. The man offers his wife to Prospero to which Vincent Price coldly replies, "I've already had that pleasure", then shoots the man with a crossbow bolt and throws the woman a sword, saying "Spare yourself, madam".

The film has a gorgeous colour scheme with some expansive castle interior sets, most notably a series of interlocked rooms each in a single colour scheme. The film comes with luxurious photography from a young Nicolas Roeg, who would only a few years later embark on his own directorial career with the likes of *Walkabout* (1970), *Don't Look Now* (1973), and *The Man Who Fell to Earth* (1976), among others.

Masque of Red Death (1989) was another version, also produced by Corman on one of his economy budgets. However, this is a drab, cheaply made film that lacks any of the vividness and atmosphere that made the 1964 version work. Vincent Price's Prospero was a study in the cruelty of power wielded for its own sake; by contrast, this film's Prospero, played by Adrian Paul, is pouty and wooden, while the script drags the character through a series of pathological meditations on the fear of dying.

At the same time, there was also another version made with The Masque of the Red Death (1989) but, while it comes with plenty of Poe references, this is Poe in name only. The story is contemporary, with Michelle McBride as a paparazzi photographer who sneaks into a ball being held by Ludwig (Herbert Lom) in his castle. Here there is no plague, and the Red Death is no more than a costume adopted by a slasher maniac who is progressively eliminating the guests.

Another telling of the story appears in *Extraordinary Tales* (2013), an animated anthology that adapts several Poe stories. This comes with the novelty of a voiceover from Roger Corman.

THE BLACK DEATH AND THE MEDIEVAL WORLDVIEW

I will start discussion here with one work that actually takes place in the modern world — namely, Isle of the Dead (1945) from producer Val Lewton. This was one of the earliest screen treatments of the Black Death.

Isle of the Dead sets up a symbolic divide that plays out in almost all subsequent film depictions of the Black Death — on one side, the world of medieval superstition and on the other the world of modern rationalism. In several films, we see characters caught between belief in a medieval religious interpretation and a modern medical secular one. In other works, we even see a literalization of the medieval worldview.

Val Lewton was a legendary producer who made a small body of horror films at RKO Radio Pictures during the 1940s with the likes of *Cat People* (1942), *I Walked with a Zombie* (1943), *The Seventh Victim* (1943), and *The Body Snatcher* (1945). Lewton's films hovered in an eerily ambiguous place, invoking in both the audience and the characters on screen an uncertainty as to whether the manifestations of the supernatural were real or merely imagined.

Taking its title from Arnold Bocklin's series of paintings, *Isle of the Dead* takes place in 1912 during the Balkan Wars. Boris Karloff plays a cruel Greek general

Boris Karloff and Katherine Emery in *Isle of the Dead* (1945).

who visits the island to pay respects to the grave of his wife, only to arrive and find the grave desecrated and the island infected with septicemic plague. Ordering the island quarantined, he comes to believe that Greek maid Thea (Ellen Drew), who tends the ill British Consul's wife, may be a *vuvoloka*, a native wolf spirit that walks the Earth in human form to drink blood.

Isle of the Dead is one of the lesser Val Lewton films. The ambiguities are established on every level — science vs. superstition, catalepsy or death, death by natural cause or *vuvoloka*, and so on. It achieves the moodiness of the other Lewton films in only isolated moments but is an interesting addition to the genre.

One of the best works about the Black Death was *The Navigator: A Medieval Odyssey* (1988) from New Zealander Vincent Ward, one of the great underappreciated directors in the world. Elsewhere, Ward has made films such as *Vigil* (1984), *Map of the Human Heart* (1992), and *What Dreams May Come* (1998).

The film opens in the year 1348 in a small village in Cumbria that is besieged by carriers of the Black Death. Young Griffin (Hamish MacFarlane) has a vision that the plague will pass the village over if the villagers make a pilgrimage to carry a cross to a city of lights and mount it on a cathedral before dawn rises. Led by these visions, several villagers tunnel down to the centre of the earth. They emerge into modern day Auckland, a place that is frightening and wholly bewildering to them as they set about to find the cathedral and complete their mission.

Lena Headey in *Anazapta* (2002).

The Navigator came out amidst the renaissance of time travel films in the mid 1980s that followed on from the successes of *The Terminator* (1984) and *Back to the Future* (1985). These others are centred around action and temporal plotting conundrums. By contrast, Vincent Ward comes from a formal arts background and constructs a vision of a completely alien modern world as seen through uncomprehending medieval eyes.

The images that Ward creates — visions of giant winged skeletons flying across gibbous moons — are arrestingly intense, almost hallucinatory in beauty. The modern world takes on a primal nightmare quality as seen through the eyes of the villagers — a submarine is thought to be a sea monster, which they ineffectually batter with oars; trucks in a junkyard and cranes with grasping claws take on the appearance of looming gargantua; Hamish MacFarlane is surrounded by multiple images of a Grim Reaper in an AIDS commercial as seen on banks of TV sets in a storefront window; even the terrifying problems presented to the uncomprehending time travellers in simply crossing the street amid traffic.

Anazapta (also known as *Black Plague*) (2002) was a British-made film from Spanish director Alberto Sciamma. The film takes place in England in the year 1348. Lena Headey is Mathilda, the wife of the local squire Sir Walter de Mellerby. Sir Walter has been captured while away fighting the French, leaving her in charge. The bishop (Ian McNeice) demands payment of taxes and will confiscate all their lands and property if they default. The bishop has carnal intentions towards Mathilda and suggests she offer herself to him to pay their debts. Others remind her that they have prisoner Jacques de Saint Armand (David La Haye), the son of a comte (governor), who would make for a worthy exchange for Sir Walter. When Mathilda mentions this to the bishop, he immediately tries to have Jacques killed. Jacques, however, begins to exert a strange influence on those around him. Meanwhile, the Black Death is striking at the court, killing people and in so doing exposing the guilty sins they all hold.

It is rare to see a film that so much gets the muck and grime of the Middle Ages. Almost the entire film takes place around a small village where the ground is muddy amid constant rain. The interiors are dark and claustrophobic, lit only by candles and the occasional colour of robes. The characters are outfitted in clothing authentic to the era and we get much focus on their unshaven faces and rotted teeth.

The alternate title *Black Plague* gives a misleading idea that this is a film about the Black Death. Certainly, the plague features and we see people dying as a result of it — although the plague seems to be oddly selective about who it affects — but it is not the primary focus of the story. Alberto Sciamma does give us one scene where we get to see a plague-infected corpse where he spares no detail showing the body covered in buboes and pustules.

In actuality, what we have more resembles a mysterious stranger film — a mini-genre that derives from Pier Paolo Pasolini's *Teorema* (1968) in which a stranger enters a town or household and exerts a strange influence, one that is frequently ambiguous and evenly divided between being miraculous and diabolic. The work that *Anazapta* comes to most resemble is the Clint Eastwood-directed Western *High Plains Drifter* (1973), which features Eastwood as a mysterious stranger who enters a small town and proceeds to disrupt everything that the townspeople hold dear as he exposes their guilty secrets, before the ending reveals he is a supernatural being. The film here remains ambiguous as to whether David La Haye is magical/supernatural, but his presence is seen as having brought supernatural retribution, in the form of the plague, down on the townspeople for the terrible crimes in their past.

Coming out around the same time were two similar films, with *Black Death* (2010) and *Season of the Witch* (2011). Both films have plots that seem almost identical at a cursory reading — they are set during the Middle Ages and involve a party of men who undertake a journey to sort out matters of witchery. Both speculate on whether the witches are real or superstition, while delivery from the Black Death is tied to the witches' actions. That said, they almost act as mirror opposites in regard to their treatment of these themes.

To start with the least of these first, we look at <u>*Season of the Witch*</u> (2011). This comes from director Dominic Sena who had previously made *Gone in 60 Seconds* (2000) and the laughable *Swordfish* (2001). The film is set in the fourteenth-century and features Nicolas Cage and Ron Perlman as soldiers returned from the Crusades who are tasked with delivering an accused witch (Claire Foy) to a

Eddie Redmayne and Sean Bean in *Black Death* (2010).

monastery so that she can be exorcised and deliver the land from the plague.

The film has a great deal of potential in terms of the issues it deals with — whether the moral justification for the Crusades of the twelfth to thirteenth centuries (where the west liberated what it considered the Holy Land of Jerusalem from the infidel (Muslim) occupiers) was a worthy one; whether the witches tortured by the Church were guilty or victims of ignorance and superstition; the question of the existence of demons; and whether the Catholic church was divinely sanctioned or a corrupt organization that wielded power with cruel autonomy.

The fascinating thing about *Season of the Witch* is that, though it is made in an age where the superstitions that dominated the Middle Ages are no longer with us, it seems to accept without question the views of the era. Demons exist and witches are regarded as having actual supernatural powers rather than being persecuted innocents. There is lip service given to how innocents were slaughtered during the Crusades, although this is reduced to a sole woman who Nicolas Cage accidentally stabbed with his sword rather than a people who were killed because they occupied what the west believed to be the Holy Land.

Similarly, the Catholic church is criticized throughout, but at the end the film accepts the notion that it had the power of the Almighty on its side, while the Church's rituals of exorcism are used to banish the demon at the climax. In its end voiceover, the film even buys into the incredulous medieval notion that the reason for the Black Plague was demonic forces. A version of *Season of the Witch* that dug beneath to question the issues it deals with would certainly have emerged as a radically different film.

You have to take *Season of the Witch* on its own terms — as a medieval fantasy film that is designed as having no greater substance or historical depth beyond what you see up on screen in terms of action set-pieces — assorted sword battles, a sequence where the party must move the cart across a flimsy rope bridge, and a climactic exorcism of the demon delivered as CGI spectacle.

In complete contrast is *Black Death* (2010). The plot has a number of similarities to *Season of the Witch*. It features Eddie Redmayne as a monk who joins a party of soldiers on a quest to find a village that has been spared the effects of the plague, reportedly because the villagers engage in necromancy and the black arts, and whose charismatic leader (Carice Van Houten) is believed to be able to raise the dead.

Where *Season of the Witch* transformed the Middle Ages into an absurd fantasy/action movie comicbook, *Black Death* gives us a portrait of the era with something that approaches a gritty realism — the plague-infected corpses in the street, the mass burnings of bodies, the flagellants, the witches burned at the stake.

During the first half, the village is built up as a place where the inhabitants engage in necromancy and have descended into barbarism. However, once the party arrives at the village, they are made welcome by the locals and the village is contrarily shown as a place that is clean, ordered, and almost utopian.

The film develops some astonishing twists. The party are imprisoned in a stockade where they are required to renounce their allegiance to God or be taken away to be executed if they refuse - especially grim is a scene where Emun Elliott swears to repudiate God before he is taken into the woods supposedly to his freedom, only to be hanged. There is also the heartbreaking scene where Eddie Redmayne is reunited with his love, Kimberly Nixon, who has been raised from the dead and, after seeing she is wandering in mind, he elects to kill her out of mercy.

Where *Black Death* gains its true power is during the scenes that come *after* that point. The film is set up as a contrast of two opposed faiths — the soldiers who act on behalf of the church vs. the pagans who have renounced Christian ways. With the exception of the purity of Eddie Redmayne's faith, the Middle Ages is portrayed with such brutality and the soldiers so harsh and cruel in their actions that it becomes hard to believe they could possibly be on the side of right.

The ingenuity of the script is to throw this on its head and reveal that both sides are wrong — the end shows Eddie Redmayne's belief that he was following the will of God to be false, but equally that the villagers are deluded, there was no resurrection from the dead, no sparing from the plague, only a group of people

following a charismatic priestess.

In contrast to *Season of the Witch*'s acceptance of medieval superstition, this is a film that boldly says there is no God, no pagan witchcraft, only the grim inevitability of the great leveller of the Black Death. There is a particularly grim epilogue where we see that the youthfully innocent Eddie Redmayne has had his soul so blackened by what he did that he goes on to become a witchfinder for the church, obsessively determined to persecute witches in order to prove what he did was right.

An absolutely fascinating work was the Estonian-made November (2017). This takes place in an unspecified medieval period. The story follows several characters, principally Liina (Rea Lest) whose father wants to marry her off to a boorish local, while she loves Hans. Hans (Jorgen Liik) meanwhile has developed a case of lust for the wife of the local squire (Jette Loona Hermanis) and conducts a deal with the Devil at the crossroads so he can have her. Liina then goes to the local witch for aid in wooing Hans.

The film opens with what is called a *kraat* — like a shuriken made up of what appear to be three axe and scythe handles with an animal skull in the midst — as it twirls across the farmyard and enters a barn and hooks a cow with a chain. The last image before the opening credits kick in is a bizarre one of the *kraat* helicoptering off through the air carrying the cow with it.

The film comes with some of the most beautiful and extraordinary B&W photography seen in some time. Director Rainert Sarnet delivers shots that render the entire screen in a luminous grey-on-grey almost as though he were filming in infrared. At other times, his stark contrast of light and shadow come with great emphasis on grime, filth, and the toothless and unshaven faces of the peasantry.

There are very few films that exist in the same mindscape as the film — ones that seem to take medieval superstition literally. The only other works that come to mind are the above mentioned *The Navigator: A Medieval Odyssey* and the work *November* most resembles, Robert Eggers' *The Witch* (2015). Sarnet fully

A kraat from *November* (2017).

embraces a medieval worldview with images of peasants spitting out digested communion wafer to make their hunting weapons more accurate because they are divinely sanctioned; of ghosts of family members that turn up on All Hallows Eve hungry for bread; of pacts with the Devil conducted at the crossroads; and where it seems natural to consult witches over matters like love spells. Especially bizarre are the *kraats*, which seem to be treated as everyday beings around the farms, where someone makes a deal with the Devil to animate creatures made up out of scythes and irons, and which come to life eager to be put to work.

The plague only forms a minor point in the film. One of the wildest images is when the peasants decide to deal with an outbreak of the plague by going to sleep in the barn wearing their pants over their heads to confuse the Devil. The Devil appears in the form of a goat and passes them by. The next morning they conduct a deal with the Devil who has taken the form of a pig, and get it to agree to pass them over and swear on the deal by having the pig place its hoof on a Bible.

A more recent treatment was Benedetta (2022) from Paul Verhoeven, the Dutch director of high-profile films like *RoboCop* (1987), *Total Recall* (1990), and *Basic Instinct* (1992).

This tells the story of the real-life figure of Benedetta Carlini (1590–1661), a novice nun at a Theatine convent in Pescia, Italy. In the film, Benedetta (played by Virginie Efira) begins to manifest stigmata. These so impress the bishop that he strips the Mother Superior (Charlotte Rampling) of her title and appoints Benedetta as the abbess. The film follows the in-house politics of the convent as those that seek to call Benedetta a fraud are viciously denounced, before Benedetta is condemned by the nuncio to be burned at the stake after it is exposed that she had a lesbian relationship with another novice (Daphne Patakia).

As with much of Paul Verhoeven's directorial output, the emphasis is on heated sexuality, violence and bloodshed, all presented with not a great deal of subtlety. The final act of the film deals with the religious perception of the Black Death in some interesting ways. Benedetta had earlier made the pronouncement that the town would be passed over if they followed her vision. The nuncio (Lambert Wilson) then insists on entering the town to condemn her, in so doing unwittingly carrying the plague with him.

As with both *Black Death* and *Season of the Witch*, *Benedetta* questions the actuality of miracles and the right of the Church. Most of the film is heavily swung on the side of scepticism, with it being shown on several occasions that Benedetta's stigmata were faked. In complete contrast, the ending tilts in the direction of the actuality of miracles and leaves suggestions of divine retribution — the nuncio and Charlotte Rampling's former mother superior both come down with the plague, while Benedetta is spared from the bonfire after manifesting more fake stigmata. If *Season of the Witch* left you feeling it missed the boat in its taking the medieval view of the world seriously, *Benedetta* leaves you confused as to which side of the coin it falls on.

We now turn to those works that take place in the modern era.

THE BLACK DEATH IN THE MODERN WORLD

<u>So Long at the Fair</u> (1950) is a British-made film that follows brother and sister David Tomlinson and Jean Simmons as they visit Paris for the real-life World's Fair of 1889. After signing into their hotel, she wakes in the morning to find he has disappeared — the desk clerk insists that she signed in alone, while the room he was in is now a bathroom. With the aid of artist Dirk Bogarde, she persists and eventually finds that her brother has become infected with the bubonic plague. He has been sequestered away in a monastery and an elaborate gaslight scheme created so as not to drive tourists away.

This was an early film co-directed by Terence Fisher, a few years before he became one of the cornerstones of the success enjoyed by UK's Hammer Films with the likes of *The Curse of Frankenstein* (1957), *The Horror of Dracula* (1958), *The Mummy* (1959), and a host of other films.

Though adapted from a novel by Anthony Thorne, this comes from an urban legend that has inspired a number of stories — Ernest Hemingway even recounts a variant of it in his novella *The Torrents of Spring* (1926). That said, this is far more of a thriller than it is a pandemic film. The major influence seems to have been Alfred Hitchcock's *The Lady Vanishes* (1938). The pandemic aspect only appears in the film's denouement.

Certainly, Fisher and co-director Antony Darnborough create some fine tension during Jean Simmons' increasingly frustrated efforts to be taken seriously or with Dirk Bogarde's attempts to steal keys and break into the hotel's safe.

In the realm of the bizarre is *The Satanic Rites of Dracula* (1973). This was the seventh Dracula film from UK's Hammer Films. Hammer had had huge success with *The Horror of Dracula* (1958) starring Christopher Lee as Count Dracula and Peter Cushing as Professor Van Helsing. The studio went on to make a string of Dracula sequels, almost all of them starring Lee who became increasingly reluctant to return to the role.

The Satanic Rites of Dracula was the second to last of Hammer's Dracula series, the last to feature Lee, and came at a point where Hammer's popularity was waning. The plots of the films had started to run out of creativity — with the entry prior to this, *Dracula A.D. 1972* (1972), Hammer had taken the step of uprooting Lee's Dracula from his usual nineteenth-century setting and bringing him into the present day in an effort to stir up the mix. *The Satanic Rites of Dracula* follows directly on from this.

The film comes with a batshit crazy plot involving satanic rituals, conspiracies among government ministers, secret agents, bikers, and hippie chicks. Peter Cushing plays the descendent of Van Helsing investigating all of this, whereupon he is led to a bacteriological research institute that has developed a more virulent form of the bubonic plague. Van Helsing eventually discovers that Dracula is alive, posing as reclusive property developer D.D. Denham, and that he is planning to release the plague as a way of wiping out humanity, thus ensuring his own death.

Epidemic (1987) was the second film from Danish director Lars von Trier. Since then, von Trier has gone on to make celebrated works such as *Breaking the Waves* (1996), *Dancer in the Dark* (2000), *Dogville* (2003), *Antichrist* (2009) and *Melancholia* (2011). The film was purportedly made on a shoestring and is von Trier's most obscure.

Much of the film is centred around two filmmakers played by von Trier and his co-writer Niels Vørsel as they set about trying to make a film after a computer error deletes the script they were working on. Interspersed with their efforts, we see various scenes from the film they start making called *Epidemic*. In these sections, we follow a young doctor Mesmer (also played by von Trier) as he leaves a walled city where a plague is killing the populace, only to find that he himself is carrying the plague.

The film has an amusing ending where, instead of handing in a completed script for their film, von Trier and Vørsel deliver a twelve-page synopsis and then bring in a hypnotist to regress a girl to plague times so that she can perform the rest — only for the actress to end up carrying the plague back to infect the present day.

Quiet Killer (aka Black Death) (1992) is a TV movie treatment that aired on the US CBS network. Kate Jackson is a public health official in New York City who detects cases of the pneumonic plague that has been brought into the city by a teenage girl who arrives on a flight (the source of infection is never specified beyond that). The assorted melodramas in a show of this type ensue — a journalist who infiltrates quarantine to get the story; the mayor's office which wants to minimize the threat due to the loss of business revenue; a senator who is infected but wants to cover up that he has been having an affair with the wife of a member of the opposition, and a climax where the senator recklessly endangers everybody by trying to escape quarantine aboard a train. For once, it is the medical staff rather than city officials who want to keep the news of the infection from getting out to prevent panic. Kate Jackson gives a speech before the mayor where she identifies the outbreak as the Plague of Justinian, which is historically the name given to what in modern times has been identified as the first strain of the Black Death that appeared in the fifth-century and spread around the Mediterranean.

Other appearances of the Black Death include the French thriller Have Mercy On Us All (Pars Vite et Reviens Tard) (2007). The film opens in the present day where a Parisian town crier receives a series of anonymous notices to be read aloud warning people of the great plague to come. Police then investigate apartment buildings around the city where every door but one in the building has been painted with a reversed number four. This is found to be a symbol used in the Middle Ages to protect houses from the plague. The inhabitants of the unmarked apartments then start to come down with outbreaks of the plague. Police find that each of the victims has been sent an envelope containing plague-infected fleas and that someone has broken in and painted the bodies in charcoal.

All of this sets up an extravagant thriller plot. The killer is eventually revealed to be a classics scholar engaged in a revenge scheme against parties responsible for the death of his father. The revelation of what is happening becomes absurdly contrived but the opening hook of the film is a provocative and intriguing one.

Another almost interesting variant was Nightwing (1979), adapted from an early novel by Martin Cruz Smith who subsequently became best known for *Gorky Park* (1981) and the ensuing series of detective thrillers featuring Arkady Renko, a detective in Soviet and post-Soviet Russia.

Nightwing features Nick Mancuso as a Native American deputy on a Hopi Indian reservation in Arizona, who investigates a series of deaths. He is caught between western law and his traditional beliefs and cannot be sure whether to take seriously the claim that the attacks were called up by an embittered medicine man who died promising to end the world. On the other hand, he faces the claims of an English scientist (David Warner) that the killings are being caused by a colony of plague-infected vampire bats that are making their way across the reservation.

Principally, *Nightwing* falls into the spate of 1970s 'animals attack' films à la *The Birds* (1963), *Frogs* (1972), *Day of the Animals* (1977), etc. As such, it is not a particularly good entry, with the film's credibility being badly sunken by some cheap and unconvincing bat effects.

On the other hand, like *Isle of the Dead* and *Black Death*, *Nightwing* has an occasionally interesting *trompe l'oeil* duality, sitting between an Indian mystical worldview and western rationalism, with Nick Mancuso's westernized deputy caught between both cultures as to whether to interpret the plague-carrying bat menace as a supernatural or a scientific one.

CHAPTER 5
LIFE AFTER EBOLA

The fascination over Ebola emerged in the 1990s. The virus first entered the public paradigm with a *New Yorker* article *Crisis in the Hot Zone* (1992) by Richard Preston. This was based on Preston's travels through Ebola-infected zones in Africa and detailed an incident in Reston, Virginia in 1989 where monkeys infected with Ebola were imported onto US soil. The response to the article gained a great deal of attention and, not long after, Preston expanded this into a book, *The Hot Zone* (1994), which became a bestseller and created considerable alarmism about Ebola.

In the book, Preston traces the first detected examples of Ebola with the Marburg Virus, named after the town in Germany where a shipment of laboratory monkeys from Africa ended up infecting thirty-one people and killing seven in 1967. Preston follows the development of the virus through various parts of Africa, most notedly the first known case with nurse Mayinga N'Seka who became infected while working at a mission hospital in Yambuku, Zaire in 1976 and travelled to Kinshasa, coming into contact with some sixty people (but infecting none of them) in her search for a hospital bed. Preston cites the virus's origin place as being the Kitum Caves in Kenya.

The bulk of the book focuses on Colonel Nancy Jaax, a veterinary pathologist at USAMRIID at Fort Detrick, Maryland, who identified Ebola in samples taken from monkeys imported from Africa via the Philippines to the Hazelton animal holding facility in Reston, Virginia. This resulted in a massive clean-up operation overseen by her husband Jerry, an army veterinarian, in which several hundred monkeys had to be euthanized. Several people working at Reston, as well as two USAMRIID lab technicians, were infected. Incredulously enough, the strain of Ebola (which was subsequently named Ebola Reston) proved to be one that was non-lethal to humans.

The book is an absorbing read. Preston spares little detail, and the depictions of the outbreaks are filled with vivid depictions of liquefying human organs, people with blank faces (caused when the muscles of the face start to dissolve) stumbling about in a zombified state, and of entire hospital rooms filled with gouts of

Cuba Gooding Jr., Kevin Spacey, and Dustin Hoffman in *Outbreak* (1995).

exploded blood. It is a far grislier, blood-drenched, and frightening read than most horror novels ever get.

The film rights to the book were immediately snapped up. A film version of *The Hot Zone* was planned in 1995 which was to go ahead under Ridley Scott, the director of *Alien* (1979), *Blade Runner* (1982), and *Gladiator* (2000). This would have starred Jodie Foster and Robert Redford as Nancy and Jerry Jaax. For varying reasons, this never emerged. The book was eventually filmed as the first season of the TV series *The Hot Zone* (2019–), which was produced by Scott — this is discussed at the end of the chapter.

Despite no film version of *The Hot Zone* happening, the public alarm over Ebola still reached film audiences. The big success was *Outbreak* (1995), which was clearly made with the intention of beating Scott's film into theatres and anticipating an Ebola films trend.

Outbreak is a fictionalized version of the Reston incident. Dustin Hoffman plays Colonel Sam Daniels, head of USAMRIID, who is sent to investigate an outbreak of haemorrhagic fever in Zaire. He is persuaded by his military superiors to regard the virus as non-lethal. However, a monkey from Zaire is brought into the US, where an employee (Patrick Dempsey) at the animal testing centre steals it. The monkey succeeds in infecting people who in turn spread the virus to those they come in contact with. All die horribly within a matter of hours. As Hoffman tries to trace the source of the outbreak, he realizes that the military are attempting to develop the virus as a bioweapon.

A VIEWING GUIDE TO THE PANDEMIC

Depictions of Plague and Pandemic on Film and TV

Outbreak is essentially *The Hot Zone* reimagined in terms of a big-budget pandemic and outbreak thriller that speculates what might have happened if one of the Reston monkeys ended up being released and infecting the population at large.

There are a good many similarities between *Outbreak* and the Reston incident. The film's contagion is referred to as Motaba Virus — like Ebola, it is a haemorrhagic virus, and has almost identical symptoms; it comes from a hot zone in Zaire; and it is carried into the US by infected monkeys after one of them is stolen by an employee at a centre that imports animals for testing. Unlike Ebola, which is carried by contaminated blood, the virus here becomes airborne.

Outbreak was made by Wolfgang Petersen, a West German director who emerged with German-made films such as *Das Boot* (1981) and *The Neverending Story* (1984) and went on to reasonable success in the US mainstream with works such as *In the Line of Fire* (1993), *Air Force One* (1997), *The Perfect Storm* (2000), and *Troy* (2004).

Petersen marshals the hardware of the epidemic genre with considerable flair — people strutting around with intent in yellow contamination suits, armadas of helicopters, military quarantines with wire fences going up, jeeps prowling the streets of small towns, bombers taking to the air, and so forth. To the mix, he adds a few tricks of his own — such as the camera diving up into air ducts and CGI effects that follow sneezed germs through the air of a cinema and down into the mouths of unsuspecting patrons.

Behind the film seems to be the belief in late 1990s American media — reflected everywhere from *JFK* (1991) to TV's *The X Files* (1993–2002, 2016–18) — that the hand of power in America has gone out of control, is being secretly manipulated from behind the scenes by something corrupt, and of the necessary fight to restore a basic moral decency. This is most dramatically demonstrated at the film's climax, with Dustin Hoffman in the skies in a helicopter in the path of an oncoming bomber that is flying a mission intended to obliterate the town, with him trying to appeal to the humanity of the crew and get them to defy the orders of a corrupt high command to spare the lives of the townspeople below. It is an extraordinarily potent image.

Outbreak was a box-office success (the twentieth top grossing film of the year in the USA according to Box-Office Mojo) and led to a number of copies. More than any other film, *Outbreak* is the one that has imprinted its imagery in the public imagination — of military cordons and quarantine by figures in contamination suits, while the images of CGI germs flying through the air have been copied by other works. A number of subsequent films have repeated the theme of the military seeking to appropriate and illegally test a virus.

The first of these copies was the TV movie <u>*Virus*</u> (1995), which aired on the US NBC network two months after *Outbreak* appeared in theatres. Nicollette Sheridan plays a junior doctor at the Centers for Disease Control who receives a promotion and is sent on her first assignment to Los Angeles to examine a case, followed by another in St Louis. She determines in both cases that this is an outbreak of Ebola. In examining the bodies, Sheridan believes there is a conspiracy but her efforts to gather evidence result in people trying to silence her and turn her into a fugitive.

The film comes from a novel by Robin Cook, a former surgeon and ophthalmologist who turned to writing fiction in the 1970s. Cook had great success with the thriller *Coma* (1977), which was adapted into a film, *Coma* (1978), that was directed by another former doctor-turned-writer Michael Crichton, author of *The Andromeda Strain* (1971) (discussed in Chapter 1). Since then Cook has maintained a successful career, turning out a series of medical-based thrillers, several of which have been adapted into TV movies.

Virus is adapted from Cook's novel *Outbreak* (1987), which depicts the Ebola outbreak in Zaire several years before Richard Preston's book. The film version has clearly been made as a work seeking to jump on the coattails of *Outbreak*.

Virus gives the appearance of those involved having done a certain amount of research about virology and contamination procedures. The main problem with most Robin Cook works is that when you've read one of his books or seen one of the film adaptations, you know the formula. There is the intern or junior doctor at a hospital/medical facility (usually a woman) who investigates an anomaly or mystery and in the process uncovers a conspiracy amongst the hospital's establishment to engage in criminal or ethically dubious activities.

Virus is no different. In this case, the eventual conspiracy is revealed to be a far-fetched one where a health provider is infecting the hospitals of a rival medical chain with outbreaks of Ebola in order to drive them out of business. The film is mostly centred around the thriller elements and dwells little on Ebola or those infected.

Armand Mastroianni (cousin of Italian actor Marcello Mastroianni) is a middle of the road director whose work has been almost entirely in B-budget video releases and TV movies (he also made the *Pandemic* (2007) miniseries discussed in Chapter 6). He delivers a couple of okay suspense sequences here. One is where Sheridan has snuck into the Level 4 containment room looking for evidence, only for someone else to enter and her only choice to avoid detection being to disconnect her air tube, leaving her with only two minutes of air supply in her suit. Another scene is where she enters the morgue to take photos and hides in a drawer alongside a corpse only to find that she is trapped and cannot get out.

Airing exactly seven weeks after *Outbreak* came out in theatres was *The X Files* episode F. Emasculata (1995). Here Mulder (David Duchovny) and Scully (Gillian Anderson) are sent to a prison in Virginia where two prisoners have escaped. As Mulder joins the manhunt for the escapees and Scully penetrates the secretive CDC

(Centers for Disease Control) quarantine, it becomes apparent that the escapees have been infected with a deadly contagion after one prisoner was sent a parcel from Costa Rica containing a leg of infected animal meat.

This is not an Ebola story. Nevertheless, it has many overlaps with the new contagion and outbreak story that was introduced by *Crisis in the Hot Zone* and *Outbreak* – in particular the prominence of the CDC. For all that, the episode demonstrates little awareness of CDC contamination procedures and shows the various scientists walking around without contamination suits and often touching the infectees with bare hands.

This is also an outbreak story as filtered through *The X Files*' standard shadowy conspiracies and cover-ups. Eventually what is going on is found to be an illegal trial set up by a pharmaceutical company. In typical *X Files* fashion, all evidence is eliminated just as Mulder prepares to expose the conspiracy.

The Burning Zone (1996–97) was an attempt to spin the basics of *Outbreak* out as a TV series. The series centered around a special task force of virologists, headed by Jeffrey Dean Morgan, who have been assembled to deal with outbreaks and biological threats. On a weekly basis, we would see the team uncover a new threat, search for a cause, and race to find a cure, all within a one-hour timeslot.

Various episodes saw the group dealing with infections that cause mass suicide and spontaneous combustion, flesh-eating bacteria spread by tattoos, and assorted other outbreaks coming from sources that included everything from ancient tombs and meteorites, contaminated blood banks, Nazis, surfers, and faith healers. In one of the more inventive episodes, the group are required to contain an outbreak aboard a 747 in mid-flight at the same time as getting the infected pilots to land.

The series suffered from dragging the outbreak and infection film through the conventions of US episodic TV. That, and its closeness to the hit success of *The X Files*, where leads Jeffrey Dean Morgan and Tamlyn Tomita were paired in a Mulder-Scully-like relationship, along with the addition of a shadowy conspiratorial cabal that was behind many of the outbreaks. The show also suffered from network interference, including dumping Morgan and Tomita after twelve episodes and promoting the secondary leads, before being cancelled after nineteen episodes and a middling reception.

Pandora's Clock (aka Doomsday Virus) (1996) was a TV miniseries that aired on the US NBC network in two two-hour time slots. The miniseries takes place aboard Quantum Airlines Flight 66 from Frankfurt to New York, which departs a couple of days before Christmas, captained by Richard Dean Anderson. Shortly into the flight, a US professor returning from Bavaria collapses with what is initially taken to be a heart attack but is then identified as an infection caught after coming in contact with a worker from a Bavarian bio-research plant. No country wants the plane to touch down and it is shuffled from Iceland to Mauritania. Meanwhile, Daphne Zuniga, a doctor employed by the CIA who has written a paper on viral transmission, is asked to consult and uncovers a conspiracy among the government to betray the plane's location to the terrorist group al-Aqba in the hopes they will shoot it down.

This is essentially a reworking of *The Cassandra Crossing* (1977), but with a plane with infectees aboard substituted for a train. The film is adapted from a novel by John Nance, a former US Air Force pilot who flew in Vietnam and the first Gulf War, who turned to writing aviation-based thrillers in the 1990s.

Pandora's Clock may count as the one pandemic work of this book that seems the least interested in the pandemic aspect. While the miniseries has clearly been mounted to jump on the coattails of *Outbreak*, the pandemic seems an unimportant aspect — one passenger aboard collapses and dies early on, although it is later determined that he was not infected with the virus. There are no scenes of the virus spreading and infecting others (although the final scene of the show casts some doubt on that) or the efforts to contain it as you usually get in these works.

Most of the show is centred around the ins and outs of the plane trying to find a place to land. The latter half becomes more a conspiracy thriller with Daphne Zuniga trying to expose corrupt doings within the CIA and US government as those responsible come hunting her. (The miniseries makes interesting viewing post-9/11 where forces within the CIA are plotting to shoot down the plane so they can declare war on Middle Eastern terrorists!)

Despite having the usual complement of characters aboard — a celebrity pastor, a US ambassador, a businessman who needs to get back for a meeting, and a journalist — the miniseries is free of the usual B-plot soap operas. Certainly, you would be hard pressed to find someone more handsome, self-confident, and calmly assuring than to have Richard Dean Anderson (aka MacGyver, 1980s TV hero to a million boy DIY tinkerers) as the captain of your craft.

The show is, however, hampered by the sedate pacing of the TV miniseries where all of the dramas that occur seem padded and timed around the commercial break — a feature film, you suspect, would have trimmed the drama to something leaner and tighter. Indeed, a much better version of the film, which does fully deal with the pandemic issues, is *The Carrier* (2015) discussed in Chapter 6.

The Hong Kong-made <u>Ebola Syndrome</u> (1996) must count as the single most offensive film listed in this book. In the opening scene alone, petty lowlife Anthony Wong is found in bed with the wife of a small-time mobster after the other man returns home unexpectedly. The wife is then ordered to urinate on Wong, while Wong is given a pair of clippers to cut his penis off. Wong manages to kill the husband by impaling him on the legs of a coffee table, whereupon he takes the clippers and cuts out the wife's tongue.

Wong then flees to South Africa and becomes an undocumented worker at a Chinese restaurant in Johannesburg. He and his boss travel to a Zulu village (all while slinging off a series of racial epithets in reference to the natives) to buy some pigs for the restaurant — only to find the village is struck with Ebola. Seemingly unconcerned, they conduct a deal for the pigs.

The point when *Ebola Syndrome* becomes completely morally irredeemable is a scene where Anthony Wong sees a native woman collapse while walking along a riverbank, and uses the opportunity to rape her. She then regains consciousness and vomits all over him, which he responds to by bashing her head in with a rock. The boss's wife attempts to dispose of Wong after finding out he is infected. Wong responds by raping her and then killing the boss by crushing his head in the restaurant's sliding door.

Wong subsequently returns to Hong Kong infected with Ebola, spreading it like a Typhoid Mary. He is eventually tracked down by the police and holds them off by spitting at them, before being shot. This feels like a film that is more interested in pushing the bad taste envelope and has had Ebola awkwardly grafted onto it because it was a buzzword that was in the news headlines at the time.

Voyage of Terror (1998) is a US TV movie that features Lindsay Wagner as a USAMRIID epidemiologist on a vacation cruise somewhere in South America with her daughter. A member of the ship's kitchen staff is bitten by a bug while on a stopover on shore and comes down infected. Lindsay quickly identifies the infection as a haemorrhagic fever similar to Ebola. She places the ship under quarantine as the US Navy surrounds it, seeking to prevent anybody aboard reaching US soil.

This is essentially *The Hot Zone* crosshatched with *The Love Boat* (1977–87). It is as though the filmmakers read *The Hot Zone* and wanted to exploit its topicality — just like Colonel Nancy Jaax, Lindsay Wagner is an epidemiologist with USAMRIID (and is also said to have been the doctor on the scene at the original Zaire outbreak). What we get is a plot where Jaax takes a luxury cruise and just happens to walk past a cabin where someone has come down with an outbreak of haemorrhagic fever. Oh, and also one where Jaax and her medical staff pick up guns and personally enter the fray to put down a crew mutiny!

This comes with assorted melodramas — Lindsay Wagner's daughter who becomes infected, the ship's captain bristles at having his authority overridden — in between assorted political drama involving double-dealing presidential aide Martin Sheen who is determined to sabotage the operation in order to disgrace the President (Brian Dennehy). At one point, Sheen issues orders to the Navy to destroy the ship, and tension mounts as the cruise ship tries to outrun a torpedo.

Contagious (1997) is another TV movie also starring Lindsay Wagner as an epidemiologist with the fictional Los Angeles Public Health Services who is called in to investigate after a man is found gutted outside his home. It is assumed that he was a drug mule who had been cut open to remove the cocaine he was carrying, but Lindsay finds that his blood was infected with cholera. As other cases of cholera begin to pop up, she realizes that these come from infected seafood that was served on board a plane flight from Bogota.

This is another film copying the basics of *Outbreak* and rather absurdly trying to create a copycat film about a cholera pandemic. Cholera certainly is a disease that has reached levels of a pandemic (and is discussed more in Chapter 7) and is deadly in its effects. Unlike Ebola or Covid, it is not a virus that is transmitted by air, touch or shared bodily fluids but comes from unsanitary conditions such as drinking water polluted by faeces. In other words, it is a disease that comes from people consuming contaminated sources (such as food and water) rather than one that is transmitted person to person. This curtails any possibility of creating drama, which is something that the film acknowledges, proceeding to ignore and treat the infectees as though they are contagious.

The film is also lumbered with a plot that has Wagner and detective Elizabeth Peña racing around the city trying to trace the source of infected cocaine brought in by the drug mule. Given that the opening scenes of the film show that the cholera was spread by infected seafood aboard the in-flight meals served on the plane from Bogota, this rather absurdly has the lead characters spending more than half the film playing catch-up with what the audience is told from the outset.

There was no direct film adaptation of *The Hot Zone* during this period — an indirect one with *Outbreak*. The nearest we did get was the TV movie *Carriers* (1998), no relation to the other pandemic film *Carriers* (2009) discussed in Chapter 3.

If Richard Preston had sued the makers of *Carriers* for blatantly stealing from his book, he would have won the court case in about five minutes flat. Judith Light plays Jaax in all but name — a virologist who works at USAMRIID and has the rank of major. Similarly, there is a plot about monkeys carrying a filovirus at an animal-importing facility where workers become infected by a bite. Like *Outbreak*, the film then speculates what would happen if Ebola got out into the general population. (Although the film makes it clear this is not Ebola — "Ebola?" Judith Light is asked at one point. "I don't think so, but it could be related.")

The plot becomes more fictional thereafter, having Judith Light head off to Gabon in search of the source of the infection, where she is joined by journalist Pamela Reed who is searching for her two daughters who have failed to return home after her ex-husband became infected. The latter sections of the film venture into the same sort of military conspiracy plotting we get in *Outbreak* where we see sinister government forces attempting to weaponize the virus and it is found that one of Pamela Reed's daughters has a natural immunity, whereupon she is hunted.

Among these post-*Outbreak*-inspired films was Thirst (1998), an NBC TV movie. This is set around a California town that is suffering from a series of mystery deaths. Adam Arkin is an engineer at the city's water filtration plant who finds out that the deaths are being caused by a mutated form of Cryptosporidium (a real-life bacteria that comes from untreated water) that has spread through the town's water supply.

The ins and outs of water filtration plants makes for a film that is about as exciting as a dramatized engineering manual. Outside of that, the film is stuck with the clichés of the outbreak movie — the corrupt mayor, the military cordon around the town, the establishment of martial law, and so on. The TV movie budget fails to depict the disaster on any wide scale — there is some rioting, but this only consists of about a dozen people scrabbling to get water bottles from the back of a truck.

The TV series *Seven Days* (1998–2001) featured a hero (Jonathan LaPaglia) who on a weekly basis would employ a time travel device on behalf of a US government agency to travel seven days back in time to prevent crises from occurring. The series featured one episode The Gettysburg Virus (1998), which seemed an odd conceptual crosshatch between *The Hot Zone* and *12 Monkeys* (1995) (see Chapter 3). In the episode, LaPaglia is required to travel back and stop a Christian radical from releasing a lethal variant of Ebola that has been stolen from USAMRIID.

Contaminated Man (2000) stars Peter Weller as an aging German worker at a bio-research facility in Budapest who is laid off following an American takeover of the plant. He demands to know why but this ends in an altercation in the laboratory, during which he spills some samples of a bio-agent over himself. William Hurt is an Environmental Protection Agency operative brought in to stop Weller as he travels across the country seeking to return to his family but inadvertently infecting everyone he comes across.

The film comes from Anthony Hickox, who had previously specialized in horror films such as *Waxwork* (1988), *Sundown: The Vampire in Retreat* (1990), *Waxwork II: Lost in Time* (1992), and *Hellraiser III: Hell On Earth* (1992). This seems an earnest attempt on Hickox's part to break away from what he has done before and make a serious thriller.

Peter Weller gives an excellent performance as the ordinary middle-aged man who is only seeking to get home to his family. However, Hickox's schlockier tendencies lurk not far beneath the surface, with the film offering up the biologically ludicrous notion of people becoming infected and undergoing complete physiological meltdowns in a matter of seconds.

One of the strangest of these outbreak films was Venomous (2001) from Fred Olen Ray, usually a low-budget director of science-fiction, horror and action films, along with a substantial output of softcore erotica. Olen Ray is a contender for the most prolific director in the world and is listed with over 160 titles to his credit since the late 1970s, including titles such as *Hollywood Chainsaw Hookers* (1988),

Scream Queen Hot Tub (1991), and *Attack of the 60 Foot Centrefolds* (1995). With *Venomous,* Ray hides behind the name of Ed Raymond, which he has used on some of his action films.

In the opening scene, we see terrorists break into and blow up a laboratory in the Mojave desert, causing rattlesnakes that were being used as test animals to escape. Treat Williams stars as a doctor in a small California desert town dealing with patients who die within a matter of hours after being bitten by snakes. In the course of the film, Treat discovers that the snakes are the ones from the laboratory and are carrying a virus that was developed by the military.

This feels like a film that is trying to crosshatch the basics of *Outbreak* with a 1970s 'nature's revenge' film à la *Frogs* (1972) or *Rattlers* (1976), which featured the animal and insect kingdom turning on humanity. There is a superbly nonsensical moment here where the scientists decide to pursue a human antidote by harvesting the antibodies that protect the snakes from the virus.

Fred Olen Ray offers up all the outbreak and military takeover clichés — the highly qualified medical specialist who has opted to return to life as a small town GP; the local authorities failing to take the menace seriously; the military conspiracy to cover up the release of the virus.

Ray throws in vehicle action sequences and car explosions at random. There is an especially ludicrous scene where a military helicopter pursues and shoots at two people as they flee in a car, only for the driver to respond by opening the trunk, retrieving a rocket launcher and shooting the helicopter down, as though a rocket launcher were the most natural form of personal protection to be carrying.

The climax is borrowed directly from *Outbreak* with the heroes struggling to stop an oncoming plane from dropping a bomb on the town — with an absurd twist added where they have to also deal with a horde of rattlers that get loose at the same time. The film also comes with the oddity of containing a number of references to *The Andromeda Strain*, including characters and institutions named after ones in that film.

Panic at Rock Island (2011) was an Australian-made TV movie. This takes place as a rock concert is held on the fictional Rock Island in Sydney Harbour. Two teens sneaking into the venue via underground tunnels come across a body, via which they unwittingly pick up and carry an infection that rapidly spreads to contaminate the concertgoers.

The threat is identified as a thread virus (one of the family of viruses that includes Marburg and Ebola) that originated in Afghanistan. Called Bactra, the virus is Ebola in all but name. In fact, the scenes with people coughing up vast gouts of blood and bleeding from their orifices makes this one of the few films discussed here that accurately depicts the symptomatology of Ebola.

Panic at Rock Island has a snappiness that makes it one of the better TV movie

The infection ward in *93 Days* (2016).

treatments. Grant Bowler is the public health official fighting local authorities who wish to minimize the threat. In one of the more unlikely variations on the B-plot melodramas that usually inhabit these works, three members of Bowler's family all happen to be on the island — his daughter works as a police officer, his son has snuck off to the concert and his concerned wife has gone to the island to help.

Playing against type, the military are the ones who step in and help Bowler quarantine the threat and deliver an antidote with almost miraculous effect — although later revelations show that they were attempting to militarize the virus as a bioweapon.

Ebola Rex (2021) vies with *Virus Shark* (2020) (discussed in Chapter 14) as being the single worst film covered in this book. It is also the only Ebola-related film released during the Covid pandemic — a point where fears about Ebola have all but vanished from the public eye. (We even get introductory scenes from Jennifer Nagle as a bad Elvira-like host cracking pandemic related jokes.) For all that Ebola has any significance to the film, it could just as easily have been called *Covid Rex*.

The film comes from Dustin Ferguson, a prolific director of micro-budget horror films. The basic plot involves a dinosaur infected with Ebola breaking loose from a laboratory in downtown Los Angeles. Ebola is of no further significance to the film than that, and in all other respects, the film is one of an assortment of B-budget dinosaur films following *Jurassic Park* (1993) — *Carnosaur* (1993), in Chapter 1, was another of these.

There is no real plot to the film, just assorted strands where things happen to different people, including Ken May as a hunter who livestreams himself hunting the dinosaur, and Erik Anthony Russo who gets abducted and taken into the shelter of his crazed survivalist neighbour (Mike Ferguson).

The film's prized piece of absurdity is the scene where Ferguson breaks into Russo's home wearing full riot gear and ventilator mask and forces Russo to get into the shower at gunpoint to "wash your ass". In another ridiculous line Ken May observes: "Even the plants have Ebola. The Ebola is infecting the environment."

Dustin Ferguson has made a sequel, *Ebola Rex Versus Murder Hornets* (2021).

TRUE-LIFE EBOLA OUTBREAKS

Finally, we turn to works that deal with real-life outbreaks of Ebola. One of the most remarkable among these was the Nigerian-made film *93 Days* (2016). This concerns itself with a real-life incident in Lagos, Nigeria in 2014 where Liberian diplomat Patrick Sawyer flew into the country infected and was taken to hospital, dying a few days later. This resulted in twenty cases and eight deaths, mostly among the medical staff that treated Sawyer.

93 Days surprises you. It is the only film about Ebola made by Africans. Every other western depiction of the Ebola outbreak that visits Africa — from *Outbreak* to *Virus*, *Ebola Syndrome, Carriers*, and *The Hot Zone* miniseries — feels like a depiction of Africa made by people who have never visited, where Africa is all mud huts, trading posts, and militia groups. Almost certainly, any English language version of the film would have stayed with these clichés. By contrast, *93 Days* feels like it could take place in a regular American city — Lagos is actually a metropolis of 21 million people — where about the only difference might be that the hospitals are cash-strapped for resources.

As opposed to the alarmism about Ebola that comes through in *The Hot Zone* book and miniseries (discussed below), *93 Days* is much more down to earth and no-nonsense. It is a film less about contamination procedures and horrors than the people infected. Not to mention there is a lot less in the way of blood vomited, gore-drenched hospital rooms, and the like. Nor do we get lots of pumped up dramatics or pieces of side melodrama, just a straightforward and well-told story about people dealing with an outbreak.

The film's most moving sections come during the latter half, which takes place in a quarantine ward as we watch various infectees dying. Even then, the film greets infection not necessarily as a death sentence but one that can be combated with a positive state of mind. Underlying the film is a sense of pride in how a nation put forward their very best and succeeded in containing a deadly outbreak.

It certainly makes for one of the better pandemic and outbreak films in this book. It is worth contrasting *93 Days* and *The Hot Zone* book and miniseries — the underlying message of *The Hot Zone* is one of fearful relief — "thank goodness we dodged the bullet" — whereas the underlying message of *93 Days* is a hopeful one: thankfulness at how a nation came together and did their best to stand up to a threat.

It seems appropriate to end this chapter with some discussion of The Hot Zone (2019), the TV series based on Richard Preston's book, which had started off the public fascination with Ebola. After the abortive 1990s film version, the project eventually ended up as a miniseries that aired on the National Geographic channel in six one-hour timeslots produced by Richard Preston and Ridley Scott.

Julianna Margulies played Nancy Jaax, the veterinary pathologist at USAMRIID, and Noah Emmerich her husband Jerry, as they deal with an outbreak of Ebola in several monkeys brought into an animal importation facility in Reston, Virginia.

The miniseries does pump up the dramatics and fictionalize a number of aspects of the real story. Topher Grace plays the equivalent of Peter Jahrling, the lab attendant who inhales a dose of the Ebola contaminant without realizing what it is. His indecision over whether or not to tell the others is drawn out over the six episodes, far more than in the book. Furthermore, while the book spends nearly its first half detailing the origins of Marburg and the history of the different Ebola strains, the miniseries condenses this into a single narrative for dramatic purposes, where Liam Cunningham plays a virus hunter encountering an outbreak in Zaire, which is depicted in a series of flashbacks.

Mostly though, the miniseries keeps to the basics of the story, details the contamination procedures at USAMRIID, presses the utmost importance of these on the audience, and tells everything with a great deal of urgency. We get a full sense of the nightmare of the scenario in a fictionalized scene where Julianna Margulies must carry infected monkey carcasses in the trunk of her car, only for the bags to start leaking and her having to stop in the middle of the highway to clean everything up. The last two episodes where the team enter the monkey house on their clean-up detail, having to do so in dim lighting amid panic as one of the monkeys manages to escape its cage, comes with a grim hellishness.

Indeed, of all the works discussed throughout this book, *93 Days* and *The Hot Zone* have to classify as the most realistic of them all for the simple reason that what is depicted is what actually happened. While other works like *The Andromeda Strain* and *Contagion* do exemplary jobs in showing decontamination and containment procedures, these simply depict the reality of the situation.

Perhaps the most concerning aspect of *The Hot Zone* is the ending. This has Margulies summoned to speak before a congressional inquiry where she gives an impassioned speech about the need for proper funding and preparedness for when something like this happens again. *The Hot Zone* aired in May 2019. Ten months later, the USA and the entire world was engulfed in a real-life pandemic of nightmarish proportions — the Covid-19 pandemic. Rather than Julianna's plea to Congress to bolster protocols and financial support, we saw the opposite effect in real life with the Trump White House making repeated attempts to defund the CDC by sometimes up to double-figure budget cuts (although these were repealed by Congress) and cutting of staff monitoring the developing situation in Wuhan. Not completely as a result, but undeniably contributing to it, the USA proved to be one of the least prepared countries for dealing with a real-world pandemic.

The Hot Zone was a success, and a follow-up series was produced with *The Hot Zone: Anthrax* (2021), which deals with the anthrax mail scare of 2001. This is covered in Chapter 2 dealing with bioterrorism.

CHAPTER 6

THE BIRD FLU AND ASSORTED OTHER OUTBREAKS

The 2000s/2010s were filled with other pandemics that pushed Ebola out of the limelight. SARS and swine flu did gain world attention but there have been no films devoted to either of these to date. The one pandemic that did make it onto screens was the H1N1 Avian Influenza epidemic after fears about it swept the world in 2002–03.

On screens at least, fears of H1N1 eclipsed the number of films made about Ebola and, if the film treatments were to be believed, it seemed on the verge of becoming a major catastrophe. This was in contrast to the actual numbers of cases, as those infected were only around several hundred and the number of deaths 450 worldwide to date.

The first of these bird flu films was The Paradise Virus (2003), a German-made film that was shot in English and directed by Brian Trenchard-Smith, a British-born director who came to fame in the Ozploitation fad during the 1970s with the likes of *The Man from Hong Kong* (1975), *Turkey Shoot* (1982), and Nicole Kidman's first film *BMX Bandits* (1983). Throughout the 1990s and 2000s, Trenchard-Smith's work was in TV movies and low-budget video releases — we previously saw him as director of *Voyage of Terror* (1998) (discussed in Chapter 5).

In the film, Melody Thomas Scott plays a virologist who takes a vacation to the fictional Barsarato Island (located in the Caribbean "between Florida and Guantanamo" — in reality location shootings in the Turks and Caicos Islands) with her teenage son. There she runs into a pandemic — in fact, before she has even arrived at her hotel from the airport — which proceeds to spread rapidly across the island.

Like many of the films made prior to the Covid-19 pandemic, this has done little research into virology or contamination procedures and its conception of a pandemic is, one suspects, largely gleaned from watching other film treatments of the subject. Thomas Scott, for instance, identifies the first infectee as having something "worse than Ebola" after giving him no more than a visual examination when he has fallen on the ground and is displaying nothing more than a minor lesion on his arm. Given that Ebola causes patients' internal organs to liquefy, and they bleed from every open orifice, this seems either absurd hyperbole or superhuman abilities to diagnose internal conditions with apparent X-ray vision on her part.

The pandemic here would appear to be related to bird flu — the first infectee is chicken farmer Dennis Banes who contracts the virus after being bitten by one of his chickens — although, unlike H1N1, this appears to be spread by contact. This plague has a phenomenally high spread rate — it is estimated that the entire island will be infected within forty-eight hours. On the other hand, while there is a virologist and CDC doctors present on the island, nobody actually suggests that anybody implement basic quarantining procedures such as staying at home and not touching others.

Even though it wasn't, *The Paradise Virus* has the feel of a TV movie. The plot slips into easy formula — the panicked spread, the US authorities (who are seen as more benevolent here than they tend to be in most other films) quarantining the island with a naval blockade as people try to flee; the girl that Melody's son is interested in coming down with the infection and getting worse as the clock ticks down to find an antidote. An antidote to the virus is eventually synthesized from the blood of a faith healer!

One of the better TV movie treatments was *Fatal Contact: Bird Flu in America* (2005), which aired on the US ABC network. In an uncanny prediction of the origins of Covid-19, this is said to have first appeared in a live animal market in Guangdong, China. A man (Ed Connelly) is fatally infected with a far more lethal strain of H5N1 while on a business trip and brings it back to the US where it spreads rapidly, killing thousands in a short space of time. The film follows Joely Richardson as a CDC virologist who tries to warn of the virus's lethality but is not listened to; Joan Cusack as the wife of the dead man who is quarantined along with their neighbourhood but organizes the community to feed all and tend the elderly; and Justina Machado as a nurse in New York City struggling to work in a hospital system so overwhelmed they have had to relocate the sick onto a subway platform.

While most TV movie treatments deal in clichés, this takes more of a sociological perspective in examining the widespread effects on society. There are all the requisite shots of contamination being spread by touch in a montage of napkins, cups, drinks, handshakes, and the like, which prefigures similar directorial effects in the more high-profile *Contagion* (2011).

The film predicts many aspects of the Covid pandemic — the inflation of prices; overflowing hospitals and, surprisingly accurately, shortages of ventilators in some hospitals. It also offers up several predictions that seem more extreme, like police walking off the job and criminals having to be released from jail and used as part of a labour force. There are also predictions that seem alarmingly believable — for example, the US government refusing to release a much-needed stockpile of

Tamiflu and keeping it in reserve for the military.

The most eyebrow-raising scene is where the US government has to put international pressure on France to release a vaccine to the rest of the world. In the reality of the Covid-19 pandemic, it turned out exactly the opposite, where international countries had to (and still have to as of this writing) place pressure on the US to release vaccines to Third World countries after the pharmaceutical manufacturers refused to release their copyright.

The next treatment was Pandemic (2007) — not to be confused with several other films with the same title including the low-budget *Pandemic* (2009) (discussed in Chapter 2), the Japanese *Pandemic* (2009) (discussed below), and the zombie film *Pandemic* (2016). This version was a TV miniseries that aired on the Hallmark Channel in two two-hour time slots.

Former *Beverly Hills 90210* regular Tiffany-Amber Theissen stars as a CDC doctor in charge at Los Angeles International Airport who quarantines a plane from Sydney, Australia after a passenger returning from holiday falls ill mid-flight. The infection is given the name Riptide Virus. However, one of the quarantined passengers sneaks out to a business meeting and the virus rapidly spreads throughout the city. The mayor (Eric Roberts) and governor (Faye Dunaway) place Los Angeles under lockdown, erecting roadblocks and instituting martial law. Also aboard the flight is drug kingpin (Michael Massee) who is being brought back into custody. His associates conduct a break-in to spring him from quarantine and he then mounts an audacious plan to hijack the shipment of antidote and demand a ransom.

This covers all the familiar cliché elements of the genre, such as the contamination innocently carried in from a foreign source (the origin of the virus is not exactly clear, but it comes from Australia, and we see dead birds, which suggests bird flu). There is the CDC wheeling into action; the passengers quarantined; the one individual who breaks out of quarantine and heads out into the city, unwittingly spreading contamination; the rapid spread of the infection; the response by civil and state authorities, culminating in the quarantining of all of Los Angeles and the institution of martial law. All of which is notedly a far more rapid and authoritarian response to when the actual pandemic broke out.

All of this is handled by Armand Mastroianni, who also made *Virus* (1995) (discussed in Chapter 5), a director who has elsewhere made only TV movies and low-budget films, in a fairly easy and predictable manner. Indeed, this is the pandemic equivalent of what gets called an airport thriller (no irony intended) — designed as a page-turner with urgent dramas, easily identifiable heroes, a cross-section of characters from all walks of life, along with a dash of human complication: FBI agent Vincent Spano's upset to find his ex-wife (Rene Ashton) is dating another man before the other man proves a jerk who abandons her when she becomes infected; a friend of Tiffany-Amber Theissen's daughter who becomes one of the infected. All that seems missing is a touch of romance in the midst of the drama.

The moment when *Pandemic* goes from a disaster movie soap opera to the ridiculous is with the plot complications that begin after the end of the first part – where an armed team breaks *into* quarantine to rescue drug kingpin Michael Massee and then take CDC head doctor (Bob Gunton) hostage. (Massee does have a nastily sadistic way of forcing Gunton's cooperation by coughing into a handkerchief and then wadding it up and taping it inside Gunton's mouth.) Massee and his gang then hijack the shipment of vaccine and decide to hold the city hostage, demanding a pardon for Massee and a ransom for the return of the shipment. At this point, a simple pandemic and outbreak drama has entered the realms of action thriller territory. The miniseries climaxes with vehicle chases racing around to stop Massee and gang amid a shootout in a warehouse.

The most high-profile outbreak drama of this era was Contagion (2011) from Steven Soderbergh, a director who has confidently worked both as an independent and a commercial filmmaker with films that include *Sex, Lies and Videotape* (1989), *Erin Brockovich* (2000), *Traffic* (2000), *Ocean's Eleven* (2001) and sequels, *Solaris* (2002), and *Magic Mike* (2012). Subsequent to this, Soderbergh also made *Kimi* (2022), a hacker thriller that takes place during the Covid-19 pandemic.

The film depicts the appearance of deadly pathogen MEV-1 that emerges in Hong Kong and rapidly spreads around the world. We see the outbreak through the eyes of various people affected – we even get to watch celebrity pseudo-science peddler Gwyneth Paltrow undergo a meltdown! – and CDC scientists working to find a cure. Much of this offers an uncanny prediction of the real thing that would occur with the Covid-19 outbreak nine years later. Indeed, during the early days of the Covid-19 pandemic in 2020, *Contagion* suddenly became the No 1 viewed title on Netflix.

The film comes with a long list of doctors and CDC scientists credited as advisors that leaves you with no doubt that Soderbergh and co. have done their homework. Foreshadowing the public health warnings about disinfection during the Covid-19 outbreak, the film leaves you with a germophobic fear of touching ordinary things. Soderbergh's camera is constantly snaking away into close-up to focus on everyday objects and highlighting the deadly things that may be lurking everywhere from doorknobs and the drinks a waiter brings, to the act of shaking hands. This is imagery that subsequently became incorporated into other outbreak films.

The emphasis is on the sobering reality of the pandemic. One only need compare *Contagion* to *Outbreak* – *Outbreak* would no doubt have pumped up the rioting and created seat-edge races against the clock to perfect a vaccine, while a TV movie or miniseries treatment would have added B plots with assorted personal mini-dramas around the edges, but Soderbergh avoids contrived dramatics. The script focuses on the chill delivery of facts and figures more so than big dramatic fireworks or images of social collapse.

The film has a strong message about such a crisis — a frustration with the governmental system and how regulations, funding issues, and inter-agency politics prevent effective management and a quick response to an outbreak. There are also digs at pharmaceutical industry pressure groups.

Also uncannily predictive is the portrayal of what US media has descended to in terms of the discussion of issues turning into invective and with character assassination supplanting hard fact. In another predictive move, Jude Law is cast as a conspiracy theory blogger who falsely advocates a homeopathic cure — and is later arrested for it. This echoes the ways that drugs like hydroxychloroquine and Ivermectin were promoted as cures during the Covid pandemic, although not quite the way in which these false claims spread like wildfire, or the explosion of online anti-vaxxer communities.

While *Contagion* became the default film that people looked to to find out what might happen during the Covid pandemic, a far better film and one that more accurately depicts the way that things did transpire was the earlier Japanese-made *Pandemic (Kansen Retto)* (2009), although this did not gain the same kind of high profile that *Contagion* did.

The film takes place at a hospital in the Izumino district of Tokyo as patients start to fall ill and die from an outbreak. The hospital is immediately placed under quarantine. It is believed that the virus is a variant of H1N1, and a search is conducted of a possibly infected farm and the livestock there culled. The hospital becomes overrun with patients, while the authorities panic as the pandemic spreads across Japan in increasingly larger numbers.

It should be noted that the real bird flu had far less devastating effect than is depicted here — 863 cases around the world between 2003 and 2021, of which 456 were fatal, according to figures published on the World Health Organization's website. In the film, the lethality is considerably exaggerated — indeed, the film has more people killed in the first few days than have been killed worldwide by bird flu in *two decades*. The symptoms of the real bird flu are relatively mild in comparison to the ones depicted here — not much more than a bad dose of the regular flu — and certainly nothing in the way of bleeding eyes (at most conjunctivitis). Later on in the film we learn that the cause is not bird flu, and that the virus appears to have originated from bats in a cave on an island in the Philippines, which draws association with Richard Preston's account in *The Hot Zone* of Ebola's origins in caves in Africa and it being spread to monkeys imported though the Philippines.

Pandemic follows many tropes established by other pandemic and outbreak films — the camera following CGI-generated germs through the air is lifted from *Outbreak*. What should be said is that while its virology is fictionalized, *Pandemic* depicts the bustle and urgency of an overrun emergency ward extremely well. The last half-hour is where the film gains its real strengths — it goes from a strong and realistic entry among the pandemic and outbreak genre to a strong and emotive one as solutions are sought and a possible radical cure is found amid various lead characters coming down with the infection and nearing death.

In fact, while people looked to *Contagion* as the film that predicted Covid-19, the lesser-known *Pandemic* gives a far more accurate portrait in many respects. It gets all the scenes of panic buying; the necessity of facemasks; of medical personnel outfitted in full-face shield masks; of hospitals being overrun trying to keep up with the infected and the staff left exhausted; the patients forced to die alone without contact with their families; and the empty city streets with the public under stay-at-home orders.

Another work around the same time was the South Korean-made *Flu (Gamgi)* (2013). This is set in Bundang, Seoul as a container of people smuggled in from Hong Kong is opened to find everyone inside dead from a fatal infection. The sole survivor makes an escape, while the two smugglers stumble out into the city, spreading the plague unawares. Hyuk Jang plays an epidemiologist who becomes involved as the hospitals are overrun with the infected to the point where authorities are forced to quarantine Bundang and set up internment camps, while fighting off pressure from the US military who want to bomb the infected area.

This wheels around the usual tropes of the genre — the outbreak from small, unnoticed beginnings; the authorities trying to deny/cover things up; the lone doctor chasing a potential cure in a nail-biting countdown. Much of these have been borrowed directly from *Outbreak* — the digital effect of germs flying through the air after they are sneezed to the lone person standing up to defy the military as bombers come to wipe out the city.

The film does a good job of mounting the imagery of the genre on a large scale — the police battering crowds as they riot in a supermarket; the military cordons on the street; the helicopters buzzing overhead; the digging of mass graves; and Hyuk Jang's almost impossible task of trying to find one person still alive who has the antidote among thousands of bodies.

Cordon (2014–16) was a Belgian-Dutch TV series that aired in two seasons for a total of twenty episodes. The series is set in South Antwerp following an infection that breaks out at a hospital after an Afghan man turns up infected with what is identified as a mutated version of the Asian bird flu. The authorities place the entire neighbourhood under lockdown and cordon it off with containers placed around all exit points.

Those trapped inside the cordon include a schoolteacher and a party of children on a field trip tour of the hospital; a lone cop and a handful other officers who struggle to maintain law and order as the situation descends into anarchy; a group of people at a data retrieval centre; a pregnant teenager whose parents run a convenience store where criminal elements muscle in and take over; an elderly couple; and the virologist who identified the disease (and may be the one who released it). Outside the containment zone, we have the police captain whose girlfriend is on the inside at the data centre who joins forces with a journalist turned conspiracy blogger in an effort to get the truth out, and the politician managing the crisis who appears to be behind the release of the virus.

The drama stretches between those infected trying to survive; possible cures, including the efforts to get one boy whose blood may hold a cure out of the zone; the anarchy and lawlessness inside the quarantine zone; the efforts to get food supplies in only to see them hijacked by the gangs; the growing attraction between the police officer and schoolteacher; and trying to expose a conspiracy to deliberately release the virus.

Cordon underwent an English language remake as <u>Containment</u> (2016), which ran for one season on the US's CW Network — the original's first season of ten episodes has been padded out to thirteen episodes. Here the action has been moved to Atlanta (home of the Centers for Disease Control), where the outbreak begins when a Syrian man turns up at the hospital. Amid speculation that the outbreak is due to a terrorist plot, the authorities place the entire neighbourhood under lockdown and cordon it off with containers.

The US version slavishly copies the first season of the Belgian-Dutch version, right down to the character names. It even reuses the same plots, sometimes shuffling events around. The dramas of the original have been fed through the formula of US episodic television with the addition of easy moral divides and solutions. Also the characters have been cleaned up — at one point, the Belgian-Dutch version has people believing they have discovered a potential cure in drinking the urine of a boy who has a seeming immunity, but that has been dropped.

Cordon is the better of the two series in most regards. The drama and characters seem rawer, while the US version feels like they have been rehashed as standard formulaic characters. The advantage the US version has is budget and casting better actors.

Containment is a passable if formulaic drama with a decent cast, but it never found sufficient interest to gain an audience and received only mediocre reviews. While *Cordon* continued for a second season, *Containment* was cancelled after thirteen episodes with the various dramas being abruptly wrapped up in the final episode.

Bird flu also turns up in <u>Postal</u> (2007) from Uwe Boll, a German-born director who lives and makes films in Canada. Boll was widely considered the world's worst living director (not an assessment this author agrees with — others are far more worthy of the title), largely due to a series of video game adaptations such as *House of the Dead* (2003), *Alone in the Dark* (2005), *BloodRayne* (2005) and their sequels. Boll's reputation rests on matters governed by a quick shooting schedule, where he rarely does more than a couple of takes, and frequently bizarrely mismatched casting choices. An online petition in 2008 begged Boll to stop making films, to which Boll responded by challenging his critics to a boxing match.

Postal is adapted from the video game that was released by Running With Scissors in 1997. In the game, the character Postal Dude undertakes various mundane tasks, which are frequently interspersed with long waits or people exhibiting rude behaviour. The player could choose to either endure these or react by unleashing their frustrations against all and sundry using the enormous arsenal of available firepower that one can pick up throughout the game. The game attracted controversy for its violence, although this is clearly intended in an over-the-top manner.

When it comes to the film version, Boll sets out to make everything in as bad a taste as possible. There's a rather funny opening with the 9/11 suicide pilots arguing with Osama bin Laden on a cellphone about the number of virgins they are supposed to be rewarded with in Heaven, getting fed up and deciding to fly to the Bahamas instead. Elsewhere, Boll throws in caricatures of trailer park rednecks, the obese, the intellectually handicapped, welfare recipients, police brutality, along with gags about Tom Cruise, Nazis, and concentration camps. At one point, Boll makes a cameo as himself where he agrees that he financed his films with Nazi gold and admits to paedophilic impulses, before the game's creator Vince Desiderio attacks him for destroying the game. None of this is particularly funny.

The film's nominal plot has Postal Dude (Zack Ward) engaged in a scheme to rob a shipment of dolls that have been infected with bird flu by al-Qaeda and intended to wipe out the US. The film ends with lookalikes of Osama bin Laden and George W. Bush skipping off into the sunset holding hands as nuclear war breaks out around them.

No more serious in its own way was the low-budget horror film *Flu Bird Horror* (2008). The plot concerns a group of teenagers from juvenile hall taken on a confidence-building course in the woods where they come under attack from giant birds. Doctors realize the birds are infected with a mutated version of the H5N1 virus, as the group try to make it out of the woods and survive the bird attacks.

This is nothing more than one of a great many low-budget monster movies that were being made for the US Syfy Channel during the era. In the real world, the avian influenza (or bird flu) epidemic is a virus infectious to humans that is carried by regular birds, whereas for the film this becomes a stepping-off point where the birds are actually transformed into vicious mutants that physically attack humans.

There was also the low-budget *Virus X* (2010), which takes place at a facility where various scientists are working to find a cure for the H1N1 virus. Unknown to them, the facility's head Dr Gravamen (Joseph Zaso) is working on behalf of wealthy backer (played by cult B-movie actress Sybil Danning who spends most of the film either in the bath or drinking champagne) who wants him to develop a weaponized strain of H1N1. Graverman has been abducting prostitutes and street people to use as test subjects. When one of the abductees gets loose into the rest of the facility, he decides to use the now-infected scientists as test subjects and locks them in.

This is a poorly made film in all regards. Everything takes place in what looks like an industrial plant with cramped rooms and suffused in heavy shadow or blue light, making it resemble a tatty 1990s cyberpunk film. The rest of the film plays out like a cheap horror film with people fleeing as an attacking infectee runs through the facility. This also features a version of H1N1 that not only makes the infected bleed out of their orifices but also burble green goo!

SMALLER SCALE PANDEMIC FILMS

All of the above deal with the widespread outbreak of pandemic or the potential threat of such. They take place on large scales as we see towns, cities, and entire countries infected and the contamination spread around the world. At the opposite end of the spectrum, there have been a number of films during the 2010s that have depicted pandemic and outbreak dramas occurring on smaller and more contained scales.

Retreat (2011) is a British-made film that takes place on an island off the coast as husband and wife Cillian Murphy and Thandie Newton get away to deal with the tensions in their marriage following her miscarriage. Their isolation is interrupted as wounded soldier Jamie Bell turns up on the island. He tells how a deadly virus has been released on the mainland and is killing everybody and immediately begins barricading the house up against infection and intruders.

The entire film takes place in a cottage on an island with a cast of three — plus one other man who turns up to pilot the boat. Director Carl Tibbetts creates a contained drama and allows the three actors, all giving top-drawer performances — especially a mercurial and unpredictable Jamie Bell — a stage to play the tensions of the situation out between them.

Here, and in *Domain* (2016) (discussed in Chapter 3), the pandemic is something that takes place off-screen for the most part (although it does make an appearance towards the end of the film). In this case, the devastating effect is imparted by another person, revealed to be an unreliable narrator. The end of the film turns things we thought were happening on their head.

REAL WORLD PANDEMICS

In _Parts Per Billion_ (2014), a viral agent used in a Middle Eastern conflict zone has become airborne and spreads around the world, killing all. The film takes place in Detroit, and we see things through the eyes of a group of interconnected individuals. These include Penn Badgley as an aspiring musician and his recently announced fiancée Teresa Palmer; Penn's aging grandfather Frank Langella, a former virologist who released information that led to the creation of the virus, and his ailing wife Gena Rowlands; and Rosario Dawson as the lawyer called to defend Langella and her husband, unsuccessful writer Josh Hartnett.

Rather than most of the other works discussed in this chapter, this is not a work depicting the effects of a pandemic on a wide scale. We certainly see the background sketched out in news clips and animated maps following the spread on TV in the background, and there are several scenes where we see bodies fallen in the street and at a hospital. However, this film is firmly focused on human dramas in the midst of the outbreak.

As such, this is a well-made effort with a fine ensemble cast all delivering strong and well-rounded characters. The film is told in a non-linear fashion that jumps back and forth between the initial stages of the pandemic and the point when the infection starts sweeping across Detroit. Much of it is concerned with the interpersonal dramas of the young people: Teresa Palmer's anxieties and possible hallucinations; Penn Badgley trying to succeed as a musician; Josh Hartnett having failed to succeed as a writer; as well as Frank Langella's guilt over his release of the information about the virus. You could almost consider it a pandemic era version of *Crash* (2005).

The British-made _The Carrier_ (2015) is set aboard a 747 flight out of London as a group of ten passengers and crew seek to escape the pandemic raging around the world and make it to Greenland, which is purported to be uninfected. However, after taking off, they discover that some of those aboard are ill. This necessitates drastic actions, from quarantining the infected on the economy deck to severing a patient's arm before infection spreads. The need for refuelling forces them to land at an airport but this leaves them open to attack by the infected who have seen the plane land and are desperate to hijack it.

This is the work about an outbreak on a plane that you wanted *Pandora's Clock* (1996) (discussed in Chapter 5) to be. The majority of the drama is contained aboard a plane (expanded to an airport runway during the latter half of the film). The script works rather well as a contained drama and keeps turning with a series of tight twists — such as dealing with the problem of how to isolate an infected person without allowing the infection to spread to the rest of the plane. There are some excellent tensions during the scenes landed at the airport and the attempt to refuel amid incursions from the infected and betrayal from within the group.

The film never specifies how the infection is spread — clearly it is not airborne as the survivors deal with it by merely confining the infected to the economy section. On the other hand, the infection does not seem to be blood- or contact-borne either, in that people conduct surgery to remove the arm of one of the infected without any kind of protection. (This is also a DIY arm removal that for some reason fails to end up with massive arterial spray.)

The only disappointment is the ending with the two potential lovers reunited on the runway after the plane takes off without them. However, as the entire thrust of the film has made clear, you wonder exactly what kind of upbeat ending this could be with the two of them left in a world that has fallen into anarchy and lawlessness, not to mention holds the possibility of infection at every turn.

Another unusual work around the same time was the British-made Containment (2015), not related or to be confused with the abovementioned TV series that came out the following year. A man (Lee Ross) wakes in the morning to find that the door of his apartment has been glued shut, as has also been the case with all of his neighbours in the building. They see people in contamination suits outside and it becomes apparent that the tenants are being contained to deal with an outbreak. Other residents break through the apartment walls and begin to organize a resistance. They capture one of the people in contamination suits but this degenerates into a furious fight between the neighbours over the single syringe of antidote she holds.

This works through the unusualness of its opening hook — one man in his apartment waking to go about his workday only to discover, bizarrely enough, that he has been glued inside his apartment. The difference of perspective makes for something interesting and unusual — the tensions that build throughout the film all logically come from the tenants trying to ascertain the situation and discover a means of escape. There is never any wider depiction of the epidemic beyond the apartment building — at most, we see figures in contamination suits trying to

contain the threat in the lot between the apartment buildings.

The Bar (El Bar) (2017) comes from Spanish director Alex de la Iglesia, known for dark comedies such as *Accion Mutante* (1993), *The Day of the Beast* (1995), *Common Wealth* (2000), *Ferpect Crime* (2004), *The Oxford Murders* (2008), and *As Luck Would Have It* (2011).

The film follows a diverse cross-section of patrons at a Madrid bar — an advertising executive comes to work on his laptop, a widow comes to play the slot machines, a homeless beggar, a retired cop, a salesman, a woman charging her phone on the way to a Tinder date. A panhandler exits the bar only to be abruptly shot in the head, as is the person who goes to their aid. A man then staggers out of the bathroom and collapses dead. As people in contamination suits clear the square outside, the group in the bar discover that the dead man is a soldier and was infected with a virus. With this comes the realization that some of them might be infected after touching the man and his belongings, which causes the group to divide in fear. A vial of antidote is discovered on the dead man, which starts a fight between people over who has the right to take it.

Most of Alex de la Iglesia's films are dark comedies that are predicated on creating a situation and putting the screws on a crosscut of characters with merciless regard. Here de la Iglesia has a good deal of fun winding up the paranoia, toying with explanations about what is going on both possible and absurd, bringing out the characters' imagined fears about why they have been confined in the bar and then whether they are infected. In the latter sections, this goes beyond black humour into a disturbing drama of human greed, with a particularly grim series of debates over who should be given the antidote and over whether it is right to kill one of the group because there are not enough doses.

A VIEWING GUIDE TO THE PANDEMIC

Depictions of Plague and Pandemic on Film and TV

Emily Kusche is taken away in *Sløborn* (2020).

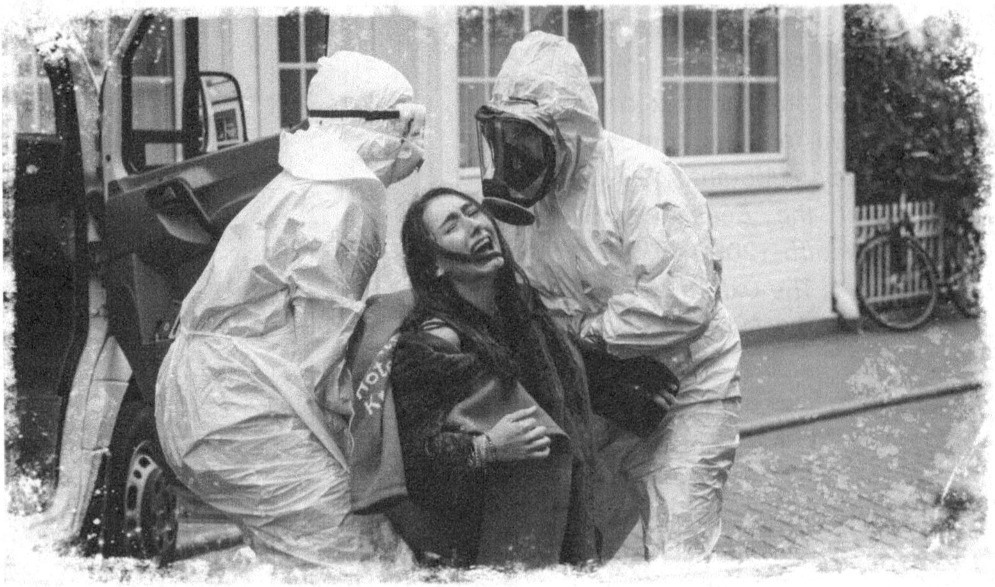

THE ARRIVAL OF COVID

And then of course came 2020, when all of the works prior to that, which had merely speculated about what a pandemic would be like, were replaced by films that were about the real thing. These we will get to in Chapter 12. However, the first works about pandemic to appear during the Covid-19 pandemic were actually two that were made *before* it.

The first of these was *Before the Fire* (aka *The Great Silence*) (2020) from director Charlie Buhler. In the film, a pandemic ravages the USA. Jenna Lyng Adams is planning to leave Los Angeles with her journalist boyfriend (Jackson Davies) who puts her on a plane but then decides at the last minute to stay behind. She finds he has sent her back to rural Georgia from where she fled an abusive family several years before. As Jenna settles in to stay with his mother, her family now come demanding her return.

Before the Fire premiered on March 7, 2020. At this point, the pandemic was in force, but the Trump White House was still debating whether the virus was a serious threat and the total death toll in the USA was only nineteen. Indeed, it was not until four days later that the World Health Organization officially listed Covid-19 as a pandemic. This makes *Before the Fire* an uncanny case of prediction.

It is interesting to contrast the predictions made by the film about a pandemic with the reality. The film overstates the socially devastating consequences —

showing panic as people attempt to flee the cities and the shutdown of domestic airlines. On the other hand, it fails to predict the key importance that was placed on avoiding transmission of infection by wearing masks and social distancing, not to mention the lunacy of the anti-masking brigade and bungling incompetence of the Trump White House's response.

The great disappointment of *Before the Fire* is that you could take the pandemic out of the film and very little of the story would be affected. It seems only there to give some kind of rationale to events. We never actually see anybody infected — after the arrival in Georgia, we get very brief scenes where local rednecks present some threat of infection and later we see abandoned military Humvees on the road but that is it. All of the actual drama is centred around the far less interesting plot of Jenna Lyng Adams (who also writes the screenplay) returning to the hometown where she grew up and being dragged back in by the redneck family she escaped.

The one other effort made before but released during the pandemic was the German TV series *Sløborn* (2020), which takes place over eight episodes. This has the distinction of being the very last work made in the model of a pandemic story influenced by Ebola and the avian bird flu.

The series takes place on the fictional island of Sløborn, located just off the north coast of Germany not far from the Danish border. It follows a diverse group of people on the island: a teenage girl who has just discovered she is pregnant to her teacher at the same time as her parents announce they are divorcing; the bullied teenage son of the police chief; a writer with substance addiction problems who has arrived on the island to deliver a lecture and is desperate for drugs and funds; a group of youths sentenced to jail who have been brought to the island on a work reform project by an ex-con, along with assorted others. An American yacht runs aground, and its passengers are found dead from the pigeon flu circling the world, but unwary teens have stolen valuables and carried the infection onto the island. Authorities arrive to contain the infection, but resistance begins as the island is about to be evacuated when it is discovered that the infected are being quarantined in death camps with no hope of survival.

While watching *Sløborn* in the midst of the Covid pandemic, what becomes evident soon into the series is that it is still drawing on a conception that was immediately outmoded by the time the show aired. The series' conception of a pandemic is drawn from the avian bird flu in all but name — it gets renamed the pigeon flu here and is said to be a mutated version of the avian bird flu that originated in India or China, and has a 100 percent fatality rate. The conception of transmission draws from the images established by *Contagion* — close-ups of hands touching contaminated surfaces and dipping into bowls of peanuts, people drinking from shared water and vodka bottles and the like. Unlike the real Covid pandemic, the belief is still that transmission will occur through surface contact as opposed to inhaled airborne particles.

There are still all the familiar images of authorities arriving in yellow contamination suits and quarantining the infected area. Although this has been one of the central images that we associate with depictions of outbreak on screen, when the real pandemic came there were almost no occasions where we saw this happening — with the exception of Wuhan and surrounding areas in China, no city areas were placed under quarantine.

Indeed, during the real world Covid pandemic, no areas were placed under martial law and no evacuation of personnel occurred, despite this being one of the recurring things that is always seen to happen during screen depictions of an outbreak. In many cases, what we saw was the exact opposite — that the apparatus of civil government had become cumbersome, and authorities were slow to act, allowing the virus to spread widely before any measures could be put in place to curb it.

Certainly, the series does predict some elements: stay-at-home orders and the implementation of contact tracing among the infected. On the other hand, when it comes to the scenes at the end where a group take over a church at gunpoint and the series champions those who defy authority and make a decision to stay on the island rather than be evacuated to death camps, it feels as though the show's makers are backing the wrong horse. In reality, those who stayed behind and defied quarantine would be the anti-maskers, the anti-vaxxers, and the Freedom Convoy truckers — groups that were castigated by the mainstream because of the extent to which their selfishness and ignorance endangered others — while the idea of government-established death camps is something that was relegated to the realms of Covid conspiracy theory. Indeed, what the film calls death camps was, more grimly, simply hospitals overrun with the infected.

Sløborn assembles its dramas with reasonable effect and brings them together at a dramatic climax. There are undeniably effective images in the latter scenes — like the grim scene when Emily Kusche breaks free and enters a ward to find it filled with the infected coughing blood everywhere and overrun by bodies to the point they are spilling onto the floor.

Sløborn was shot between August and December of 2019 but did not air until July 2020, right at the height of the first wave of the Covid-19 pandemic. At the point that the series was made, it is worth noting that most people in the western world had not experienced a real pandemic. Few were old enough to remember the Spanish flu epidemic; smallpox had its last recognized case in 1977; cholera has not travelled out of developing countries in the twentieth-century; Ebola and the avian bird flu never moved out of isolated regions of Africa and Asia; AIDS certainly spread around the world and was a concern but for many years was (wrongly) seen as being a disease that was confined to the gay community.

Sløborn can be considered a kind of demarcation point. Prior to it, every work has been a fictional representation of what *might* happen in a time of plague; not so the films and TV shows that follow it. Hereafter, such themes would be tackled by people who actually lived through a real-life pandemic.

CHAPTER 7

ASSORTED OTHER PANDEMICS

CHOLERA

Quarantined (1970) was a TV movie that aired on the US ABC network. The director Leo Penn had spent his time working in TV hospital dramas of the day, including episodes of *Dr Kildare* (1961–66), *Ben Casey* (1961–66), and *Marcus Welby M.D.* (1969–76), among other shows, and this simply seems an extension of these same earnest dramas.

The setting is a family-run hospital somewhere in rural California. It is the sort of amiable hospital that you could easily see located in Andy Griffith's Mayberry, where the personal touch and homespun decency always wins out and the handsome doctor (Gary Collins) personally lifts the actress patient (Susan Farrell) from her bed to her wheelchair and escorts her arm-in-arm to her waiting driver at the end.

There are assorted melodramas — a young boy who needs an operation; the actress who needs a kidney transplant (eventually provided by a fan who seems to have benign stalkery tendencies); and the youngest son of the family of doctors that run the hospital, who feels that his having attained a medical degree has still not earned him the respect of the rest of the family.

Amid these, the staff elects to place the hospital into quarantine after the boy's father collapses, infected with cholera. The biggest drama in the show is the surgical staff having to conduct the kidney transplant during the midst of a power cut. The actual outbreak is wrapped up with anticlimactic lack of drama — it simply being announced that there have been no new outbreaks for five days.

The entirety of *Quarantined* would be over in five minutes flat if the filmmakers had done even a modicum of research about the outbreak in question. Cholera is certainly a highly infectious disease. It emerges primarily from sources of drinking water contaminated by faeces. However, it is not a disease transmitted by person to person contact. In other words, the entire premise of the film — being placed in quarantine for fear of spreading infection — would disappear; the doctors should be less concerned with putting up a cordon and instead should be tracing the source of the infection, be it in the water or food the patients are consuming.

Death in Venice (1971) comes from Italian director Luchino Visconti. The film is set in the early years of the twentieth-century as German composer Gustav von Aschenbach (Dirk Bogarde) visits Venice for a health cure. In the hotel where he is staying, he becomes obsessed with a teenage boy (Björn Andresen) who is staying there with his family. The boy leads Bogarde on a taunting, possibly seductive, trail through the streets. At the same time, Bogarde becomes aware that the city is infected with a cholera epidemic and that the staff of the hotel and residents of the city are keeping this a secret.

Death in Venice is a beautifully made work. It received a special award at the Cannes film festival as well as being nominated for Best Film, Best Director, and Dirk Bogarde as Best Actor at that year's BAFTA Awards, while in recent years it has been celebrated as a gay classic.

Certainly, *Death in Venice* is an exquisitely made and photographed film — the architectural splendour of Venice; of rich old hotels in period dressing — against which the boy drifts as a seemingly impossible ideal of beauty. Counter to this sits imagery of death and decay — Dirk Bogarde with his undefined medical condition; the classical beauty of the city hiding the outbreak of cholera — we see the streets being sprayed in disinfectant and at one point what look like bodies being burned out in the open, giving the proceedings an almost apocalyptic air. And through this, Bogarde's pursuit of the boy becomes a dance, the boy's actions increasingly teasing.

The contrast is never made more apt than in the image of the aging Dirk Bogarde being given a makeover by a barber, putting on a buttonhole carnation, powdering and rouging his face in a grotesque attempt to seem more youthful as he goes forth in pursuit of his ideal of beauty, before expiring on a sun chair on the beach, his hair dye melting in ugly black streaks down his face, while the boy and his family play not far away.

Cholera also appears as a pandemic in the TV movie *Contagious* (1997), which is discussed in Chapter 5. Here, cholera is brought into the US via food served on a plane flight from Bogota. Like *Quarantined*, the film makes the mistake of trying to treat cholera as a disease that is transmissible from person to person.

SMALLPOX

The first depiction of a smallpox epidemic on screen occurred in *The Killer That Stalked New York* (1950), which is discussed in Chapter 1. This was one of the earliest depictions of a pandemic and was a fictionalized account of the real-life smallpox outbreak in New York in 1947 and the massive vaccination efforts undertaken by city authorities to combat this. Smallpox also briefly turns up in several episodes of the TV series *Survivors* (1975–77) (discussed in Chapter 4), an outbreak among a small group of people having otherwise survived a pandemic of a different sort.

The Yugoslav-made Variola Vera (1982) is based on the true-life smallpox epidemic that struck the country in 1972 (the last recorded outbreak of smallpox in Europe). The initial infection was brought into the country by an imam returning from a trip to the Middle East. The outbreak rapidly spread among the staff at the Belgrade hospital where he was admitted and out into the community. The government instituted martial law, quarantining some neighbourhoods and mounting a campaign to vaccinate the entire population. In total, 175 people were infected and thirty-five died.

This has similarities to other films, such as *93 Days* (2016) (discussed in Chapter 5), *Virus* (2019) discussed later in this chapter), *Chinese Doctors* (2021) and *This England* (2022) (discussed in Chapter 12) in depicting a true-life outbreak and efforts to contain it. (The title *Variola Vera* is the official Latin medical term for smallpox.)

While these other true-life films end up being nationalistic works that applaud the efforts of the medical staff to combat the epidemic, *Variola Vera* goes the other way with what appears to be an overwhelming cynicism. Without quite coming out and saying it, it holds an implied criticism of what would have been the Communist government of Yugoslavia at the time. The whole system seems in the process of running down — far fewer supplies of vaccine are delivered to the hospital than required, the majority of which ends up in the wrong hands (and veins).

The drama of the film is contained in the Belgrade hospital as it is placed under quarantine and the staff and patients confined inside. Rather than nobly struggling above and beyond the call of duty, as in other based-on-true-life films, everyone seems to be going stir crazy in isolation. We see doctors sexually assaulting nurses, nurses stealing medicines to support drug habits and staff horsing around. The outbreak is eventually quashed but it seems to happen in spite of anything the medical staff or government does.

Smallpox: Silent Weapon (2002) is a British-made mockumentary — a work of fiction that poses as a documentary — about a smallpox pandemic that spreads through the UK and USA with devastating impact, killing sixty million people. The film exists in two cuts: the two-hour long original and a truncated US version of eighty-nine minutes (the one seen here) that removes some of the British-set scenes to place the focus on an American family.

In vox pop fashion, numerous people are interviewed, ranging from survivors and those who lost family members, to doctors, FBI, and crisis management officials. What adds an uncanny realism is the mixing of actors alongside real-life figures such as Reverend Al Sharpton, BBC presenter Gavin Esler, and former Soviet microbiologist Ken Alibek.

It is worth noting that *Smallpox: Silent Weapon* was released only five months after 9/11, as well as the anthrax mail scare in the USA that occurred a matter of weeks after that (discussed in Chapter 3). As was the case with the anthrax scare, there was the eagerness of authorities to blame the outbreak on Middle Eastern terrorists. Here, the film sketches out an all-too-believable scenario in which the outbreak is seen as having originated from Russian biowarfare laboratories and unemployed biochemists eager to sell their services in the aftermath of the collapse of the Soviet Union. In the end, though, the film places the blame on an individual whose purposes and motives are deliberately left obscure.

This contains some uncanny reflections and predictions of the real-life Covid pandemic nearly two decades later. A surprising prediction that no other film has touched on is the importance of essential workers — the film here has transit employees protesting their need for vaccination because they are frontline workers. One aspect that becomes rather hilarious when contrasted with the Freedom Convoys in 2022, led by truckers in various countries against vaccine mandates, are the scenes with truckers protesting *in favour* of wanting to be vaccinated!

The film also predicts other aspects like stay-at-home orders — where we see some communities going so far as to board people up in their homes — and overwhelmed hospitals. Somewhat more in the realm of fiction is the lack of sufficient vaccines and the need to dilute existing supplies, leading to reduced efficacy in some cases.

Smallpox also appears in the *Containment* episode of the British TV series *Eleventh Hour* (2006) from Granada Television. The series consisted of four ninety-minute episodes, featuring Patrick Stewart as Ian Hood, a scientific advisor to the British government, who investigates various scientific mysteries accompanied by a special branch officer (Ashley Jensen). The series later underwent a US remake with *Eleventh Hour* (2008–09) with Rufus Sewell inheriting the role, which lasted for a single season of eighteen one-hour episodes.

This episode has Patrick Stewart investigating a worker on a church reconstruction project who has become infected. The cause is speculated as being everything from the bodies beneath the church to Chinese sweatshop workers. In his investigation, Stewart finds that the real cause is a refrigeration facility that allowed a series of smallpox-infected archaeological samples to thaw, releasing the disease to the wider community.

This is a solid story, driven by Patrick Stewart's charisma and moral authority.

You do a double-take at the lack of some quarantine procedures, including people handling samples and other materials with their bare hands. On the other hand, the episode does one of the best variants on the cliché of the person escaping quarantine and trying to return to his family. Particularly good is a scene where Patrick Stewart bars a door preventing the infected man (Michael Begley) from returning home: "I just want to see my children," Begley protests. "So does the virus inside you," Stewart retorts.

Milkmaids (2022) is an episode of the US anthology TV series *American Horror Stories*. The story takes place in 1757 in a pilgrim town that is beset by smallpox. Celeste (Julia Schlaepfer) is a prostitute who is infected but remains immune. Her customers come to her to suckle on the pus of her sores in the belief it will grant them immunity. She is viciously condemned by the pastor Walter (Seth Gabel) who believes he has discovered his own cure — eating the hearts of corpses — and inspires his congregation to indulge. Celeste falls in love with the milkmaid Delilah (Addison Timlin) who realizes that she and Celeste share an immunity due to having consumed cowpox vaccine from the milk.

The story has some basis in fact — cowpox, a virus that infects cattle and can be carried to humans, was once used as a vaccine against smallpox, although the episode has this happening some forty years before its use was first recorded. The episode primarily offers a horror focus — images of men suckling on pus-oozing sores, and the devouring of hearts taken from corpses. In between that, there is a biting critique of religious judgement and hypocrisy vs. scientific methodology.

BSE (MAD COW DISEASE)

BSE, or Bovine Spongiform Encephalopathy to give it the full technical name, more commonly Mad Cow Disease, is a disease that affects cattle. It is a neurodegenerative disease that eventually causes loss of motor function in the affected cattle. People eating meat from BSE-infected cattle can become affected by Creutzfeldt–Jakob Disease, which causes a series of mental degenerative conditions that are eventually fatal.

Natural Lies (1992) was a BBC TV miniseries in three one-hour episodes. Bob Peck plays a London advertising executive who learns that a friend has committed suicide. Disbelieving the official diagnosis, he digs deeper and believes that she was murdered due to her involvement with an environmentalist organization where she was endeavouring to expose a cover-up by the British meat industry over the fact that mad cow disease had entered the food chain.

Natural Lies falls far too much in the shadow of the BBC miniseries *Edge of Darkness* (1985), one of the great TV works of the 1980s in which Bob Peck played an almost identical character — a police inspector grieving the shooting of his daughter, an anti-nuclear activist, who then goes on a trail to find the persons responsible, which leads him into the shadowy corridors of power in the British government and their backroom deals with the nuclear power industry. *Natural Lies* substitutes a murdered friend and the British beef industry for Peck's daughter and the nuclear power industry, but both plots operate in very similar ways.

Natural Lies is more concerned with being a Wronged Man thriller — with Bob Peck seeking information from Manic Pixie Dream Girl Arkie Whiteley, finding her dead body dumped in his home and then forced to go on the run from police and hired killers — than with exposing the meat industry and dangers of BSE. Nevertheless, there is a fine scene where Peck invades a food industry conference to stand up with a slideshow display of meat industry practices that cause the assembled diners to start exiting en masse — a scene that can be guaranteed to leave a viewer contemplating wanting to give up meat-eating for life.

The miniseries was predictive in many ways. A mere two years after it came out, the British health authorities began to report cases of Creutzfeldt–Jakob disease found in humans, with the first death resulting from such in 1995. This led to the mass slaughter of infected cattle and bans placed on British beef around the world for a number of years after. More than 170 people in the UK died of Creutzfeldt-Jakob Disease in the two decades following.

VRSA (VANCOMYCIN-RESISTANT STAPHYLOCOCCUS AUREUS)

Vancomycin is an antibiotic drug used for dealing with life-threatening bacterial infections and is commonly used as the last resort in cases when other drugs do not work. There is a concern that some patients can develop a resistance to the use of vancomycin, leaving doctors with no means of combatting severe life-threatening diseases. One of those resistances comes from the bacteria Staphylococcus Aureus.

Another work influenced by *Edge of Darkness* was *Fields of Gold* (2002), a BBC miniseries in four one-hour episodes. This follows Phil Davis as a newspaper journalist and Anna Friel as his assigned photographer as they investigate what appears to be a series of suspicious deaths of patients under a doctor (Mark Strong) at a country hospital. The investigation leads to a conspiracy that has ties to big business and the halls of government. It becomes apparent that the doctor was conducting illicit trials of an experimental antibiotic yet to be officially approved, in an effort to combat a VRSA outbreak at the hospital. The plague is traced to a nearby farm where a company has grown an experimental strain of genetically modified wheat, and the discovery that the farmer (Max Beesley) has infected the crop as a protest against genetically modified foods.

This is an overly complicated plot — starting with an investigation into a doctor up to no good, onto illicit deals by Big Pharma and a government cover-up about an outbreak, to finally arrive at an anti-GM foods polemic that is delivered with the wild hysteria of a placard-waving protestor.

For the most part, this is a solid entry perhaps notable for a great cast including then unknown Benedict Cumberbatch as a junior reporter, not to mention Phil Davis giving one of the most venomously caustic and unlikeable lead performances that one has ever seen in a film or TV series.

NIPAH VIRUS

Nipah Virus is a zoonotic transmission (one passed to humans from animals). It is usually caught from fruit bats or pigs but can also be transmitted by contact with infected human patients. It produces fevers, disorientation and confusion, and in more severe cases seizures and encephalitis. According to the CDC, death occurs in forty to seventy percent of cases. There have been assorted outbreaks in India, Bangladesh, Malaysia, and South-East Asia since the virus was detected in 1999, with an estimated 100 fatalities.

Virus (2019) is an Indian-made film, not to be confused with other entries by that name, the post-apocalyptic *Virus* (1980) (discussed in Chapter 4) and the Ebola TV movie *Virus* (1996) (discussed in Chapter 5). Nor for that matter *Virus* (1999), in which Jamie Lee Curtis fights an alien bio-machine.

This is based on a true-life incident that occurred in the Kozhikode district of Kerala, India between May and June of 2018. The incident began when an infected patient was brought into a hospital and died soon after. The infection spread to a number of medical staff tending the patient and others with whom they had come into contact. A total of nineteen were infected, resulting in seventeen deaths before the virus was contained. The source was eventually traced to fruit bats.

Virus resembles *93 Days* (2016), about a true-life Ebola outbreak in Nigeria, discussed in Chapter 5. Both films chart a real-life outbreak that occurred in a community and follow through the initially detected cases, the medical response, and the ways in which civil authorities handled the crisis. As such, *Virus* keeps to the facts, figures and medical details and delivers a solid, no-nonsense depiction of the outbreak.

REAL WORLD PANDEMICS

AIDS AND HIV

AIDS and HIV are virally transmitted conditions, and the AIDS crisis of the 1980s and nineties is widely accepted as being a pandemic. On the other hand, it seems more difficult to slot films about AIDS under the same umbrella as those about the Black Death, Covid-19, Ebola, and bird flu. It may be telling that in all other texts on pandemic films, none, as of writing this book, mention films about AIDS.

The main difference, I suspect, is that films about the AIDS pandemic are almost always tragic stories about individuals struggling to keep going, whereas pandemic films are generally seen to be about attempts to combat an outbreak, and urgent containment situations. I am not aware of any film about the AIDS pandemic that breaks away from the personal approach for a medical or sociological perspective.

Another part might simply be bias — unconscious or otherwise — in that some critics see AIDS films as gay films and place them in a niche bracket. Regardless, there have been a number of non-gay AIDS films, such as *Boys on the Side* (1995) and *Precious* (2009). A by no means exhaustive list of excellent works about the AIDS pandemic would include *Longtime Companion* (1989), *The Living End* (1992), *And the Band Played On* (1993), *Philadelphia* (1993), *Jeffrey* (1995), *Rent* (2005), *Dallas Buyers Club* (2013), *The Normal Heart* (2014), *120 BPM* (2017), *Bohemian Rhapsody* (2018), and the TV miniseries *It's a Sin* (2021).

My personal favourite is the TV miniseries <u>Angels in America</u> (2003). Based on Tony Kushner's Pulitzer and Tony Award-winning play, it tells the story of several gay men in New York in the mid 1980s, with Al Pacino as real-life conservative politician Roy Cohn, who hid his condition. A surreal fantasia, it incorporates the appearance of ghosts, angels, and Mormon theology through some flat-out great writing.

ASSORTED HORROR TREATMENTS

<u>*Cabin Fever*</u> (2002) was the first film from Eli Roth, subsequently to establish himself as a leading horror director with *Hostel* (2005), *The Green Inferno* (2013), and other works.

The film concerns five college friends who go to a cabin in the woods for the weekend. Their idyll is interrupted when a strange man approaches the cabin, vomiting blood everywhere. They drive him off with guns and sticks — only for the man's body to fall into the nearby lake. In drinking the contaminated water, they are infected with a contagious, skin-eating disease.

This is an unapologetic horror film that quickly aims for blood-glistening shock images — Jordan Ladd with her face rotted to the teeth, vicious dog attacks,

An infected Najarra Townsend in *Contracted* (2013).

various bodily meltdowns — all overlaid with a wryly sarcastic sense of humour. Roth delivers two well directed scenes — one where Rider Strong finally gets to make it with Jordan Ladd only for his fingers probing down below to reveal a shock mass of blood and gore, and a sequence where Cerina Vincent shaves her legs in the bath and unwittingly starts gashing her sores open.

This was followed by two sequels: *Cabin Fever 2: Spring Fever* (2009), in which the infection is carried down river to a bottled water company and causes a prom to undergo meltdown, and *Cabin Fever: Patient Zero* (2014) set amid a bachelor party on an island in the Dominican Republic. Both of these sequels upped the amount of gore-drenched horror. *Cabin Fever* (2016) was a pointless remake of the original that entirely missed Roth's sense of humour.

In a similar vein, *Contracted* (2013) stars Najarra Townsend as an LA waitress who has drunken sex with a guy in the back of a car, only to wake up the next morning and find she is infected with something nasty.

This is a film built around Najarra Townsend's progressive physical collapse — at first rashes on the skin, then thickets of hair falling out from the back of her head, her nails falling out, her teeth rotting, and her eyes turning red and then yellow. The background of the film is constantly filled with imagery that suggests a link to sexually transmitted disease.

Contracted: Phase II (2015) was a sequel that follows Matt Mercer as one of Najarra's friends who becomes infected. This offers copious meltdowns and blood vomiting, but without even half the impact of the original.

On the low-budget side was *Epidemic* (2018), which takes place at a birthday party in Chesterbrook, Pennsylvania. Almost all of the action gives the impression it was simply shot in someone's house with non-professional actors. The virus (?) — it is not clear what it is — certainly operates with lethal effect and there are some gory meltdowns as people are contaminated and killed.

What it sorely lacks are explanations. The nearest we get to understanding the infection is a closet in a basement where Gina Destra finds a cubby hole into a small room where she accidentally smashes a container. What a lethal bio-agent is doing sitting in a regular suburban basement is never made clear.

PART THREE

PANDEMICS OF A MORE OUTLANDISH NATURE

PANDEMICS

of a More Outlandish Nature

Zombies overrun a shopping mall in *Dawn of the Dead* (1978).

CHAPTER 8

THE ZOMBIE APOCALYPSE

Zombies are creatures that have returned from the dead. On movie screens, the term 'zombie' has different meanings. The universally accepted version of the zombie these days is a reanimated corpse that has returned to life, mindless and hungry for the flesh of the living. It was not always that way, but this characterization has come to eclipse all other usages of the term.

The word 'zombie' originated in West African voodoo. In voodoo, a zombie is supposedly a person who is reanimated from the dead by ritual and blankly shuffles about. Initially spelt 'zombi', the term was first recorded in Brazil by the poet Robert Southey in 1819. It entered English usage during the 1920s with several US newspaper articles, closely followed by books offering sensationalized accounts of Caribbean voodoo rituals.

The first screen depiction of a zombie appeared not long after *White Zombie* (1932) – where it was a creature animated by voodoo. Here and in other depictions for a number of years, the zombie was seen as dull, slowly shuffling, and mindless, often under the control of another person – either a voodoo practitioner or a mad scientist, or even alien invaders as in *Plan 9 from Outer Space* (1959). There was little in these voodoo zombie portrayals about the resurrected dead coming out of their graves and certainly no flesh-eating aspect. This depiction stayed with the horror genre for the next three decades.

Things changed with George Romero's *Night of the Living Dead* (1968), an apocalyptic film in which the dead everywhere return to life. It is crucial to note that the term zombie is not used in the film itself but was applied afterwards – coined by the magazine *Cahiers du Cinema* – and stuck. *Night of the Living Dead* gave birth to a vast industry of films in which the zombie has returned from the dead due to a viral or biowarfare outbreak, or scientific accident – in Romero's film, it is as a result of a virus brought back by a Venus space probe.

The crucial elements that Romero added were that the zombies were an aggregate attacking force, that they were hungry for the flesh of the living, and that only a bullet to the head or destruction of the brain could stop them. In the films that followed, the zombie outbreak is frequently depicted as being apocalyptic in nature and spelling the end of society. Since 1968, the zombie film has become overloaded with hundreds of entries, both serious and comedic. Many cities around the world even hold annual Zombie Walks where attendees dress in makeup and costume and stumble through the streets.

It should be stressed that not all zombie films are about viral outbreaks and pandemics. There are plentiful examples where zombies are created by supernatural means, as in *The Evil Dead* (1981), or where no explanation is offered at all. Nevertheless, the analogy between viral pandemic and the zombie apocalypse is not lost — many works have the zombies caused by viral outbreak or biowarfare spill, while others draw connections between the zombie bite and the spread of infection.

The zombie film has become overloaded with such a vast shuffling (occasionally fast-moving) horde of entries that this book would quadruple in size if one were to list all of them, even if we reduce the list to only those that feature viral pandemics. So rather than overweigh the book with discussions about zombie films, what I has opted for is an overview of the genre and a listing of major and significant examples.

THE BEGINNINGS OF THE MODERN ZOMBIE FILM

The voodoo zombie does not concern us here so we will begin discussion with George A. Romero's Night of the Living Dead (1968), the work that created the modern depiction of the zombie as a stumbling, flesh-eating figure. The plot centres around a group of people who take refuge in a farmhouse as the dead begin rising from their graves. This becomes an apocalyptic siege as the farmhouse is surrounded by the dead who are trying to break in and devour them — although just as much threat is presented by the bickering amongst those inside over the best means of survival.

The film was shot on a $114,000 budget outside Pittsburgh by Romero, who had previously only directed commercials. The result has the stark power of a social parable. The bleakness of the ending where Duane Jones survives the night and emerges to greet the sheriff's posse, only to be shot by them as a zombie, is an absolute classic. Many have since read the film as an allegory for either Vietnam protests, civil rights protests, or the youth rebellion of the 1960s, embodying the era's sense of society coming to devour itself.

Night of the Living Dead proved highly influential and became a cult film within a short space of time. It saw several sequels (discussed below) and copies, although the zombie genre we all recognize did not fully gain its feet for another decade.

A VIEWING GUIDE TO THE PANDEMIC

Depictions of Plague and Pandemic on Film and TV

"They're coming to get you, Barbara." Zombies on the prowl in *Night of the Living Dead* (1968).

One of the oddities that came in the immediate aftermath of *Night of the Living Dead* worth mentioning was *I Drink Your Blood* (1970). This concerns a group of hippies known as The Sons and Daughters of Satan. After the Sons and Daughters force-feed his grandfather a tab of LSD, young Pete (Riley Mills) swears vengeance and takes a syringe of the blood from a rabid dog, injects it into meat pies, and gives these to the hippies. This causes the hippies to become rabid and go on a killing rampage. The film ends with the hippies in a showdown against redneck construction workers who are also infected with rabies.

A decade after the original, George Romero followed *Night of the Living Dead* with *Dawn of the Dead* (1978). This focuses on four survivors who take refuge from the zombies in a shopping mall. Here, the stark Vietnam-era nightmare of the original has turned into a siege that is often broadly comedic. The film is a satire on modern consumerism — rather than bickering over the best means of survival, the survivors find all the material wealth they want and revel in the luxury offered inside the mall, while the dead gather outside, ineffectually pressing against the closed doors. The group's idyll is overturned when a group of bikers discover the mall and invade their consumerist paradise.

The crucial thing that Romero did for the zombie film with *Dawn of the Dead* was to introduce copious gore and splatter delivered at previously unseen levels. The fun of the film is watching the numerous creative ways in which zombies are dispatched thanks to what were then state of the art makeup effects created by Tom Savini. This made Savini a cult figure and spawned an industry of makeup effects-driven films that proceeded to take over the horror genre throughout the 1980s. It is from here that the real popularity of zombie films started to grow.

Romero subsequently returned to zombies with Day of the Dead (1985), which contains his best writing of the series. This is a frightening parable that takes place among a group of survivors gathered in a vast underground bunker where the tensions between military and civilians, and the one woman of the group, sit on a hair trigger. At the same time, a full-blown mad scientist experiments with finding ways to humanize the zombies in a lab.

Tom Savini's gore effects are at their most polished, the razor tensions and confrontations that come in the dialogue and performances are electrifying. In the midst of this, we start to see some humanizing of the zombies — in particular, the character of Bub (played by Howard Sherman) who dimly recalls aspects of his past life.

However, *Day of the Dead* was only a middling box-office success and Romero abandoned further plans to make more zombie films for another two decades. In the interim, Romero did oversee a passable colour remake of the original film in the trilogy with Night of the Living Dead (1990), directed by effects man Tom Savini.

Around the same time, there was Return of the Living Dead (1985). This emerged out of a complicated legal split between Romero and his co-writer/co-producers over ownership of the title *Night of the Living Dead*. The others sold their half of the copyright, and it ended up in the directorial hands of Dan O'Bannon, the screenwriter of *Alien* (1979) and *Lifeforce* (1985) (discussed in Chapter 9).

O'Bannon gives Romero's original a hilarious black comedy spin and a furious punk soundtrack. The film is set at a mortuary where the characters accidentally release a canister of military nerve gas that was supposedly the inspiration for the zombies in *Night of the Living Dead*, only for the dead to return to life and overrun the morgue and neighbouring cemetery.

The film is noted for coining the idea of fast-moving zombies and their chanting of the word "brains!" This also spawned several sequels with the unfunny *Return of the Living Dead Part II* (1988) and the quite interesting *Return of the Living Dead III* (1993), plus a couple of shabby revivals in the 2000s.

The most enthusiastic country to leap on the bandwagon created by Romero's zombies was Italy, which produced a host of ultra-gory zombie copycats during the early 1980s. The first of these was Lucio Fulci's Zombi 2 (1979). *Dawn of the Dead* had been titled *Zombi* in Italy and Fulci's film was released with a title that posed as a sequel, although it was renamed *Zombie Flesh Eaters* for English language release. The film deals with an outbreak after a ship filled with zombies sails into

New York. A group heads to a Caribbean island in search of where the zombies originated. Mostly, the film is notable for some extremely gory scenes, including a zombie wrestling with and devouring a shark.

The oddest among these Italian copies was Cannibal Apocalypse aka Cannibals in the Streets (Apocalisse Domani) (1980). John Saxon plays a Green Beret who returns home from the Vietnam War to find one of his colleagues (John Morghen) has gone on a killing spree, biting people. Morghen has contracted a virus that causes the infectee and anyone they bite to become cannibalistic. The cause is traced back to their imprisonment in a Viet Cong village. Beyond a novel approach, this does little more than focus on gory cannibalism scenes.

Another entry among these Italian films was Hell of the Living Dead aka Zombie Creeping Flesh (Virus: L'Inferno dei Morti Viventi) (1980), which is a routine entry in all regards, about people encountering an outbreak in Papua New Guinea. The original Italian title, which translates as *Virus: Hell of the Living Dead*, gives the misleading impression that this is a film about a viral zombie apocalypse whereas the zombies are in fact created by a chemical spill.

However, the film is significant for other reasons. Forty years later it was re-edited by Charles Band with a rifftrack (redubbing movies with comedy lines) as *Corona Zombies* (2020) (discussed in Chapter 12) and became the first film to be released during the Covid-19 pandemic. The zombie outbreak was rewritten as being due to the coronavirus.

THE 2000S REVIVAL

The zombie film underwent a massive revival in the 2000s. The first of these was Resident Evil (2002), based on the Capcom video game that first appeared in 1996 and has to date spawned more than twenty-five sequels and spinoffs. *Resident Evil* drew from the George Romero 'Dead' films and was the first of what subsequently became referred to as survival horror games, in which players fought zombies amid a great deal of gore and splatter.

The film version of *Resident Evil* opens with an amnesiac Alice (Milla Jovovich) waking up in a mansion with no memory of who she is. Armed soldiers arrive and drag her with them down into the laboratory complex of the Umbrella Corporation located beneath the mansion. There, they discover that the corporation's AI, the Red Queen, has gone amok, unleashing the T-Virus, which has turned all in the complex into zombies and assorted mutants.

The film was a success and generated a surprising number of sequels with *Resident Evil: Apocalypse* (2004), *Resident Evil: Extinction* (2007), *Resident Evil: Afterlife* (2010), *Resident Evil: Retribution* (2012), and *Resident Evil: The Final*

Chapter (2016), as well as a prequel/reboot *Resident Evil: Welcome to Raccoon City* (2021), with all but the last featuring Milla Jovovich. Paul W.S. Anderson, a director known primarily for other videogame adaptations such as *Mortal Kombat* (1995) and *Monster Hunter* (2020), directed all but the second and third films of the series. There were also three anime films with *Resident Evil: Degeneration* (2008), *Resident Evil: Damnation* (2012), and *Resident Evil: Vendetta* (2017), as well as the anime TV series *Resident Evil: Infinite Darkness* (2021) and a live-action TV series *Resident Evil* (2022).

The *Resident Evil* films take place with minimal plot. They consist of assorted action set-pieces with Milla Jovovich (usually) in kick-ass action mode taking on a series of zombies, and increasingly larger mutations, in action that moves out from the Umbrella Corporation laboratory to the surrounding Raccoon City and eventually the entire post-apocalyptic world. The films have little beyond action poses and monster scenes — it often feels that what happens is interchangeable and the films can be viewed in any order. That said, they are among the most popular of all the films covered in this book in terms of box-office revenue.

The film that led the way in the zombie revival of the 2000s was <u>28 Days Later</u> (2002) from British director Danny Boyle, best known for works like *Trainspotting* (1996) and *Slumdog Millionaire* (2008), with a script from Alex Garland who went on to direct *Ex Machina* (2015), *Men* (2022), and *Civil War* (2024).

The film takes place as animal rights activists break into a research laboratory and free a group of monkeys infected with the deadly Rage virus. Twenty-eight days later, Jim (Cillian Murphy), a bicycle courier who was struck in a hit-and-run, comes out of a coma, only to find the hospital and the rest of London deserted. Society has collapsed and the city is overrun by the infected who have been turned into maddened, red-eyed zombies. The film follows Cillian and a handful of survivors as they try to make it to safety.

28 Days Later is a film that draws much on what has gone before. It falls very much into a genre of post-apocalyptic films about survivors making their way through deserted cities. Most notedly, the scenes with Cillian Murphy waking up in hospital and exiting into a deserted London invite comparison with John Wyndham's novel *The Day of the Triffids* (1951), which has influenced a number of works in this book and opens as a man wakes from an eye operation to find all of London deserted and the survivors blinded.

Even more so, the second half of the film — the scenes with the civilians entering a military enclave; the soldiers verbally harassing the women of the group; and the zombie kept chained up for experimental purposes — has been directly lifted from George Romero's *Day of the Dead*. Danny Boyle offers up images of the survivors raiding supermarkets and leaving useless credit cards behind to pay for everything — while amusing, you cannot help but be reminded of the far more potent images of the survivors in an abandoned shopping mall in *Dawn of the Dead*.

The zombie scenes are shot in fast edits that make the action seem blurred and hard to follow. Boyle does a decent job of sustaining suspense, particularly during a hair-raising scene in a tunnel where the group try to change the tire on a taxi as the zombies close in.

There is little discussion of the nature of the virus — the notion of an infection that can cause an entire metabolic change in the space of ten seconds is medically ludicrous. The end of the film buys into the wish-fulfillment notion that underlies many survivalist films, of an almost miraculous restoration of the status quo, but this is so generic that we never even learn where the fighter plane that flies over at the end comes from.

28 Days Later is a passable revival of zombie themes, although I am in a minority opinion in preferring the sequel 28 Weeks Later (2007), where Spanish director Juan Carlos Fresnadillo inherits the director's chair. This is set during the attempted reconstruction of society, only for the Rage-infected to breach a Green Zone that has been erected around London. The assorted scenes of people fleeing for their lives amid zombies spilling over everywhere are handled with a great deal of seat-edge tension.

Another big hit of this era was the remake of Dawn of the Dead (2004). This was the first film from Zack Snyder who has subsequently become a high-profile director of comicbook adaptations such as *300* (2007), *Watchmen* (2009), *Man of Steel* (2013), *Batman V Superman: Dawn of Justice* (2016), and *Justice League* (2017), along with one unrelated zombie film, *Army of the Dead* (2021). It also has a script from James Gunn, who subsequently became a director known for Marvel's *Guardians of the Galaxy* films and *The Suicide Squad* (2021).

Like the original, the film is centred around a group of characters who take refuge in a mall from the zombie horde outside. The character complement is upped from four to fifteen, the invading bikers are dropped, and the zombies are now fast-moving. What is more noticeable is that the film becomes merely a survival drama — dropped entirely is Romero's satire where the survivors built their own materialist utopia inside the mall. The parade of novelty gore effects that made the original a cult hit has also been watered down. The 2004 *Dawn of the Dead* was a disappointment, but it did herald a massive revival of the zombie film.

This revival brought renewed focus on George Romero. Since then, almost every possible connection to Romero and his original trilogy of zombie films has been rehashed in some way. There have been two crappy remakes of *Day of the Dead* plus a sequel and a TV series, while *Return of the Living Dead* was revived for two tatty sequels. Romero had earlier overseen the 1990 remake of *Night of the Living Dead* and there were two further cheap remakes. Due to *Night of the Living Dead* being in the public domain due to lapsed copyright, there have also been a number of films

PANDEMICS

of a More Outlandish Nature

with connection in title only making spurious claim to be sequels and prequels, even *Night of the Living Dead: Reanimated* (2009), which retells the original and is comprised of fan-contributed animated clips and artwork, and an animated remake *Night of the Animated Dead* (2021).

Romero himself was brought back to make three other zombie films with *Land of the Dead* (2005), *Diary of the Dead* (2007), and *Survival of the Dead* (2009). The best of these was *Diary of the Dead*, which retells the outbreak of the zombie apocalypse in terms of a found footage film. In *Land of the Dead,* Romero returns to social satire and digs his teeth into conservative America, with Dennis Hopper leading a group of the entitled in a walled enclave that has shut the zombies out. Both *Land of the Dead* and *Survival of the Dead* end with the hard to accept argument that the dead and the living have equal right to coexist.

An enormous success that contributed to the popularity of zombie films during the 2010s was the US TV series *The Walking Dead* (2010–22). This follows a diverse group of characters in the Atlanta area through the initial aftermath of the apocalypse, and their efforts to create a shelter — in a farmhouse, in an abandoned prison, and eventually as three different neighbouring communities. At the same time, they are fighting the vast army of the dead that lurks outside. This is alongside other human threats in the form of marauders, cannibals, and militant groups, as well as dissent from within the communities, which often proves as deadly as the massed horde of undead.

The series never gives us any origins of the outbreak. However, towards the end of the second season, we meet a scientist who reveals that the zombies are created by a dormant virus in the human brain that is activated after death, bringing the body back to life.

While most individual zombie films have slid into repetitive moves or self-parody in the 2010s, the advantage of *The Walking Dead* is that it takes place as a fierce survival drama among an ongoing ensemble of characters. It is, if you like, *Survivors* but with the addition of zombies — although unlike *Survivors,* it takes the group until the sixth season to set up their own community and attempt to reconstruct some type of society. Unfortunately, after around the ninth season, the series started to taper off. Due to a rapidly growing cast, characters would not turn up for half a season, leaving you struggling to remember whether or not they had been killed.

The popularity of the zombie film in the 2000/2010s has led to an enormous outpouring of films even when restricting the list solely to those that have some direct pandemic theme. A sampling of titles that do might include the Irish zombie film Dead Meat (2004) where the zombies are created by an outbreak of mad cow disease; Flight of the Living Dead: Outbreak on a Plane (2007) set aboard a plane as it is overrun by zombies created by a mutated malaria virus; Against the Dark (2009) with Steven Seagal pitted against blood-drinking zombies; and World War Z (2013), a big-budget film with Brad Pitt in a globe-trotting chase to find the source of the infection and an eventual cure.

One oddity that specifically tied itself to real world pandemics was the Hong Kong-made Ebola Zombies (2015). The plot centres around a group of criminals who mount a heist on a jewellery store. As this goes wrong, they pursue the fleeing staff into the neighbouring rooms where a scientist is experimenting to create a cure for SARS (which, we are amusingly told, stands for Sudden Aggressive Reanimated Syndrome) and to a lesser extent Ebola, during the course of which he has found a way to reanimate the dead. Expectedly, the zombies he has created escape to overrun the city. The film contains several minutes of footage from the pro-democracy protests in Hong Kong (against rule by mainland China), creating an interesting political metaphor between the populace and zombies: "If we can't control what we do, how different are we from living corpses?"

COMEDY TREATMENTS AND THE GONZO ZOMBIE FILM

Into the 1990s, the zombie film began to increasingly head in the direction of comedy approaches — a move that began with *Return of the Living Dead*. One of the key films — in fact, the ultimate zombie comedy — was Peter Jackson's Braindead (1992) (released as *Dead Alive* in the US). Set in New Zealand in the 1950s, it features a zombie outbreak that begins after Tim Balme's dear mum (Elizabeth Moody) receives a bite from a Sumatran rat monkey while on a visit to the zoo. Balme cannot bear the thought of burying her and brings her home, a

Tim Balme surrounded by zombies in Peter Jackson's *Braindead* (1992).

decision which proceeds to go sideways with catastrophic results.

The film features record levels of gore and bloodshed, including a transcendentally surreal scene where Tim Balme wades into battle against the zombies armed with a lawnmower, drenching an entire room in showers of blood.

The film and its wilfully absurd sense of humour has to be seen to be believed. It is Peter Jackson in his early days and is far more fun than many of his subsequent, CGI-heavy, works where his desire to be taken seriously as a filmmaker or to experiment with new technology started to weigh down his films.

It is worth touching on the odd entry among these comedy treatments. There was the charming British entry *Harold's Going Stiff* (2011) in which men across the country have been infected with Onset Rigor Disease, which causes their joints to stiffen and their mental faculties to degenerate, while at more advanced levels they become crazed and attack others. The image of zombies treated as seniors and placed in a geriatric home is rather delightful. Another appealing effort was the US-made *Cooties* (2014) where the teachers at a high school are forced to lay siege as a group of schoolchildren become infected and go on the attack.

Night of Something Strange (2016) is a low-budget entry that feels like a film made by a bunch of drunken adolescents trying to out-gross each other after an all-weekend beer party. The film's one interesting distinction is that the zombie infection is a sexually transmitted disease. There are assorted gross scenes where this is depicted.

Amid this, there has also been the rise of what one might term the gonzo zombie film — works that opt for deliberately ridiculous titles, puns, or incongruous conceptual mashups where zombies are thrown together with the most unlikely things. The feeling you get with most of these is that the limited number of plots available to the regular zombie film has become so creatively exhausted that filmmakers are left turning to wilfully absurd combinations in a desire for some novelty.

Some of these gonzo zombie films that can be included here are the insistently crass *Poultrygeist: Night of the Chicken Dead* (2006) from Troma Films where the infection is carried by mutant chickens; the Japanese-made *Attack Girls' Swim Team vs. the Undead* (2007) featuring a girls high school swim team fighting against zombies; *Attack of the Vegan Zombies!* (2009) where the zombies are created by infected wine; the popular mainstream comedy *Scouts Guide to the Zombie Apocalypse* (2015); and *Attack of the Southern Fried Zombies* (2017) involving zombies created by an experimental serum to curb runway foliage.

Shaun of the Dead (2004) from Edgar Wright and co-writer/star Simon Pegg is very much a tongue-in-cheek affair. While the film fails to give an origin for its pandemic and thus falls outside the remit for this book, it can be considered the mainspring of the modern comedy zombie film.

NEW AND ORIGINAL TREATMENTS

Amidst this, there have also been some highly original works. One of these was the Canadian-made *Pontypool* (2008) from director Bruce McDonald. This is set at a radio station in the tiny titular Ontario town. During the morning broadcast, DJ Stephen McHattie receives reports of locals who are becoming crazed and attacking others. It is explained that the townspeople are infected with a virus that hides inside certain words of the English language. The infectee initially stumbles over and then mindlessly repeats words, before becoming a zombie that needs to attack others to pass on the virus. As the infected surround the studio, McHattie and his crew take siege and continue broadcasting, knowing that the very words he uses could also transmit the virus to the outside world.

This is the zombie apocalypse creatively reconceived in terms of meme theory — an idea popularized by scientists like Richard Dawkins and Susan Blackmore that regards certain concepts as akin to biological organisms (such as viruses) that

PANDEMICS
of a More Outlandish Nature

Radio DJ Stephen McHattie in *Pontypool* (2008).

pass from mind to mind. The film comes with effectively contained tension, all before the rather amusing climax where McHattie resolves the problem by switching to speaking in French. (This plays out more amusingly in Canada where the country is divided linguistically and culturally between French-speaking Quebec and English-speaking regions everywhere else.)

Another interesting effort was the Spanish *[Rec]* (2007) made by directors Jaume Balaguero and Paco Plaza. This is a found footage film that follows a news team as they profile a local fire station and follow the firefighters on a callout to an apartment building. As the group arrives, the apartment is hit by a zombie infection among the tenants, which rapidly spreads throughout the building. With a great deal of frenzied tension, the film follows the camera crew as they try to survive while they are locked inside as the authorities quarantine the building.

The novelty of *[Rec]* is that it borrows from the zombie film in every way and yet the eventual explanation comes down to a case of demonic possession. The original infection comes from a priest in one of the apartments who had isolated the virus from a possessed girl. The film performs an odd conceptual juggling act that tries to mix a spiritual condition (demonic possession) with an infection spread by saliva and treated as contamination by authorities.

[Rec] was an international hit and Jaume Balaguero and Paco Plaza made three Spanish-language sequels between them with *[Rec]²* (2009), *[Rec]³: Genesis* (2012), and *[Rec]⁴: Apocalypse* (2014). There was also an English language remake with *Quarantine* (2008).

A VIEWING GUIDE TO THE PANDEMIC

Depictions of Plague and Pandemic on Film and TV

Amid the massive onslaught of zombie films during the 2000s/2010s, there have been some strong and intelligent entries worthy of note. *Maggie* (2015) is a low-key effort with Arnold Schwarzenegger in a surprisingly serious, non-action role as a family man who is trying to maintain a semblance of normality and protect his daughter (Abigail Breslin), who is affected by the Necroambulist Virus that is slowly turning her into a zombie.

The Girl With All the Gifts (2016) is one of the most unique. It takes place at a military enclave in England where the zombie apocalypse rages outside. Within the base, there are a group of children that are intelligent but also have a hunger for human flesh and are forced to wear muzzles. As the zombies overrun the enclave, a party of soldiers make an escape along with one of the children (Sennia Nanua). The journey becomes an extraordinary one where the group's reaction to what is a zombie is turned on its head and we come to be affected by the humanity that Sennia displays.

Here Alone (2016) is an unusual effort, much of it a one-person film focused on Lucy Walters as she tries to survive on her own in the woods. We get the impression that society has collapsed following an unspecified pandemic. We follow her attempts to create shelter, scavenge food, and create a tentative connection with a father and his daughter that she meets. It is only gradually that the film starts to pull back and reveal it is a zombie film.

A similar approach was taken by the Danish-made *What We Become (Sorgenfri)* (2015), which is set in a sleepy residential neighbourhood in Sorgenfri, just north of Copenhagen. Authorities abruptly arrive and wall the area off, declaring a pandemic. Residents are ordered to stay inside their homes at gunpoint, and those that try to escape are shot. This wheels into play the usual imagery of the pandemic film: the neighbourhood being quarantined, SWAT teams prowling the streets and shooting those who try to make an escape, and houses being covered in plastic. It is only near the end that it becomes apparent that the infection is a zombie outbreak.

Cargo (2017) was an affecting Australian-made entry with Martin Freeman as a father crossing the Australian Outback with an infant daughter in a backpack. After receiving the zombie bite, he has forty-eight hours before he succumbs and tries to spend his remaining time finding a home for his daughter.

One of the most conceptually ingenious of these films was the Irish-made The Cured (2017). The film is set in Dublin after the world has been devastated by a zombie plague called the Maze Virus. A cure has been found that is effective in seventy-five percent of cases — the downside of this is that those cured return to life remembering everything they did as zombies. The film follows one of the Cured (Sam Kelley) as he tries to slot back into life, facing prejudice against his kind all around — he was a barrister but is now forced to do only menial work as a cleaner. He moves in with his brother's wife (Ellen Page), keeping it a secret that he killed and ate his brother.

There have been several zombie works to emerge out of the era of the Covid pandemic with *Corona Zombies* (2020) (see Chapter 12), *Covid-21: Lethal Virus* (2021), and *Virus: 32* (2022) (see Chapter 14), although most of these are simply regular zombie films with a virus/pandemic slapped on. The one major work to adapt to the Covid era was the South Korean Happiness (2020), a twelve episode TV series that aired on Netflix.

In the latter half of the 2010s, the South Korean zombie film exploded on screens following the international hit of the ferociously entertaining *Train to Busan* (2016). The pandemic era also brought *#Alive* (2020), a charming film about the relationship that forms between a guy and girl trapped in different apartments on either side of a street during a zombie apocalypse, and the hit TV series *All Of Us Are Dead* (2022–). However, none of these offer any explanations for the origin of their respective zombie outbreaks.

Happiness concerns Next, a new brand of cold pill released during the Covid pandemic, which has the unintended effect of turning those that take it into a zombie. This is a different zombie than most — one that is triggered by drinking water leading to the desire to devour human blood, although some of the infected are able to control this and appear normal.

The series borrows the basic premise of *Cordon* or *Containment* (both discussed in Chapter 6). The setting is an apartment building where authorities have cordoned off the area and nobody is allowed in or out. Those trapped inside include two police officers who have gotten married so as to qualify for a decent apartment; a doctor who has just used the pretext of the zombie outbreak to murder his wife; a lawyer; a social media influencer; a man who remains behind a mask throughout before being revealed to be a wanted serial killer in later episodes; and the building's janitorial staff. As with *Cordon/Containment*, it seems that the authorities monitoring the situation are duplicitous and may be responsible for deliberately unleashing the contaminant while using the quarantine zone as a giant experiment.

As with *Cordon/Containment*, it seems that once people are locked inside these quarantine zones it is the standard practice for the authorities to abandon them without even basic provisions. As a result, much of the series centres around the tenants' squabbles over food and water supplies. Here, the film approaches something of the savage apocalyptic social satire of *High-Rise* (2015) with the development of a hierarchy between those in the more expensive apartments on the higher floors and the janitorial staff who are stranded in the building. Some of the best episodes centre around the vicious in-fighting over resources between groups or of the scheming by the murderous doctor to wipe out evidence of his crimes by letting the zombies in.

CHAPTER 9

VAMPIRISM AS PANDEMIC

The vampire is a fictional character that originates in folklore and mythology. It is a human being that has returned from the dead and preys on human blood. It is immortal unless killed. It has vulnerabilities to the crucifix, daylight, and holy water and can be dispatched by being staked through the heart. Its appearance is with fangs and very pale skin, sometimes with red eyes. It can be handsome or voluptuous, or rat-like and cadaverous. In certain interpretations, it has even been known to sparkle. It can wield great hypnotic abilities on its victims and transform into bats, wolves, and other animals.

The vampire appears in many world mythologies. There is the common misconception that Bram Stoker created the vampire, which is not the case, but he did popularize it in his novel *Dracula* (1897). In his novel, Stoker brought together a series of disparate elements from folklore to lay down the key aspects of what have since come to be regarded as vampire lore—the vampire's aversion to crucifixes, the need to kill it with a stake through the heart, its coming from Transylvania, and the need to live in a coffin of its native earth. Some films change various aspects of this or strip out the supernatural elements and offer medical/scientific explanations, but these aspects remain at the core of what is accepted as vampire lore.

The iconic image of the vampire in dinner suit and cape with a thick East European accent, was created with Bela Lugosi in Universal's *Dracula* (1931), which was the second Hollywood vampire film and the fourth vampire film made in all. This is the image of the vampire that has remained in the public imagination, despite hundreds of other treatments, and is one that has been much copied and parodied.

The vampire film certainly has overlap with the general umbrella of the films discussed here. It is adjacent to the zombie film (discussed in Chapter 8) in that both feature former human beings resurrected from the dead who pass their respective infection on to others via a bite. However, while a great many zombie films easily slot into being plague and pandemic films and frequently adopt the imagery of pandemic cinema, vampire films almost never do.

A VIEWING GUIDE TO THE PANDEMIC

Depictions of Plague and Pandemic on Film and TV

Klaus Kinski's Dracula feasts on Isabelle Adjani's neck in *Nosferatu the Vampyre* (1979).

The zombie stumbles about and infects anybody it bites. In contrast, the vampire is more selective — in most vampire films, the focus is on the process whereby the vampire targets who it bites, or else on those fighting against the vampire. The metaphor that the vampire film operates on is less one of an apocalyptic society-wide outbreak than it is of sexual seduction (although this is not always the case). It is difficult, for example, to conceive of a vampire film where, instead of being armed with stakes and crucifixes, the vampire hunters come outfitted with syringes and contamination suits. The obvious pandemic-related metaphor for vampirism would surely have been AIDS and sexually-transmitted disease but, while literary scholars have discussed the links between vampirism and sexually-transmitted disease in Stoker's novel, no films have taken up the challenge to explore likewise.

The second vampire film ever made was the German Nosferatu (Nosferatu — Eine Symphonie des Grauens) (1922) from director F.W. Murnau (who is discussed in Chapter 4). This was an unauthorized adaptation of Bram Stoker's *Dracula*. Stoker's widow sued and demanded that all copies of the film be destroyed, although prints did survive and give us one of the great early vampire films. *Nosferatu* is now regarded as one of the classics of the German Expressionist era.

Stoker's version of *Dracula* concerns the eponymous count from Transylvania who relocates to England where he preys on the wives of a group of Englishmen, transforming them into vampires. The novel, and most film adaptations of *Dracula,* are vehicles for much sexual metaphor about adultery (Dracula preys on other men's wives), repressed female sexuality in the Victorian era (one of the things Dracula does is make the women much more voluptuous and wanton), and the breaking of taboos.

In *Nosferatu,* however, Murnau drops all the sexual metaphors of the vampire. Max Schreck plays a character who is renamed Count Orlok. He is made up to resemble a rat — bald and pale-faced, with protruding ears, exaggerated eyebrows, two extended front teeth, and a spindly gait. Schreck wears a long black mandarin coat and keeps his hands with their six-inch fingernails in front of him.

Murnau creates a mood that feels as though the film has stepped over into a twilight zone where a medieval worldview still prevails. Here, Dracula is not seen as a sensual seducer but as a figure associated with the Black Death — he arrives in the sleepy town of Bremen accompanied by hordes of rats, while his devouring of the blood of the locals is akin to the spread of the plague.

These images of Dracula as a metaphor for the plague are retained in Werner Herzog's worthwhile remake, Nosferatu the Vampyre (1979). Around this time, the German-born Herzog had gained a reputation as a director who would go to extraordinary lengths to make films such as *Aguirre, The Wrath of God* (1977) and *Fitzcarraldo* (1982), in which he trekked into the Amazonian rainforest, recruiting native tribes as extras, building entire settlements, and winching a ship over the side of a mountain.

In Herzog's version of *Nosferatu*, his regular collaborator Klaus Kinski inherits the Max Schreck role. The crepuscular look of the character is still retained but Herzog was able to openly call the character Dracula due to the novel now being in the public domain. In contrast to Murnau, Herzog makes a far more realistic film. He drops Murnau's medieval worldview and any sense of Dracula as a supernatural being. He does retain Murnau's imagery of Dracula as a metaphor for the plague, being surrounded by an army of rats that overrun the sleepy town of Bremen.

Most vampire films are of the supernatural variety and do not concern us here. There is the odd one that is of interest in regard to our discussion. One of these is Lifeforce (1985), which comes from Tobe Hooper, director of *The Texas Chain Saw Massacre* (1974) and *Poltergeist* (1982), with a script from Dan O'Bannon, the author of *Alien* (1979) and director of *Return of the Living Dead* (1985) (discussed in Chapter 8).

Lifeforce is a conceptually audacious reimagining of the vampire film. It concerns a space shuttle mission to Halley's Comet that discovers an alien ship containing hundreds of bodies in suspended animation. Things go wrong after the shuttle crew return with three of the alien bodies. The aliens turn out to be vampires that devour human lifeforce and can hop between bodies, reducing their victims to withered husks unless they suck the souls of others.

This is one of the few vampire films that deploys the imagery of pandemic as we see the vampire infection spread to cover London within a matter of hours — even the British Prime Minister is shown furtively vampirizing his secretary behind a filing cabinet!

I AM LEGEND

One of the more interestingly exotic vampiric outbreaks is the one that occurs in Richard Matheson's novel *I Am Legend* (1954) and the three films adapted from it. During his lifetime (1926–2013), Matheson was a renowned science-fiction, horror and fantasy author who was responsible for *The Incredible Shrinking Man* (1957), the book that became Vincent Ward's *What Dreams May Come* (1998), the screenplays for most of the Roger Corman's Edgar Allan Poe films, and assorted episodes of the original *Twilight Zone* (1959–63) and *Star Trek* (1966–69), among a good many other works.

I Am Legend concerns Robert Neville, who appears to be the last man left alive on Earth after a plague has turned everybody else into vampires. By day, Neville scours the city, searching for nests of the vampires and staking them, while trying to research the nature of the plague. By night, he barricades himself in his home, which he keeps covered in garlic and crucifixes, as the vampires gather outside, pleading with him to come out and join them. Eventually he is captured and sentenced to be executed, going off with the realization that he will now be seen by this new breed of vampires as a mythological monster in the same way that he perceives them — the 'legend' of the book's title. Or as *Station Eleven* (2021–22) (see Chapter 14) puts it: "to the monsters, we are monsters."

The first film adaptation of *I Am Legend* was The Last Man on Earth (1964) starring Vincent Price as Robert Neville (changed to Morgan for the film). This was shot in Italy and came with a script from Richard Matheson, who was dissatisfied with the result and substituted the pseudonym Logan Swanson. (This is unrelated to the earlier pandemic film of the same title *The Last Man on Earth* [1924], discussed in Chapter 11.)

The Last Man on Earth is generally regarded as a disappointment, although it is more interesting than most people credit it. It changes some minor aspects and pads the one-person drama out with some flashbacks to before the outbreak, including turning Neville/Morgan into a biochemist who creates a cure to the plague (something retained by all the other film versions). It is also the only faithful adaptation of the book to date, as well as the only version that keeps the

Robert Neville (Vincent Price) stakes vampires in *The Last Man on Earth* (1964).

remarkable end twist intact.

The Last Man on Earth works in occasional moments. There is an effectiveness to the ritual that Vincent Price goes through in the opening scenes, replacing the garlic and mirrors around the house, sharpening stakes on a lathe, replenishing his supply of garlic out of the walk-in freezer of a department store and staking various vampires throughout the city, then returning home and taking a nap before his alarm goes off and he gets up to see the vampires gathered outside calling "come out, come out". It is a near perfect adaptation of the opening scenes of the book.

What nearly kills the film is Sidney Salkow's dull direction. The vampires seem a weak threat. The film does have an undeniable atmosphere and moodiness during the outdoor locations (shot in Rome), which are aided a great deal by the B&W photography. On the other hand, none of this takes us inside the protagonist's loneliness and internal struggle. There is nothing of the paranoid sense in the book of a man isolated and alone, hounded nightly by the vampires' taunts for him to come out to them.

Vincent Price also seems miscast — his fruity overwrought hand-wringing style of acting is not suited to the part. Neville is an internal role with almost no dialogue, a character who is consumed by loneliness, not something suited to Price's very theatrical form of anguish.

Charlton Heston in *The Omega Man* (1971).

The second version of *I Am Legend* was The Omega Man (1971) from director Boris Sagal. The film is set in 1975 with Charlton Heston inheriting the role of Robert Neville. This is a radically different story to the one in Matheson's book and *The Last Man on Earth*. It is as though vampires were considered too much of a B-movie concept by the producers — as a result they have been eliminated and rewritten as mutants that shun the sunlight.

The mutants are now also conceived as a cult that wants to destroy all remnants of technology, this change no doubt being inspired by the public fascination with Charles Manson: the trial of the cult leader and his followers, the so-called Family, had only completed its sentencing four months before the film came out. The film even borrows the name for its own cult, The Family. It makes no real sense. It is difficult to see what prevents the mutants from simply breaking into Neville's home — in the book they are unable to do so because of garlic and mirrors.

The film keeps and expands on the idea introduced in *The Last Man on Earth* that Neville was a biochemist who created a cure for the plague and survived because he injected himself with it. Now there is also a plot about Charlton Heston encountering another survivor (Rosalind Cash), a subplot that does come from the book, although here he uses his blood to provide a vaccine.

Boris Sagal does a reasonable job of creating a sense of isolation as Heston prowls the empty streets of Los Angeles. The film opens on a great series of images — panoramic wide-angle views looking down from the sky on the deserted streets; Heston's car breaking down and him simply taking a brand new one from a showroom, driving through the plate glass window; imagining hearing telephones ringing in his head; an armoured car left open and abandoned with useless money blowing in the wind.

On the other hand, the film casts Heston in square-jawed hero mode. As a result, we get no sense of Neville's loneliness and despair. Instead, we get Heston dressing for dinner in a velvet frock coat and making wisecracks with a bust of Caesar over a game of chess. This feels like a betrayal of the book, where Neville was someone utterly haunted by loneliness. We do get scenes of the mutants begging Neville to come out but no corresponding sense of his utter isolation.

The film plays on our association with Heston as star of 1950s Biblical movies, ending with him dying in a Christ-like crucifixion pose where his blood has symbolically been shed to save the world in the form of the vaccine he has synthesized. Elsewhere it's a different sort of Heston: at one point he sits in an abandoned cinema watching and reminiscing over *Woodstock* (1970). Here, and in other scenes, the film seems to tap into the politics of the love generation with Paul Koslo as an *Easy Rider* (1969)-type biker anti-hero, or Rosalind Cash with bandana and machine-gun drawing an association with the Black Power movement. The interesting idea the film offers is in saying that civilization has fallen and that the hope of the future lies in political radicals and anti-establishment youth figures of the 1960s — ironic given the ultra-conservative political stance taken by Heston in his later years.

The third film version of the book was *I Am Legend* (2007) with Will Smith cast as Robert Neville, the sole human left alive in New York City after a reengineered virus that was designed to eliminate cancer has instead killed off humanity and turned the survivors into mutant creatures.

Though this is the only film version to return to the title of the book, it is more a remake of *The Omega Man* than an actual adaptation of Richard Matheson's book. The various changes that *The Omega Man* made to the novel have been retained — the vampires being replaced by mutants that have an allergy to light, and Neville being a former military officer who comes up with an antidote and survives because he injects himself with it.

Indeed, this feels like a film written by people who have never even read the book. It becomes the old question of — if they bought the rights to a book and threw most of it out, then why not just write their own original work? What we have is *I Am Legend* reimagined in terms of the then-recent success of *28 Days Later* (2002) (discussed in Chapter 8).

One of the most potent images of the novel was the image of the last man on Earth locked in his home as the vampires gathered outside each night, inviting him to come out to them. Even *The Omega Man* kept that, but it is missing here. Indeed, the mutants even fail to find Will Smith's home until the very end. The essence of Matheson's book is its sense of one man defending himself against the world outside his door; the film is now only a story about a man hiding and hoping that the mutants don't find where he lives. Indeed, Will Smith's Neville is such an all-round nice guy that this version fails to even give us any scenes of him tracking down and eliminating the mutants.

Director Francis Lawrence (who later went on to handle the *Hunger Games* sequels) and the visual effects team take maximum opportunity to depict a devastated New York City with various landmarks lying in ruins or overgrown. There is one glorious image of Smith shooting golf balls off the wing of a fighter plane on the deck of an abandoned aircraft carrier. There is also the captivating opening scene with Smith hunting a deer with a rifle in a sports car through the streets and into Central Park, before lions emerge to pounce on his target.

The film also ends as *The Omega Man* did, with Neville sacrificing himself so his blood can save humanity. It's an absurdly optimistic end, one where we see survivor Alice Braga (in the equivalent of the Rosalind Cash role) entering the gates of an enclave and being welcomed by other survivors in a perfect small town USA setting beyond. One can also note that when the film explains the title 'I Am Legend' in the end voiceover narration, it completely reverses it from what it meant in the book. In the book, what it meant was that in his campaign to eliminate the vampires Neville was now a legend to the new race of vampires, in the same sense that the vampire was regarded as a mythic monster by humanity; here, it is merely taken to mean that Neville is a legend in the heroic sense of having sacrificed his life to save humanity.

RECENT TAKES

An interesting attempt to offer a science-fictional explanation for the vampire was Ultraviolet (2006). This comes from Kurt Wimmer, a screenwriter known for *Sphere* (1998), *The Thomas Crown Affair* (1999), *Salt* (2010), and the remakes of *Total Recall* (2012) and *Point Break* (2015), as well as previously directing the dystopian film *Equilibrium* (2002).

The film is set in the future following an outbreak of the experimental HGV virus, which has caused some of the population to mutate into what are called Hemophages that have vampire-like characteristics. The human populace placed most of the Hemophages in concentration camps but those that have survived have formed a rebel underground. Milla Jovovich of *Resident Evil* fame plays Violet Song Jat Shariff, a Hemophage rebel who comes into possession of a 'package' — a human boy who carries a virus that will eliminate all the Hemophages when released. Much action ensues in a fight between rebels and authorities over possession of the package.

This is a film that comes with a conceptually challenging story and some great world-building. The main problem is that the distributors reportedly hacked something like twenty minutes of footage out of the film, dropping much in the way of reference to vampires.

All that remains is a stunningly designed film that can be mostly noted for its preposterous action sequences — like when Milla Jovovich is engaged in a motorcycle chase and operates an anti-gravity device that allows her to race horizontally along the side of a building at a ninety degree angle to the street, before zooming vertically up the building where she smashes through a helicopter and the windows of the building opposite. Or of Milla standing in the midst of gunfire and remaining untouched while she shoots down her opponents by the dozens as they seem to stand still to be attacked.

V-Wars (2019) was a US TV series based on a 2014–15 IDW comicbook series by Jonathan Maberry and Alan Robinson. The series ran on Netflix for ten episodes before being cancelled. The storyline features Ian Somerhalder as a scientist who discovers the existence of a vampire virus that has been uncovered in the Arctic as a result of melting polar ice caps. This rapidly spreads until humanity is pitted in a full-on war with the vampires. After his friend becomes one of the first infected, Somerhalder joins assorted vampire hunters while struggling to contain the virus and find a cure.

This emerged as a tedious mix of modern vampire movie clichés plus elements that were being set up for an ongoing series that never ended up being resolved. Even a few episodes into the show, it became apparent that nobody in the writing department cared about consistency or basic believability and the rest seemed to coast along on recycled clichés.

Coming out at the same time as *V-Wars* was *The Passage* (2019), based on a trilogy of books by Justin Cronin. This aired on the Fox network and suffered a similar fate in being cancelled after ten episodes. Henry Ian Cusick is a scientist who runs Project Noah, conducting experiments (originally to cure his dementia-ridden wife) with a virus taken from a creature found in a cave in Bolivia. The virus miraculously cures all diseases but turns infectees into vampires, which are referred to as virals. Ten-year-old orphan Saniyya Sidney is chosen as a test subject. However, Mark Paul Gosselaar, the FBI agent tasked with protecting Saniyya, rebels and goes on the run with her. The death row inmates who were being used as test subjects for the virus break free and the infection spreads.

This has the same problems as *V-Wars* did — a variety of characters set up only for the show to be abruptly curtailed leaving unresolved plot strands — although it is the better made of the two. Cronin's books have an ambitious arc that stretches between the present and ninety-three years in the future where the virals have overrun the world, but the series never makes it beyond the present.

Vampire Virus (2020) comes from Charlie Steeds, a British director who has made a reasonable output of modest B-budget horror entries. This feels like a work that was made as a regular vampire film and had mention of a virus added to it to take advantage of the topicality of the Covid-19 pandemic when it came out.

The film features Natalie Martins as a modern girl who is dragged off for a night out by her girlfriends in the hope of spicing up her dull stay-at-home life. In a nightclub, she is seduced by the exotic Jessica Alonzo, a nurse who was bitten by a girl in a Romanian asylum in the opening scenes. Natalie wakes up the next morning with a black infection growing from a cut on her stomach that leaves her with vampire-like symptoms. It turns out that Jessica is also wanted by the police for a series of vampire killings across the city and is trying to build an army of vampires.

This is a standard vampire movie with the addition of some steamy eroticism that barely tiptoes up to a PG-rated line. The oddness is seeing the traditional elements of vampirism conflated with the idea of vampirism as a virus — where the infection on Natalie's stomach also apparently leaves her with the ability to cast no reflection, for instance.

The era of the Covid pandemic brought one other vampire film with Vampirus (2022). This takes place in Chicago during the first thirty days of the lockdown. Ashley Marie Jones plays a vampire who rents an apartment and is befriended by her upstairs neighbour (Michael Holding). He wants to pursue a relationship with her. After discovering her secret, he persuades her to let him aid her in procuring victims for the blood she needs.

This is another micro-budgeted film, a number of which were made by enterprising filmmakers during the pandemic, and it is better than many of the others. It should be clarified that this is not a film where vampirism is treated as a viral contagion but simply a kitchen sink work about a vampire living during the pandemic.

Vampirus seems made without much of a plot and most of it appears to have been improvised, which ends up being a little too freeform to work. Certainly, Ashley Marie Jones has great presence, including a unique second-person perspective where she breaks the fourth wall to directly address the viewer. On the other hand, Michael Holding seems to talk in an endless blather that strains patience. (Not to mention, he goes most of the way through the film masked up but wearing it beneath his nose, which has precisely the same effect as wearing no mask at all.) That said, director Ryan Ohm brings everything together for an undeniably grim and effective ending.

CHAPTER 10

MASS INSANITY OUTBREAKS

This chapter discusses a body of films that deal with outbreaks of mass insanity among the populace. Not all of the explanations for the mass insanity that occur in these films implicate viral outbreaks — there are a number of other works not included here that give the cause as everything from toxic waste to environmental leaks.

The mass insanity outbreak genre began with *The Crazies* (1973), which was the fourth film directed by George A. Romero, creator of the modern zombie film with *Night of the Living Dead* (1968) (discussed in Chapter 8). *The Crazies* is one of the most underrated of Romero's work.

The film is set in Evans City, Pennsylvania. Soldiers arrive, quickly establish martial law and round up the populace in the high school. It is revealed that a military plane went down in the area a few days earlier and released a viral bioweapon that drives people insane. The contaminant has sunk down into the artesian wells where it has infected the town's water system. As the townspeople start to become infected, five people try to escape to freedom but their efforts face disruption from within as members of the group start to succumb to the virus's effects.

Romero propels us through the scenario with a grim urgency. The film is filled with some great shock images — the grandmother who sits knitting and then smilingly turns to stab one of her needles into an enquiring soldier; the priest who sets himself on fire; or the little child watching as her mother is shot and then torched by soldiers.

However, the most impressive images in the film become the internal psychological horrors — the subtlety that comes in watching the party's inner weakening — of the gung ho relish with which one of the group starts shooting up soldiers; or when another starts raving about protecting his daughter from men and is then found trying to molest her himself; and how the daughter starts flirting with a ring of soldiers who simply shoot her when she refuses to stop.

The end of the film emulates the same black irony that came in the classic ending of *Night of the Living Dead*. W.G. MacMillan discovers he has natural immunity and disguises himself in a contamination suit to get past the soldiers, only to be shot at by crazies thinking he is a real soldier. He is then thrown in the high school but dismissed by the medics. "Shall we check this one for immunities?" "Are you kidding?" Meanwhile, the only person who does discover an antidote ends up being shot, thought to be a rioter.

The film later underwent a remake as The Crazies (2010), which expanded Romero's original with a big budget, special effects, and a recognizable name cast. This repeats the same essential plot of a town (relocated to an Iowa farming community) that is placed under martial law by soldiers in contamination suits following a plane crash that has spilled a contaminant into the town water supply.

On the other hand, new director Breck Eisner has no real interest in depicting any outbreak of mass insanity. Eisner's emphasis is less on the psychological manifestations of madness and far more on gory dispatches — shooting in the head, people cut up with a surgical saw, pitchforked, and so on. There is nothing as effective or disturbing as the scenes in the original, with the old lady with the knitting needle, or the girl flirting with soldiers as she is gunned down. In fact, what we have seems no more than a regular zombie film. The bleak ending of the original has been dropped in favour of something more upbeat — despite the entire town being obliterated by a nuclear weapon, the protagonists survive when they are blown free in a semi-trailer cab.

The second film on the topic of mass insanity was *Impulse* (1984) in which Meg Tilly returns to her hometown in the Midwestern US. Here she discovers the townspeople are being affected by a contamination that is breaking down inhibitions and causing eruptions of bizarre, violent behaviour everywhere — a man breaks his fingers because Meg will not dance with him, the sheriff starts shooting at a mischief-making kid with a semi-automatic rifle. While this is an effective, low-key entry in the genre, the explanation here is a toxic waste leak that has been unleashed following an earthquake and thus it falls outside the purview of pandemic films.

Next up was *Warning Sign* (1985), which comes from Hal Barwood and Matthew Robbins, two former Steven Spielberg associates who branched out on their own to write and direct a number of films together, the best of these being the Disney dragon film *Dragonslayer* (1981) and the cute UFO film *Batteries Not Included* (1987).

The film takes place at the BioTek agronomic research lab in Utah, which is secretly a front for a facility conducting bacteriological warfare research. A test tube containing a deadly virus ends up being accidentally knocked onto the floor in a lab and the contents released as it is trodden underfoot. As a biohazard alert is triggered, security head Kathleen Quinlan is forced to seal the establishment off, leaving some ninety people trapped inside. The military enter the facility to find the virus has infected the research staff and turned them into crazed killers.

PANDEMICS

of a More Outlandish Nature

While *Warning Sign* was pegged as a zombie film in its day, it feels as though it has been conceived as a conceptual amalgamation of *The Crazies* and *The Andromeda Strain* (1971) (discussed in Chapter 1). It begins deceptively, starting out as though it is a hard science-driven drama in the vein of *The Andromeda Strain*, detailing the technical minutiae of the decontamination procedures, the biohazard security procedures, and so forth. None of this is particularly original if one has seen other films in this genre but director Hal Barwood moves it along with fine thriller pacing.

About the halfway point, Barwood turns everything on its head and *Warning Sign* becomes a horror film. The introduction of the infected crazies comes in a series of eerily suspenseful moves — a video monitor showing a lab previously filled with dead bodies to now be empty; a security camera closing in on a circuit box as a chillingly understated voice comes from off-screen, "It's awfully bright in here. The light hurts my eyes," whereupon an axe crashes into the box and the screen goes black.

As the military team enters the lab complex, there is the eerie sense of not knowing what it is they will encounter. The film develops an undeniable effectiveness in the scene where the team encounter head scientist Richard Dysart standing at the end of a corridor, all of which is effectively contrasted with the insistence from the voices of the people in the monitoring van over the radio urging them to retreat, before the scene erupts into frenzied chaos.

Primal Rage (1988) was an Italian-made horror film shot on location in the US. Mitch Watson is a crusading campus newspaper journalist — he comes out with lines like "gonzo journalism is like eating without a colon — you don't know how it is going to come out". In search of an article, Mitch breaks into the laboratory where Bo Svenson's professor has been conducting experiments in an attempt to regenerate brain tissue. However, the flash from the camera causes the baboon that Svenson has been experimenting on to panic and bite Mitch. Infected with the Rage Virus, Mitch stumbles across the campus where the infection causes him to erupt in bursts of violent temper and attack others. Those he bites in turn become infected and the virus rapidly spreads among the students.

I cover the Italian zombie film in Chapter 8 dealing with the zombie apocalypse. This is a zombie film in all but name, where the emphasis is on gory meltdowns and dispatches. The name of the virus — Rage — may well have inspired *28 Days Later* (2002), which is covered in Chapter 8. Otherwise, this is a negligible treatment.

Alien Cargo (1999) is an Australian-made production in which Jason London and Missy Crider play crewmembers and lovers who are awoken out of cryogenic suspension aboard a spaceship travelling from Titan to Mars. They find that they have been asleep for a year rather than several weeks and that the other crew members are missing. They quickly find themselves at one another's throats, trying to kill each other. They discover this to be due to the other crew members bringing on board an infection of alien origin that turns the human brain homicidal.

Dead Air (2009) was a directorial outing from actor Corbin Bernsen, best known for his regular role on TV's *L.A. Law* (1986–94). The film features Bill Moseley as a popular radio talk show host who is live on air as Middle Eastern terrorists release a deadly airborne viral agent that causes those infected to start bleeding from the eyes and then begin frenziedly attacking others. Moseley keeps broadcasting as the studio comes under attack by the infected. *Pontypool* (discussed in Chapter 8) did a far better job of conducting the same premise and this is no more than another zombie film.

Salvage (2009) is a British entry set in Liverpool. The story follows several domestic dramas — principally teenager Linzey Cocker's upset at walking in on her mother (Neve McIntosh) having sex with a man she picked up at a bar — before these are abruptly turned on their heads as soldiers surround the area and everybody is ordered to stay inside their homes. The soldiers are dealing with a threat that may have emerged from a shipping container found washed up on a nearby beach and is infecting people, turning them into crazed killers. This starts extremely well but falters — we are never given enough explanation for what is going on, nor a clear idea of the threat people are facing.

Patient Zero (2012) is a US film from director Brian T. Jaynes and follows Brandon Slagle and Amanda Phillips as a couple who both work at an agricultural research laboratory. They settle in for a regular workday only for a contamination breach to occur and the laboratory to be sealed off. During the course of this, Amanda learns that the agricultural research laboratory is a front for the US Department of Defense. Scientists at the laboratory have developed a virus that causes people to frenziedly kill everybody they come into contact with.

This is a solid set-up that seems like a low-budget version of the much superior *Warning Sign*. The main problem is that the film does nothing remarkable with the scenes of the outbreak and develops little tension out of people being attacked by crazed infectees or the attempts to escape the facility.

Truth (2014) is a low-budget film from director Michael Cramer. William McNamara is a professor at a New Mexico university who offers a group of students extra credit to go hiking with video cameras to investigate a mysterious abandoned hospital that does not register on satellite photos of the area. What they do not know is that this is the site where prisoners were taken from an early 2000s government experiment with the nanotech-engineered virus Veritas PVH-13. The virus was designed to get Guantanamo Bay prisoners to tell the truth — something that proved extremely successful for the first forty-eight hours before having drastic side effects. The students wake up the following morning to find the hospital surrounded by armed soldiers who shoot anybody who exits the building. As they try to find a way out, they begin to be affected by the virus.

Steve Yuen faces mass insanity in an office building in *Mayhem* (2017).

From the opening credits that play out over a montage of 9/11 news clips, amid mention of CIA-enhanced interrogation techniques and Guantanamo prisoners, not to mention a bold declarative title like *Truth*, there is the feeling that the film has travelled well into conspiracy theory territory.

All the talk about truth-telling viruses leads you to imagine something like an epidemic version of *Liar Liar* (1997), a comedy where Jim Carrey was the recipient of a curse that forced him to be honest. In actuality, what we get is just a regular mass insanity film where the truth-telling virus does no more than bring out people's true selves. The film never does a particularly good job of making the idea work. Much of the latter half simply concerns various members of the group running around the abandoned hospital trying to find a means to escape.

GLEEFUL MAYHEM

Mayhem (2017) is demented fun. It comes from Joe Lynch, who has mostly worked in the horror genre. The film follows Steven Yuen as a corporate lawyer who is fired after finding his boss has framed him for refusing to take the fall for her screw-up. Just as he is about to be evicted from the premises by security, the building is surrounded by SWAT teams. It has been discovered that ID7, a virus that breaks down people's inhibitions and allows them to give in to every impulse, has been released into the ventilation system. In rapid course, the people in the building descend into violence and anarchy as Yuen and client Samantha Weaving seek to escape.

While the other films included here are works of horror about the unaffected fighting those who have succumbed, this throws back its heels and has fun. Joe Lynch and his cast launch into the mayhem with a great deal of relish. Steven Yuen and Samantha Weaving seem to be having the time of their lives stalking about the office fighting off the infected with nail guns, hammers, power saws, and screwdrivers.

An equal amount of fun can be had with *Mom & Dad* (2017) from Brian Taylor, previously the co-director of the *Crank* films as one-half of the partnership known as Neveldine-Taylor. This concerns an outbreak that is spreading across the US, causing parents to start trying to kill their children.

The film is filled with jolt scenes like that of parents waiting outside the school gates and then abruptly tearing apart one child who scales the fence, before bursting onto the sports field en masse and attacking their children — including visions of one father suffocating his daughter with a plastic bin liner and another parent impaling their child with a flag marker.

The background of the film is littered with other such moments — a delivery room scene where a woman gives birth and immediately wants to kill the baby; the mother in the street who shoves her child in a stroller out into the path of a car.

The film features Nicolas Cage in full crazy man mode and Selma Blair as his wife. The story follows their two children (Anne Winters and Zackary Arthur) under siege in the cellar as Cage and Blair are trying to cut down the door with saws or hooking up the gas to suffocate them. There is an appealing black humour to the film — like when grandparents Lance Henriksen and Marilyn Dodds Frank turn up and go from reacting in horror at people attacking a child, to then almost immediately trying to kill them.

The sole mass insanity film of the Covid pandemic era has been the Taiwanese-made *The Sadness (Ku Bei)* (2021). This follows a couple (Berant Zhu and Regina Leu) who go about their day amid warnings on the news about the outbreak of the Alvin Virus.

After driving her to work on his scooter, Berant stops off at a cafe where an elderly woman abruptly throws cooking fat over the chef's face and then tears his melting flesh off with her fingers, while in the background one diner stabs another with a fork. Out on the street, a motorist gleefully runs the elderly woman down at the same time as people jump out of the windows of apartment buildings. Back home, Berant is attacked by the neighbour who snips his fingers off with garden shears.

Things become even more extreme as Regina takes the subway home, where an outbreak ends up with the entire subway car drenched in blood. She helps a fellow passenger who has been stabbed in the eye get to a hospital only for the ER room to erupt into mayhem amid which the staff engage in an orgy covered in blood. Even the Taiwanese President is shown forcing a hand grenade into a rival's mouth during a live press conference.

Like *Mayhem* and *Mom & Dad*, this is a horror film that goes for the throat. Director Rob Jabbaz pushes everything to a brutal and blood-drenched extreme, with highly entertaining results.

CHAPTER 11
MORE EXOTIC OUTBREAKS

PANDEMICS THAT ELIMINATE ONE OF THE GENDERS

The silent The Last Man on Earth (1924) — not to be confused with the Vincent Price-starring *The Last Man on Earth* (1964) discussed in Chapter 9 — was the first film on the topic of the world in the aftermath of a pandemic. It was also the first film on the theme of one or other genders being wiped out by a virus.

The Last Man on Earth and its remake are among a handful of films discussed in the book where I have not been able to find viewing copies. In matters of description, I bow to Wikipedia and the Internet Movie Database.

The film features Earle Foxe as a man who proposes to a woman who turns him down, saying she wouldn't marry him if he was "the last man on Earth." Foxe departs for a remote island to get over the rebuff only for the rest of the world to be struck by a plague known as masculitis, which kills off all males. Ten years later, Foxe is found and brought back to civilization. There, he immediately becomes a prized asset, fought over by the women who have taken over society in the absence of men. At the end of the film, he reunites with the woman who earlier rejected him, and they happily settle down together.

Everything is played as a comedy based around making fun of traditional gender roles. As the first film to depict the world in the aftermath of a pandemic, it is not particularly auspicious. Nevertheless, the theme of a plague that wipes out gender lines has played out in a number of other works since then, both comical and serious.

The Last Man on Earth underwent a sound remake as *It's Great to Be Alive* (1933) where this time it became a musical. Raul Roulien inherited the role of the last man on Earth who is now an aviator who crashes in the South Pacific, while Gloria Stuart, later of *Titanic* (1997) fame, played the love interest.

The next entry was *Percy's Progress* (1974) (released in the US as *It's Not the Size That Counts*). This was the sequel to the earlier British sex comedy *Percy* (1971). In the first film, Hywel Bennett receives the world's first penis transplant and then undertakes a series of softcore romps as he sets out on a quest to find out the donor of his new member.

In the sequel, Leigh Lawson takes over the role of Percy, who has decided to escape the constant pressures of female attention by heading out to sea aboard a yacht. While he is away, a US bomber containing the PX-123 toxin explodes over the ocean, infecting the world's water supplies and making all men impotent. After a year at sea subsisting on champagne, Percy returns to land the only virile man left on Earth, whereupon his penis becomes a prized asset sought by every nation, not to mention every woman, in the world.

In other works such as *Light of My Life* and *Y: The Last Man* (both discussed below), the premise of the last man or woman left on Earth (or at least the last fertile one) has served as the basis of a series of stark future scenarios. Here the film is merely an opportunity to throw in as many atrocious double entendres as possible in between Leigh Lawson engaging in assorted bedroom romps.

It would be seventy-five years between *The Last Man on Earth* and the first serious treatment of the theme with the US TV movie *The Last Man on Planet Earth* (1999). This is set sometime in the future after a bioweapon employed during a Middle Eastern war, intended to wipe out all enemy combatants on the battlefield with a Y chromosome, ended up spreading and killing off all men on the planet. The remaining few unaffected men were regarded as violent and dangerous and either hunted down or placed in quarantine zones.

Amid this, Julie Bowen plays a scientist driven by her curiosity (she spends her free time languishing in hologram fantasies of incredibly buff men) who decides to genetically engineer the first man seen in many years. The man (Paul Francis) becomes the source of much fear and is hunted by law enforcement, at the same time as being sought by the curious, and at one point even imprisoned as a sex worker in a brothel.

Written by Kenneth Biller, a former producer on 1990s *Star Trek* TV series, this has a fairly solid set-up — indeed, the idea of an all-woman world where everybody with a Y chromosome has been wiped out prefigures the *Y: The Last Man* comicbook (discussed below) by several years.

The main problem with the film is that it has been produced as typical US TV movie filler. It has been afforded a medium budget, and a perfectly okay cast, but all of the dramatics and the social scenario of such a world are delivered with the uninspired hand of a conveyor belt TV director.

On a more serious level, there was the standout *Light of My Life* (2019) directed, written by and starring actor Casey Affleck (the younger brother of the better-known Ben Affleck). The setting is several years after the collapse of society due to the QT Virus, which has killed off all women. Casey plays a father whose daughter Anna Pniowsky has remained unaffected. The two live in the woods where he insists that

A VIEWING GUIDE TO THE PANDEMIC

Depictions of Plague and Pandemic on Film and TV

Casey Affleck and daughter Anna Pniowsky in *Light of My Life* (2019).

she cut her hair short and introduces her to everybody as his son. However, in their attempts to find refuge, her existence is discovered and draws the attention of others.

Casey Affleck creates a beautiful story of a father and daughter. We are reminded of the relationship between father and son in the not dissimilar post-apocalyptic *The Road* (2009), although I would argue that Affleck actually does a better job of crafting the relationship between parent and child.

The film is shot with a soft tenderness — often in two shots, or scenes filmed by candlelight. Affleck is eccentric enough to give us a twelve-minute long opening scene that is an almost entirely unbroken shot looking down on him and Anna Pniowsky lying side-by-side in a tent as he tells a highly creative interpretation of the story of Noah's Ark. Many of the scenes are just Affleck turning the camera on himself — one of the best of these is a hilarious scene that goes on for several minutes as he awkwardly tries to tell Anna Pniowsky about the birds and the bees.

It becomes a subtle film with many small and understated touches. Affleck keeps details about what happened to a minimum. We piece things together from the newspaper headlines, where we learn that all of the women in the world have been killed. It is only after we see this that other touches early in the show — Casey Affleck's insistence to the man they meet in the woods that Anna Pniowsky is his son and the man's casually tossed-off comment "that's a comely boy" — become apparent. The dialogue is often surprisingly thoughtful, not to mention Affleck offers up the nicest carjacking ever depicted on screen.

Light of My Life came out just two months before Only (2019), which takes place after a comet has brought a worldwide cloud of ash that has caused all women to become infected and die. This has a near-identical plot in which Leslie Odom, Jr. tries to keep his still alive wife, Frieda Pinto, a secret. The two films could almost be sequel/prequel — *Only* is set during and in the immediate aftermath of the outbreak, while *Light of My Life* is set following the collapse of society.

The idea of the comet passing by causing a worldwide catastrophe is another example of an idea lifted from John Wyndham's *The Day of the Triffids* (1951) — a plague of blindness for Wyndham, the death of all women here. The script is a little vague on the details — it is not exactly clear, for instance, how we go from debris in the wake of a comet to a worldwide plague that is transmitted by men. The science nitpicker in me also tends to think that the amount of ash we see coming down would leave such an amount of particulate matter in the atmosphere that it would have far more serious environmental consequences, akin to the oft-theorized nuclear winter.

Only premiered in April 2019 but was not released to digital platforms until March 2020, right at the point where the Covid-19 lockdown went into effect. As a result, there seems to be something uncannily predictive to it. Although the film didn't know about any of this when it was made, its images of empty streets and parking lots, or of people scouring bare supermarket shelves for supplies, could almost be taken from TV news footage after the outbreak of coronavirus. These sit alongside scenes of Frieda Pinto and Leslie Odom, Jr. in quarantine in their apartment socially distancing themselves from one another, reduced to eating canned and packaged food, wearing face masks and contamination suits, with plastic sheeting over the door and everything from outside having to be disinfected.

Where *Only* works far less effectively than *Light of My Life* is that director Takashi Doscher seems to have primarily wanted to make a film about the relationship between two people who connect despite not being able to touch. For the most part, the film takes place in a series of intimate and often beautifully filmed vignettes. The downside is that these come as glimpses and images more than they do pieces of drama that we are engaged in. The film is also hindered by being shot in non-linear order.

The theme of a pandemic that wipes out all men was explored by two TV series that came out around the same time; both were made during the Covid-19 pandemic. The first of these was developed from *Y: The Last Man* (2002–08), a comicbook series created by Brian K. Vaughan and published in sixty issues from Vertigo Entertainment. In the comic's story, the escape artist Yorick Brown becomes the sole man left alive after a disease kills off every human and animal

A VIEWING GUIDE TO THE PANDEMIC

Depictions of Plague and Pandemic on Film and TV

Ben Schnetzer as Yorick Brown in *Y: The Last Man* (2021).

in the world that has a Y chromosome. He becomes a prized commodity in the now woman-dominated world. This is a variant on the 1924 *The Last Man on Earth* but treated with far more stark seriousness in its depiction of such a world.

The comicbook series garnered considerable acclaim and received several awards. After several abortive attempts to conduct a film adaptation, the comicbook eventually reached screens as the TV series Y: The Last Man (2021). Unlike the comicbook's lengthy print run, this only lasted for ten episodes on the US FX network before it was cancelled.

The series started with promise. It is reasonably faithful to the comicbook, albeit updated to now add issues of trans identity to the question of who survives. On the other hand, while the comicbook held great writing that made it a classic, the TV series failed to deliver the same in a sufficiently compelling package that stood it above the rest of the post-pandemic, post-apocalyptic series. It was *Y: The Last Man* reduced to formulaic US TV writing.

Things were played for more comedic effect in the New Zealand-made TV series Creamerie (2021–), which could easily be set a few years along from the timeline proposed by *Y: The Last Man*. It takes place among a matriarchy established on a rural farm. There, a lottery has been established to select which of the women can give birth using the leftover contents of sperm banks. Some members of the community discover one man still alive and fairly predictable comedic complications occur as they try to keep his existence a secret. As of this writing, only six episodes have been produced and it is not clear if the series will continue for a second season.

One of the most bizarre entries in this entire volume is Crimes of the Future (1970), the first full-length film from Canadian director David Cronenberg, who we previously discussed with *Rabid* (1977) in Chapter 1. This is set in a future where a disorder known as Rouge's Malady has killed off all women over pubertal age. Dr Adrian Tripod (Ronald Mlodzik) observes the conditions that have emerged in the survivors, including random mutating organs and the production of a froth known as Rouge's Foam that people like to lick.

In his next film *Shivers/They Came from Within* (1975), Cronenberg was pegged as a horror director and worked in the genre for the next decade plus. In his earlier works, here and in *Stereo* (1969), you get the impression that Cronenberg was intending to head along a career path making arthouse films. Though by its title, *Crimes of the Future* is pegged as a science-fiction film, it belongs more to the surrealist tradition.

It proves mind-boggling trying to get a grip on the film. In terms of camera set-ups, it is a strangely abstract and static work. Cronenberg shot the entire film without dialogue — the soundtrack was dubbed afterwards with Ronald Mlodzik's dry deadpan voice describing everything in the mock tones of a scientific paper.

Ronald Mlodzik in *Crimes of the Future* (1970).

Accompanying all of this is an extremely experimental score made up of percussive effects, rattling noises, chirruping, and bird calls.

The film is filled with people engaged in obsessive alien behaviours. In the opening moments, two men in lab coats run after another man — when Ronald Mlodzik comes across them a little later, they are lying on the grass painting their fingernails. On the soundtrack, Mlodzik talks about Rouge's Foam and then we see him creeping up the side of the bed of the man the lab assistants were running after earlier, taking the foam off the man's chest and excitedly licking it from his hand. The scenes at the Metaphysical Import/Export Company contain an amusing little pantomime where Ronald Mlodzik goes around and shows employees bags of socks and underwear, and they place them out on the floor in patterns.

Cronenberg has a great deal of fun parodying academic doublespeak and coming up with the names of strange-sounding institutions that Ronald Mlodzik keeps passing through to be hired — The House of Skin, The Oceanic Podiatry Group, The Institute of Neo-Venereal Diseases, Metaphysical Import/Export, The Gynaecological Research Foundation. There are all the coolly detached lines in reverence of the scientific process, and the fetishistic interest in bodily mutation and medical science that runs through Cronenberg's horror works.

There is also an incredibly dry sense of humour to the film. "His nurse says his disease is possibly a form of creative cancer," says Mlodzik of one patient. This is followed by a hilarious piece of narration about the colleague whose body keeps manifesting strange organs of unknown purpose that are then removed, only for the disease to drive the patient to break into the specimen room to steal the organs back.

Of course, the ending the film arrives at, where the only solution to save humanity seems to be the impregnation of a five-year-old girl, is fairly way out. It caused a moderate degree of controversy at the time, with the film receiving various reviews calling it 'distasteful'. It is difficult to imagine *Crimes of the Future* being made in the 2010s/20s where the likely upshot would be calls for its banning and every distributor and theatrical chain refusing to show it. Cronenberg later made an unrelated film with the same title, *Crimes of the Future* (2022), which also concerns patients manifesting new organs.

PANDEMICS THAT AFFECT THE SENSES OR MIND

One of the most interesting splinters of the treatments of plague and pandemic themes comes in a cluster of films dealing with plagues that have unusual effects on humanity, in particular impairing one or the other of the senses or state of the mind.

PANDEMICS

of a More Outlandish Nature

Mark Ruffalo and Julianne Moore (front) lead the escape from the detention ward in *Blindness* (2008).

The first of these films was Blindness (2008), an internationally financed production from Brazilian director Fernando Meirelles, best known for the international hit of his third film *City of God* (2002), and featuring a reasonable cast, including Julianne Moore, Mark Ruffalo, Gael Garcia Bernal, Danny Glover, and Sandra Oh.

The film takes place in an unspecified city as people are suddenly affected by a plague that rapidly spreads among the population causing blindness. The infected are placed inside a detention centre. However, as the situation outside deteriorates, the facility is abandoned and conditions inside become a tyrannical nightmare as one of the men (Gael Garcia Bernal) establishes dictatorial control over the other internees.

Blindness is adapted from a 1995 novel by José Saramago, although one might argue it bears a smiliarity to John Wyndham's *The Day of the Triffids*, a novel which exerts influence over a surprising number of works discussed throughout this book. Wyndham's novel concerned an outbreak of blindness after people around the world view a meteorite shower, resulting in the collapse of civilization into anarchy. *Blindness* never goes so far as to have the survivors picked off by man-eating plants, as Wyndham proceeded to do, but the two works share much in common.

Wyndham's book was largely concerned with examining different models of how best to put civilization back together and the search for a place where British middle-class decency could establish itself when other social models failed. By contrast, *Blindness* has more in common with the Stanford Prison Experiment — the study conducted by psychology professor Phillip Zimbardo in 1971 where he created an artificial prison and divided students up into jailers and inmates. This ended with him having to halt the experiment when the treatment of prisoners by those designated as guards became too extreme. In a similar manner, *Blindness* concerns itself with the conditions that ensue when people are confined together, and of how a liberal outlook and the decency that Wyndham upheld is rendered useless in the face of cruel authoritarianism.

The film's most powerful sections begin once the characters are confined in the detention facility, and we start to see the cohesion of social order collapsing. Director Meirelles creates compelling images — the slow dissolves as the facility is filled and we see it overflowing with refuse and litter, or of people simply walking past without clothes on. The film becomes especially charged with the introduction of Gael Garcia Bernal and his establishment of a tyrannical dictatorship, confiscating food supplies and demanding valuables, and then the women of the other wards, as payment. These scenes are drawn with a maximum amount of grim effect as we see Mark Ruffalo's protestations of fairness being ignored and people having to confront the moral repercussions of what they are required to do. This culminates in an orgy scene shot in an amazing montage of blurred and out-of-focus camerawork, where Meirelles lets the indistinct half-lit shapes of bodies and accompanying sounds do all the work for him.

The film is equally remarkable once the survivors emerge into the outside world where the entire city is in a state of chaos and covered in litter. There is a highly effective scene where Julianne Moore (who can still see) enters a supermarket where *everything* has been trashed and finds an undisturbed cache of food, only to be mobbed as the blind smell what she is carrying. There are other beautifully evocative scenes — like the moment where aging Danny Glover and young Alice Braga admit attraction for one another, ask if they are alone and conclude from the silence that they are, only for the camera to pull back to show everyone else in the room sitting there staying quiet.

Perfect Sense (2011) is an international production made by British director David Mackenzie. Set in Glasgow, it depicts the progressive social collapse that occurs as a pandemic causes people to gradually lose each of their senses — at first their sense of smell, followed by taste, hearing, and eventually sight. We see this through the eyes of epidemiologist Eva Green and chef Ewan McGregor, who works in a restaurant across from her as they connect and strike up a relationship.

Some of the most remarkable images in the film are where we see people trying to pick up and continue on with normal life after the loss of each sense — how after the loss of taste, restaurants continue on by offering up variations based on temperature and texture; or of Eva Green and Ewan McGregor together in the bath playfully eating shaving cream and soap. In the world after the loss of hearing (where even the soundtrack mutes), we have a remarkable scene where Ewan McGregor goes to a concert where people are playing musical instruments and the attendees place their heads up against vast speakers near the front, where the dull, distant vibrations prove the nearest they can get to hearing something.

In the film's final scenes, the whole world loses its sense of sight. This occurs just as Eva Green and Ewan McGregor run back into one another's arms and reconcile. It is implied that people will be left with just the ability to touch one another. I did wonder what the social ramifications of this would be: when people only have the sense of touch, how does society not completely collapse overnight? How could a society possibly organize, let alone communicate? With no sense of sight, smell or taste, how do people go about finding food anymore? If the two lovers are together (as we see at the ending of the film), there must be some point, they would break contact — to find food, go to the bathroom, or some such — so how would they find one another again? Despite the powerful upbeat note the film ends on, this is a scenario that would surely doom humanity to mass starvation within a matter of days.

The Last Days (Los Ultimos Dias) (2013) comes from Spanish brothers Alex and David Pastor who previously made the powerful *Carriers* (2009) (discussed in Chapter 3). This film takes place after the world has been struck by a plague known as The Panic, which may have been caused by a volcanic eruption. This has left the population in an extreme state of agoraphobia, mortally afraid of going out of doors. We follow Quim Gutierrez as a Barcelona office worker who has been trapped inside his office building along with his co-workers for the last three months.

The film opens as a group of dishevelled people queue in the office for rations. With their supplies dwindling, Quim Gutierrez leads efforts to break through into the subway tunnels and sewers beneath the building. The full effect of what has happened does not become clear until they travel down into the subway and arrive at the first platform, where dozens of people shelter in a makeshift refugee encampment, and we discover a whole society that has relocated underground.

The film is filled with potent images — the visit to an apartment where we see that the family living there have hung a line of dead birds on a clothesline (presumably so they can eat them); the man who is found to have been living inside the office and is evicted from the building by security only to have a heart attack once he is thrown out onto the street; the woman who elects to be burned alive in a supermarket rather than escape through the fire exit door.

A VIEWING GUIDE TO THE PANDEMIC

Depictions of Plague and Pandemic on Film and TV

The film arrives at an appealing uplift where Quim Gutierrez makes a titanic struggle out into the open to reunite with his love Marta Etura. In a series of cuts, we then see that they have given birth to a baby and the child has grown up and is able to go into the outside world unaffected — in the final images, we see it join a group of other children as they run off to play in the now overgrown ruins of the city.

Little Fish (2020) is set in a world that has been affected by the NIA (Neuroinflammatory Affliction) virus that causes people to lose their memory. The story follows Olivia Cooke as she realizes that her husband Jack O'Connell has become affected and is gradually starting to forget things. The narrative flips back and forward in non-linear order just like memory itself.

There are brief but undeniably effective glimpses of how this affects the rest of the world — stories of a fisherman swimming to shore because he is unable to remember how to pilot his boat; a woman who keeps jogging because she doesn't remember where her home is; a man attacking his girlfriend, believing her an intruder because he doesn't recognize her anymore.

Mostly, the film is a small, intimate relationship drama told through the eyes of Olivia Cooke as she watches husband Jack O'Connell losing his memory. Amid this, there are some great pieces of writing — like the jolt that comes as Olivia explains to Jack that this is the third time they have had the same argument about their rescue dog. One of the most powerful scenes is where Jack tells Olivia he is losing it, how he has been masking it and of all the things that she means to him.

There were two similar films made around the same time on the theme of the world affected by outbreaks of mass amnesia with *Embers* (2015) and *Apples* (2020). However, in neither of these is the cause specified as being a pandemic.

The TV series *Star Trek: Deep Space Nine* (1993–99) offers up one episode worthy of inclusion here. This was *Babel* (1993), the fourth aired episode in total and one of the best among the fairly negligible first two seasons of the series.

In the story, a weapon hidden in the structure of the Deep Space Nine station is accidentally activated when Chief O'Brien (Colm Meaney) repairs the replicators. This releases a virus that proceeds to affect people aboard the station with aphasia — a medical condition where there is a disconnect between the brain and the capacity for language — causing everybody to start babbling in an unintelligible word salad.

One of the strangest entries in this entire volume is the comedy *What's So Bad About Feeling Good?* (1968). In the film, a toucan is brought to New York City aboard a Greek freighter. The toucan is carrying an airborne virus that causes euphoria and happiness. The happiness virus infects boyfriend and girlfriend George Peppard and Mary Tyler Moore who live in a garbage dump along with a group of beatnik artists dedicated to experiencing the true misery of life. After becoming infected, they get jobs and happily set about adopting regular middle-class lifestyles.

PANDEMICS

of a More Outlandish Nature

George Peppard and Mary Tyler Moore as a beatnik couple in *What's So Bad About Feeling Good?* (1968).

Most comedies act as liberating anarchic fantasies that poke fun at the people who take themselves too seriously, or allow the child within loose to run amok and cause chaos. However, this acts as completely the opposite. Where in just about any other comedy one would expect the happiness virus to allow people to indulge in wacky behaviour, here the toucan operates as a force of conservatism, causing people to adopt traditional lifestyles.

To place things in context, *What's So Bad About Feeling Good?* came out just after the legendary Summer of Love (1967) where youth everywhere were throwing off the social expectations of their parents. The film can be seen as an establishment reaction to 1960s youth rebellion. The film's subtext is extraordinary — not to mention profoundly insulting — in its equation of a middle-class lifestyle with happiness and by corollary its caricaturing of the bohemian lifestyle with unhappiness. Furthermore, happiness is equated with people getting married and singing America The Beautiful. Also, when the infected beatniks become middle-class, they develop a conscience and start telling the truth, as though counter-cultural people and those who are depressed are naturally amoral and dishonest. It is a glib and smug film.

A VIEWING GUIDE TO THE PANDEMIC

Depictions of Plague and Pandemic on Film and TV

NON-VIRAL PANDEMICS

I will briefly touch here on a couple of films about pandemics and outbreaks that come from non-viral sources, although I will limit these as this opens the door to a large body of other films. Casting the net any wider, we would, for instance, have to include *Alien* (1979) and its assorted sequels and imitators, where people become infected by a parasitic alien organism.

The Invasion (2007) was the third remake of *Invasion of the Body Snatchers* (1956), the classic film about the subversion of small town America by alien body snatchers that come in the form of pods which form into identical duplicates of humans, all except for their emotions. In the original, Kevin McCarthy is a GP who leads a group of people as they try to escape while the town around them is taken over by the pod people. The 1956 film is one of the classic science-fiction works and creates an unbeatable mood of paranoia and fear. The other two versions, *Invasion of the Body Snatchers* (1978) and *Body Snatchers* (1993), also offer solid and well above average variations on the plot.

In this version, the pods are replaced by biological contamination brought back by a returning space shuttle. Nicole Kidman is a Washington, D.C. psychiatrist who gradually realizes that people are being taken over as they sleep and turned into something alien and emotionless.

This is a disappointing version lacking in the paranoid nightmare-fuelled atmosphere of the original or even its 1978 and 1993 remakes — it is the weakest of all four versions. In one of the more amusing touches, the body snatchers mass distribute the infection by setting up a fake countrywide vaccination scheme.

Splinter (2008) concerns a couple on a camping trip, as well as an escaped convict and his girlfriend, who end up at a gas station in the middle of nowhere. There they have to deal with a plant-based infection that causes the infectee to erupt in spikes. They are forced to barricade themselves inside the gas station as the plant creatures infect them and others. Director Toby Wilkins generates an at-times unbearable level of tension and a series of outlandish creature effects.

There was also the South Korean *Deranged (Yeon-ga-si)* (2012), in which people across the country become infected with a parasitic organism known as a horsehair worm. The infected are driven to frantically consume water. The film starts in an everyday manner, before a montage of jump scenes as we watch the infected throwing themselves into rivers, fountains, pools, even fish tanks. The infected are quarantined in a school gymnasium as the government tries to find a vaccine. Hope seems to be offered in the drug Windazole, only to find that the manufacturer has discontinued production, leading to a desperate scrabble for remaining supplies.

The latter sections of the film concern themselves less with the infection and more with the unscrupulous dealings of the pharmaceutical company in withdrawing and hoarding supplies of Windazole, at the same time refusing to release their copyright on the drug to allow more to be manufactured.

What I did like about the film was its constantly raising the stakes on the hero (Kim Myeong-min) and his attempts to get supplies of the drug for his family. He finds a small supply only to lose this when a mob attacks him; he then discovers the company's stockpile only for the warehouse to go up in flames. This reaches an epic level at the climax, which involves Kim bursting into a warehouse in a truck to commandeer chemical supplies to make more antidote. At the same time, the President is just about to sign the contract that will pay billions to the crooked pharmaceutical company; while in the school gymnasium, Kim's wife (Jung-hee Moon) uses her body to hold back a frenzied mob of infected wanting to trigger the sprinklers that will kill them all.

One oddity that can be briefly included here is the Danish-made *Possessed (Besat)* (1999) about a virologist on a chase across Europe in search of an Ebola-like infection — only to find that what he is tracking is a body-hopping parasite that is the embodiment of the Devil.

MISCELLANEOUS

Finally, I will briefly touch upon some other odd plagues and pandemics that have turned up on screens.

Mauvais Sang (1986) was the second film from French director Leos Carax who subsequently went on to make acclaimed works like *Holy Motors* (2012) and *Annette* (2021). This takes place in a near future where the world has been affected by SYPO, a virus that causes people to have sex without love. Denis Lavant is a petty cardsharp drawn into a scheme to steal a vaccine, during the course of which he ends up in a romantic entanglement with a young Juliette Binoche. The film is visually extraordinary, as all of Carax's films are. However, the virus is merely a background detail and of minor significance — we never see it infect anybody, for instance.

The Hole (Dong) (1998) comes from Taiwanese director Tsai Ming-Liang. It was one of a series of films funded by French companies and made by various directors around the world to celebrate the millennium. I must confess that I have found Tsai's other films a major endurance fest in their infuriating lack of plot and his penchant for frequent long, static shots that go on for minutes at a time. *The Hole* is no different.

In a premise not dissimilar to *The Last Days,* the film is set on January 1, 2000, as Taipei is plagued by a virus that causes people to lock themselves away in darkness. This is merely backdrop and the rest of the film is almost like a play that takes place on a single set. It begins after a plumber leaves a hole between an upstairs and downstairs apartment during maintenance work. The man upstairs (Lee Kang-Sheng) takes great delight in tormenting the woman in the apartment below (Yang Kuei-Mei) through the hole. All of this happens in the dullest way possible. The virus is mentioned at the start of the film but does not feature again thereafter.

In a similar vein, there was ***It's All About Love*** (2003) from Thomas Vinterberg, the Danish director known for *The Celebration* (1998) and *The Hunt* (2012). This takes place in the year 2021 where the world has been experiencing strange phenomena — random localized weather changes, a Ugandan village where gravity has stopped, people dying from a plague that causes loneliness. The plot centres around Joaquin Phoenix as he tries to reconcile with his ex-wife, played by Claire Danes. The loneliness plague and these other elements sit around the edge of the film without any explanation and are of little significance to the plot.

PART FOUR

THE ERA OF THE COVID-19 PANDEMIC

CHAPTER 12
LIFE DURING LOCKDOWN: THE FILMS OF THE COVID-19 PANDEMIC

In watching the films made during the pandemic, I became intrigued as to how the usual logistics of making a film world work amid quarantine and social distancing restrictions. Most post-production work on a film — editing, visual effects, music, and ADR/voice dubbing — can be conducted remotely. However, a certain amount of any live-action film has to actually be shot with people in front of and behind cameras.

Naturally, with the entire populace being advised to remain six feet apart from others and/or stay indoors, this presents considerable logistical hurdles. Filmmakers soon came up with inventive ways of dealing with this — films shot remotely or with performances delivered by Facetime or Zoom. In other cases, films were shot with reduced casts and crew.

While the pandemic did present a series of hurdles to filmmakers, it failed to stop the industry in its tracks and many productions found ways to keep on filming. There were reports of Covid infection striking and shutting down the sets of a number of films such as *The Card Counter* (2021), *The Batman* (2022), and *Jurassic Park: Dominion* (2022), while other productions like *Death on the Nile* (2022), *Fantastic Beasts: The Secrets of Dumbledore* (2022), and *Mission: Impossible — Dead Reckoning Part One* (2023) had to arrange alternate locations when the original intended locales went into lockdown. By mid-2021, shoots had largely normalized with the industry-wide establishment of Covid bubbles and Covid safety advisors.

The pandemic was a period that also saw the biggest sea change in the distribution of films since the closure of commercial video stores in the 2000s. With most businesses around the world forced to shut down during lockdown, this also meant the closure of theatrical venues. This saw a number of films either abandoning any hope of theatrical release and going straight to streaming platforms, or else delaying release until reopening. Viewing figures for streaming media dramatically increased, by something like thirty-one percent according to the BBC. Theatres eventually reopened with masking protocols and seating gaps in place, but audience figures were still way down even after many areas in the US reopened — global box-office recorded a mere $12.4 billion in earnings in 2020, rising to $21.3 billion in 2021 but nowhere near the $42.5 billion gross in 2019. This demonstrates a major shift in the ways that audiences were now choosing to view films — a clear preference for the isolation of one's own home rather than shared spaces.

Films made during the pandemic can be divided into two types — those that acknowledge the pandemic's existence, and those that pretend it doesn't exist. The majority of films and TV made during the 2021 season fall into the latter category and give the appearance of taking place in an alternate reality where the pandemic never occurred. This makes sense in that Hollywood stars whose faces are their livelihood don't want to give performances hidden behind masks. We do not concern ourselves with those films here.

There have been some films such as *Borat: Subsequent Moviefilm* (2020), *Drive My Car* (2021), *Zeros and Ones* (2021), and *Kimi* (2022) in which aspects of the pandemic, principally images of people masked, have been incorporated. However, this is merely background detail, and the films cannot be said to be *about* the Covid pandemic. These too we will leave aside. Instead, we will concern ourselves in this and the next two chapters with films and TV that depict the Covid pandemic as a core plot element.

THE FIRST FILMS OF THE COVID PANDEMIC

It is a debate as to what can be considered the first film dealing with the Covid pandemic. The first film to be *released* was Corona Zombies (2020). The World Health Organization officially recognized the virus as a pandemic on March 11, 2020; the film was released one month later on April 10, 2020.

Corona Zombies comes from director/producer Charles Band, who has a long history producing and occasionally directing low-budget horror films since the 1970s. As the head of studios like Empire and Full Moon Productions, Band has produced multiple series of low-budget films including the *Ghoulies, Trancers, Subspecies, Puppetmaster, The Gingerdead Man*, and *Evil Bong* films.

The film gets around Covid restrictions by shooting all of its scenes inside an apartment and having only a single actress (Cody Renee Cameron) on screen for the running time, as well as one other (Robin Sidney) whose performance is literally phoned in — she is only a voice on the end of a phone.

For the rest of the film, Band has cheated and simply recycled footage from the Italian zombie film *Hell of the Living Dead* (1980), which is discussed in Chapter 8, plus several minutes from the Band-produced *Zombies vs Strippers* (2012). The recycled scenes are laid over with a comedy rifftrack à la *Mystery Science Theater 3000* (1988–99, 2017–18), making fun of issues like toilet paper shortages, the virus's origins in Wuhan ("I like the rap group" says Cody Renee Cameron), hand-washing, and pandemic buzzwords such as 'social distancing' and 'flattening the curve'. Most of the jokes are hit and miss, if not downright lame. There is a negligible plot, although most of the film consists of the abovementioned recycled footage, which we are told is airing on TV news broadcasts that Cody Renee Cameron is watching.

Before 2020 was out, Band, Cody Renee Cameron and Robin Sidney reteamed to make two sequels with *Barbie & Kendra Save the Tiger King* (2020) and *Barbie & Kendra Storm Area 51* (2020).

Corona Zombies was certainly the first Covid film to be released. On the other hand, depending on what you define as being the earliest — when a film was shot or when it was released — <u>*Corona*</u> (2020) becomes another strong contender for being the first Covid film. This was made by Mostafa Keshvari, an Iranian expatriate who lives in Canada. Keshvari shot the film in February of 2020, before the official announcement of the pandemic, but it was not released until August of 2020 after several other Covid-related films had come out.

Keshvari's film takes place entirely in an apartment building elevator as it becomes stuck between floors. Those trapped inside include: the lift's technician; the building's owner and his pregnant wife who is about to go into labour; a wheelchair-ridden racist with a swastika tattooed on his head; a teenager glued to her cellphone; one tenant who is a parking meter attendant, and a Chinese woman who speaks no English. There have been rumours about someone in the building being infected with Covid. When the Chinese woman begins coughing, the others assume she is infected, and the situation becomes one of suspicion and fear.

Keshvari's unique method of shooting the film is to employ what is called the long take — where the entire film (or sections of a film) has been shot in a single unbroken take with no cuts. This is a highly ambitious form of filmmaking that has been employed in only a select few films. The first of these was Alfred Hitchcock's *Rope* (1948) and modern examples include *Russian Ark* (2002), *Cut* (2010), *Silent House* (2011), *Fish & Cat* (2013), *Victoria* (2015), *King Dave* (2016), and *Rendez-Vous* (2019), before the genre was hilariously parodied by the Japanese *One Cut of the Dead* (2017).

Surprisingly, a number of other films made during the pandemic used the long take, or at least limited versions of it. Others (all discussed here and in the next chapter) include *Help* (2021) with its twenty-six minutes single scene, while both

Together (2021) and *Coastal Elites* (2020) are shot as several long monologues with cuts. *Safer at Home* (2021), discussed in the next chapter, tries to give the impression it is taking place in real-time and is shot as a long take, although it does use cuts.

As Keshvari recounted to me, he shot his film over the space of two days after a month of rehearsals with his cast, using only a single set. The script was largely improvised with the cast being given general notes of where things were to go.

The set-up of the film, with people trapped in an elevator, reminds of a non-supernatural version of *The Night Chronicles 1: Devil* (2010). As with these types of contained-location thrillers, everyone present undergoes some kind of soul-baring exposure/self-examination, while things the group think to be the case, especially in regard to the Chinese woman, are turned on their head. Keshvari stated that his primary intention was to make a film about racism — the opening credit dedicates the film "to the victims of Coronavirus and Xenophobia."

The film certainly predicts the racist backlash against the Chinese, who were scapegoated as being responsible for the pandemic and even attacked in some areas. On the other hand, the film fails to quite predict key aspects of the pandemic like the importance of masking — one of the more amusing parts is seeing the group get into the elevator unmasked, with only a single mask between them, and then debate over who most deserves to have it.

A number of the films that were shot during the peak of the pandemic did so with minimal casts and crew, and with the action contained to a single or minimal number of locations. Most of these films dispensed with scenes involving large crowds and extras or physical effects and action scenes. These limitations produced a series of smaller, much more intimate films.

Some films dealt with these limitations in clever ways. *Dune Drifter* (2020), for instance, was a British-made space opera that managed to shoot an entire space battle in the living room of its director's apartment.

Far more ambitious was *Zero Contact* (2022), which boasts of being shot in seventeen countries during lockdown. All of the actors, Anthony Hopkins among them, delivered their performances via Zoom with none, as the title states, ever meeting in person. This in itself is not a Covid film, and no depiction of the pandemic occurs. The plot is instead focused on a group of people around the world who have been left parts of a Quantum Initiative following the death of Hopkins' tech guru, and the debate via teleconferencing on the potentially dangerous ramifications of activating it.

Host (2020), from newcomer British director Rob Savage, has a fairly simple premise about a group of people in lockdown isolation, who conduct a séance via a conference call on Zoom and accidentally summon a supernatural entity. It is essentially *Unfriended* (2014) for the era of Covid. That film came with a unique approach as it took place across social media, the film screen replaced by a computer screen on which various video and instant messenger windows appeared as the characters interacted. A number of other films of the Covid era — *The Gone Game* (2020), *The 12 Day Tale of the Monster That Dies in 8* (2020) (both discussed in Chapter 13), and *Safer at Home* — have also employed the computer-screen-as-film-screen approach.

Operating with a largely improvised script, Rob Savage and his actors created the film remotely in their own homes during the midst of lockdown, each setting up their own lighting and doing their own makeup, even arranging their own effects scenes. All of this added up to produce a modestly effective ghost story.

Influenced by *Host* was the also British-made *The Lockdown Hauntings* (2021). The end credits boast how "This film was shot during the first UK lockdown for Covid 19 ... by one man" — the one man in question being director Howard J. Ford, previously known for the zombie film *The Dead* (2010).

The film opens with Tony Todd, delivering his entire performance by Facetime, giving an ominous warning about entities having been unleashed during the isolation of lockdown. Todd's opening dialogue, and warnings of supernatural beings wandering the deserted cities in the absence of people, conjures something undeniably imaginative, effectively aided by Ford's montage tour of empty city streets.

However, the film belies this initial promise and merely shifts between scenes where various girls walk around their respective homes as an invisible force throws cutlery and crockery about before they are strangled by an invisible entity. This is interspersed with scenes where a police detective (Angela Dixon) conducts an investigation (mostly from her home by internet) and talks to some experts. That is about the sum of the film. *Host* did the same thing with low-tech effects but built up a spooky story; here, almost the whole film consists of scenes where girls get kitchenware thrown at them.

The Gone Game (2020) was a Bollywood TV miniseries consisting of four half-hour episodes that appeared on India's Voot network fairly soon into the pandemic (August 2020). The series was filmed almost entirely remotely with the assorted cast members in their own homes. Like *Host*, it has been shot in a way intended to give the impression it is all taking place across social media video conferencing apps and messenger programs (although this is mostly an effect created in post-production).

The story takes place between various family members and their assorted spouses between Mumbai and New Delhi in the early days of the pandemic (March-April of 2020). One of the group, Sahil (Arjun Mathur), comes down with Covid symptoms and has to be admitted to hospital. They are then told he has died there and the body had to be cremated. Sahil's wife and others can find no record of his being at the hospital. They then receive phone calls from Sahil that are abruptly curtailed, only to learn that he had no phone with him in the hospital, before the phone is later found in his wife's car.

This is a solid effort that builds up a good mystery — quite a reasonable part of the story is dependent on modern technologies like video and messaging apps, GPS location tracking, mapping devices, and remote CCTV cameras. The series eventually provides solutions but also arrives at an open ending clearly intended to pave the way for a second season.

Released in September 2020 (although set in the first few months of 2020) was *Coastal Elites* (2020), a ninety-minute TV movie that aired on HBO. This came from Jay Roach, better known as a comedy director with the Austin Powers films and *Meet the Parents* (2000) and sequels, whose output since then has often taken an interest in contemporary US politics. As with *Host* and *The Gone Game*, the film was shot remotely with the actors in isolation.

For the most part, *Coastal Elites* is *not* a film about the Covid pandemic, rather one that expresses a liberal disgust with US President Donald Trump and his legion of MAGA followers. The film consists of five monologues where the respective actors address the camera: Bette Midler is a retired Jewish teacher who has been arrested for snatching the hat of a MAGA follower and expresses her anger at the contempt and ignorance the man represents; Dan Levy is a gay actor who discusses his experience at auditioning for a film featuring the first gay superhero and being asked to play a clichéd gay caricature; Sarah Paulson is a maker of meditation videos who recounts her experience of going home to visit her MAGA-supporting family for the holiday season.

The writing — which comes from playwright Paul Rudnick who also wrote *Jeffrey* (1995) and *In & Out* (1997) — is sharp and incisive, with all the actors giving standout performances. The most devastating episode is the third one, *The Blonde Cloud*, where Issa Rae plays an African American college friend of Ivanka Trump who was invited to a White House dinner where Ivanka took her aside, seeking her support in order to obtain street cred with African American communities. The peeling apart of Ivanka and her world of privilege leaves you drop-jawed.

Though Covid is mentioned in several of the monologues, the only episode to feature it as a plot element is the final one, *President Miriam*. This is narrated by Kaitlin Dever as an ER nurse treating Covid patients, who tells how she found hope amidst the chaos in the brassy attitude of Bette Midler's character, who had become an infected patient.

A VIEWING GUIDE TO THE PANDEMIC

Depictions of Plague and Pandemic on Film and TV

TALES FROM THE FRONTLINE

The films discussed in this section opt for very different depictions of pandemic than every other work throughout this book. Almost all of the films discussed elsewhere are about outbreaks, the people infected, and the race of authorities and medical personnel to contain the threat and/or find a cure. Contrarily, almost every one of the Covid films are not about people infected but about people under lockdown and quarantined — they are works about the effects of isolation rather than outbreak dramas. We discuss the films about lockdown and isolation in Chapter 13.

Surprisingly, only a handful of Covid films depict anybody becoming infected (although we do get a few more where people suspect they might be infected). There are only a few works among these that take the perspective of almost every other pandemic film in following the medical staff and governmental officials in trying to deal with the outbreak. We discuss those films in this section.

<u>*Chinese Doctors*</u> (2021) is a Chinese-made film about the initial outbreak of the coronavirus in Wuhan and the efforts to contain it. The film starts with the appearance of the first cases, the rapid spread of infection, leading to strict government measures blocking travel to and from the region, and then the conversion of existing wards to house patients, followed by the construction of new hospitals. The greatest focus, however, is on the dedication of the doctors and medical staff working in extreme circumstances and often beyond the point of exhaustion.

Chinese Doctors resembles works like *93 Days* (2016) (discussed in Chapter 5) and *Virus* (2019) (discussed in Chapter 7) in that it is a work of nationalistic pride, about how the authorities and the medical staff give their utmost and triumph over adversity. *Chinese Doctors* does all of this on steroids and in effect becomes a propaganda piece for the government of the People's Republic of China.

Chinese Doctors (2021).

Facts and figures appear on screen throughout citing the number of lives saved, including the number of people over the age of 100 who made a full recovery, the rapidity with which new hospitals were built, the equipment contributed from other parts of the country, and so on. When the hospital head calls for staff to volunteer their services, a surge of triumphal music usually reserved for national anthems comes on the soundtrack, as everyone in the room rises to their feet. There is a lengthy ending involving much gratitude and tribute to the personnel who worked on the frontline.

China is a country where emphasis is placed on subsuming individuality as part of group identity, as well as the importance of family tradition. Thus, it seems nothing here for one infected person to be arrested on the spot, while on the other hand it seems a great personal affront to have to ask relatives for permission to conduct an autopsy. You cannot help but think if this were a western-made film, the situation would be reversed — autopsies on the dead are a matter of routine without the need for family approval, while the arrest of infectees would be seen as an example of authoritarian police overreach.

The way the pandemic spread to the rest of the world never gets a look in. There is a brief depiction of the arrival of US observers in Wuhan but the sole dialogue they get is to express amazement at the authorities persuading a population of eleven million to stay indoors. Noticeably, the film's triumph comes with the reduction of numbers of infected in China to zero and the reopening of Wuhan in April 2020—a point when the number of cases was rising to nightmare proportions around the rest of the world.

On the other hand, while the film's patriotic flag-waving makes it a hard swallow at times, *Chinese Doctors* is fairly good at depicting the nightmare that went on in the hospitals in the midst of the pandemic. We get glimpses of some of the situations faced: shortages of oxygen tanks or PPE masks for medical staff; the infected in massive lines being turned away and rioting for available hospital beds; exhausted medical staff with their faces and hands scoured from wearing masks; power cuts in the ER as staff try to deal with multiple arresting patients at once; the problems presented in performing a C-section on an infected pregnant woman.

Embrace Again (2021) is another Chinese-made effort. Like *Chinese Doctors*, it takes place in Wuhan shortly after the city went into quarantine in January of 2020 and ends with the official lifting of the lockdown in April of 2020.

The film centres around a group of characters who join one man's attempts to organize volunteers to distribute food during the lockdown. We follow various of these people as they connect — a takeout delivery motorcycle courier who befriends a piano teacher and dreams of romance; the organizer of the volunteer effort who is estranged from his family; an elderly retired doctor and his unspoken love for a woman; and a man who re-evaluates his relationship after his wife confronts him over being too preoccupied with business and ignoring his family.

These are all stories told with warm affection. Like *Scenes from an Empty Church* and *Stuck Together* (both 2021) (discussed in Chapter 13), this is a film about connections made and strengthened through adversity. The film rarely shows the tragic side of things until the end, when we learn that some of the characters we met throughout have died. This ends the film on a saddening note, although the reopening of Wuhan — where we see the streets going from empty and doused in antiseptics to filled with life and vehicles once again — is seen as a positive uplift.

Chinese Doctors would make a great double-bill with *This England* (2022), a TV miniseries of six episodes of fifty minutes to one hour, that aired on the UK's Sky channel. Both *Chinese Doctors* and *This England* take almost identical approaches — they depict one country's handling of the pandemic, showing the overloading of the hospital system with infectees and the government's response.

However, in terms of what they have to say about this, the works are mirror opposites. *Chinese Doctors* is a propagandist work of national pride that lauds the efforts of the Chinese government in handling the crisis in Wuhan. By contrast, *This England* is deeply condemnatory of the government of Prime Minister Boris Johnson and its handling of the pandemic in Britain.

This England comes from director Michael Winterbottom, who produces, writes all the episodes, and shares directing duties with three others. Winterbottom has been responsible for often highly political films such as *Welcome to Sarajevo* (1997), *24 Hour Party People* (2002), *The Road to Guantanamo* (2006), and *A Mighty Heart* (2007).

The miniseries opens with Boris Johnson winning a second term as Prime Minister in December 2019 and follows through to the arrival of the pandemic and Johnson's government's disastrously unprepared response. The series ends in May 2021 with the press revelations that Chief Adviser Dominic Cummings, one of the chief architects of the pandemic response, broke travel restrictions to be with his family during lockdown. In some ways, the series, which aired in September 2022, was made too early and does not cover subsequent developments such as the Partygate scandal where Johnson and other members of his cabinet attended Christmas parties in contravention of lockdown regulations, as well as Johnson being forced to resign in July 2022 after his handling of misconduct allegations against Chief Whip Chris Pincher, although these do get a brief title card mention at the end of the last episode.

The series contrasts assorted cabinet discussions with the home life of Boris Johnson (Kenneth Branagh giving an awards-worthy performance) and his girlfriend, later wife, Carrie Symonds (Ophelia Lovibond) and the announcement of her pregnancy. These alternate with a montage of scenes that move between homes and hospitals as we see the infection spread and medical staff trying to deal with the mass hospitalizations. The series delivers this with undeniably sobering effect.

Just like *Chinese Doctors*, the show offers a dense quoting of infection statistics (reported numbers of cases appear on screen alongside the actual number of infections) and depicts the government apparatus being wheeled into operation. Unlike the unquestioning praise of the Chinese government and its controversial Covid Zero policy in *Chinese Doctors*, Winterbottom and his production team are damning of the numerous failings of the Johnson government.

The series covers everything: the government's ignoring or diminishing of warnings from experts; the failure to provide adequate PPE equipment and ventilators to hospitals; the slowness to go into full lockdown; the lack of proper testing procedures; the release of elderly patients from general hospitals into aged care facilities without testing them first, leading to rapid spread of the pandemic; the construction of the Nightingale hospital in London to house up to 4000 acute patients and its closure after treating only fifty-four infectees; and the blatant untruths told about the number of tests conducted.

One of the most damning things that the series has to say is how key decisions in the government were placed in the hands of image consultants and spin doctors as opposed to ministry officials with actual hands-on experience of crisis situations.

Jodie Comer in *Help* (2021).

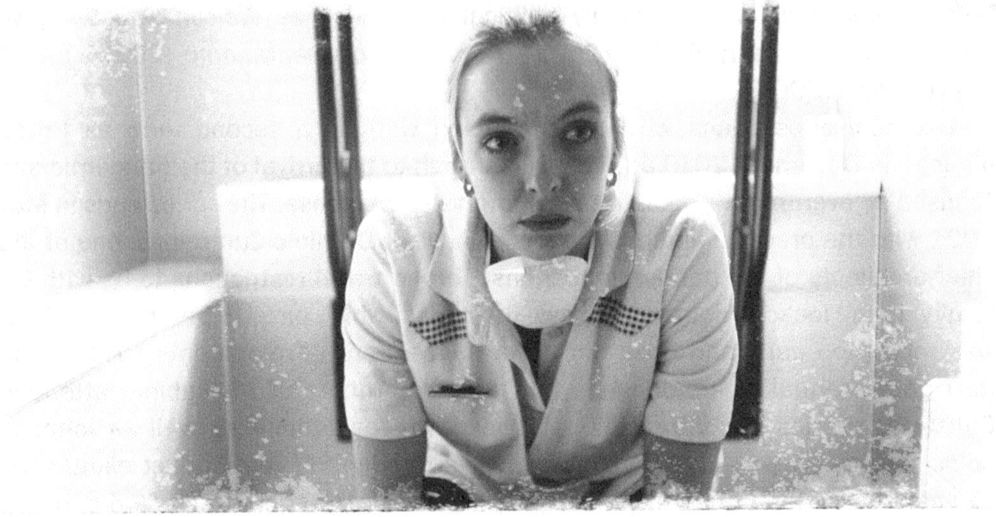

The series offers stark images of focus groups being held to test out new slogans, contrasted with grim scenes of infections spiralling and the infected struggling on ventilators.

The single best work about the Covid pandemic viewed in the course of writing this book was Help (2021), a TV movie that aired on the UK's Channel 4. This stars Jodie Comer, who accepts a job as a care aide at a retirement centre somewhere in the Liverpool area. The setting is April of 2020, just as Covid was spreading across the UK. The film follows Jodie's adjustment to the job, and her connecting with the various patients, in particular Stephen Graham as a man in his late forties who suffers early-onset Alzheimer's. As the infected begin to overload regular hospitals, aged patients are sent to the home, bringing infection with them, which rapidly spreads throughout the facility.

Jodie Comer and Stephen Graham, despite giving performances through accents so thick they could be used to cut logs, are both at the peak of their game here. Director Marc Munden often opts for handheld camerawork that ventures into unusually personal close-up, giving a singular intimacy to the film.

The film conveys extremely well the sense people had in the early part of the pandemic, where everybody was struggling with partial or erroneous information about the correct methods of dealing with the outbreak. Like *Together* (discussed in Chapter 13), *Help* directly confronts the way the NHS was overburdened during the pandemic and how infected elderly patients were dumped into private care homes, resulting in a massive spike of deaths during the first several months.

The most extraordinary scene in the film is a twenty-six minutes long take. This has Jodie Comer alone on night shift at the facility after every other staff member is either ill or unable to come in, as she tries to get help for one infected patient from various emergency lines to no avail, and is left having to rely on Stephen Graham with his wavering mental faculties. The scene has a raw impact that none of the other films listed here do, in depicting the desperation that hospital staff experienced on the frontline. It is a film that leaves you emotionally devastated.

COMEDY TREATMENTS

Stuck Together (Huit Rue de l'Humanite) (2021) is a French-made effort from comedy actor/director Danny Boon. This is set in a Paris apartment building and follows the lives of various tenants during the lockdown. Boon plays a man paranoid with fear over every possible source of infection, while the film's co-writer Laurence Arné, plays his lawyer wife, trying to work from home. Also present is the building's bullish owner, who has made his money in vape stores and is struggling to handle his children while his wife is away; a scientist who is experimenting to find a vaccine; a man who livestreams an exercise channel while trying to keep his pregnant wife a secret from his legion of female followers; an elderly bar owner who copes with the mandated closure of her business by repackaging her supplies of alcohol as hand sanitizer; and the husband of the building's concierge anguishing after his wife's hospitalization with Covid.

The film creates comically self-absorbed characters and situations without ever doing anything to wind them up or produce anything other than a vague amusement. There's the odd line that survives subtitled translation — "You're asymptomatic", "No, I'm a Catholic."

Like *Embrace Again* and *Scenes from a Church* (see Chapter 13) this places its hope in a community connection — of the bunch of oddballs finding a common togetherness and this uniting them through eventual tragedy. The film arrives at an ending that is a shamelessly sentimental emotional uplift.

Sheer Pandemic (2022) is a comedy treatment from US directors Grant Davis and Chason Laing. This concerns a filmmaker (co-director Chason Laing) and a fitness trainer (Kris Clinton), both rendered unemployed by the lockdown, who sign on to a shady scheme by Laing's uncle (co-director Grant Davis) to sell blackmarket supplies of hoarded toilet paper and hand sanitizer in order to make ends meet. The uncle also conducts sales of unregistered guns — these two sidelines become mixed up when a sale to an underworld figure ends up with the governor's kidnapped daughter hiding in their vehicle.

This is a comedy that aims at easy targets — jokes about essential workers, toilet paper hoarding, Russian mobsters hacking the US election — without particularly funny results. On the other hand, the latter half of the film twists and

A VIEWING GUIDE TO THE PANDEMIC

Depictions of Plague and Pandemic on Film and TV

Police take over running the school in *South Park's Pandemic Special* (2021).

turns in some ways that prove appealing — where the two guys conducting a deal to offload hand sanitizer come up against gangbangers wanting guns; the kidnapped child seeking refuge in their car; Chason Laing being shot but, unable to go to hospital, having to get help from Kris Clinton who faints at the sight of blood; all amid their inept attempts to rescue the kid. As the kid, Shiloh Laing, daughter of Chason, had a perfect line in bored, deadpan sarcasm.

The animated TV series *South Park* (1997–) has become a hit on the US's Comedy Channel for its willingness to satirize almost any topic under the sun, frequently entering into the offensive and bad taste. The show devoted its entire twenty-fourth season to dealing with Covid, beginning with the extended forty-five-minute *Pandemic Special* (2021).

In their wilfully ridiculous and surreal way, creators Trey Parker and Matt Stone sink their teeth into the pandemic. It appears that Stan's father caused the virus due to having sex with animals while on a visit to Wuhan accompanied by Mickey Mouse (who is the premier of China). With the teachers absent from school, the police are hired as replacements but end up gunning down students and then claiming these are virus-related deaths. Stan's father sells a cure for the virus by ejaculating into the marijuana he sells but finds this is causing anyone who smokes it to grow a moustache. After a call from Cartman, Donald Trump says he doesn't want to intervene in the pandemic because it is fulfilling his campaign promise to kill off Mexicans.

Next up was the *Vaccination Special*, where the regular characters end up procuring all the supplies of vaccine in town, while QAnon conspirators step in to act as tutors to children on home quarantine. This was followed by *Post Covid* and

Post Covid: The Return of Covid, which take place in the future: we encounter the now grown-up versions of the kids as they return to South Park for the funeral of Kenny who died from the coronavirus Delta Plus Rewards Program variant after attempting to perfect time travel.

South Park is a show like *The Simpsons* (1989–) that has stuck around for a phenomenal length of time. Both shows have a satiric bite and a willingness to make fun of topical issues that have gained them a large fanbase. It is also generally agreed that after twenty years on air both shows are getting well past their sell-by dates. During its heyday, *South Park* produced episodes that were hilariously on target — Tom Cruise even sued to have one episode taken off the air. On the other hand, given the devastating impact that the virus has had on society, when the last two episodes end up padding their time with very contemporary jokes about NFTs and the existence of *Space Jam: A New Legacy* (2021), it feels like a satiric show taking aim at a broad canvas and falling far from target.

7 Days (2021) is a US-made film centred around two people who meet for a date via an Indian matrimony site. He (Karan Soni who also co-writes the script) is traditional-minded and uptight, while she (Geraldine Viswanathan) is more carefree and westernized. Lockdown comes into effect, meaning that his transport out of town is cancelled and he is forced to stay over at her apartment for three days to wait for an available rental car. They quickly conclude that they are not a suitable match, but the enforced togetherness ends up creating a connection. She then becomes infected with Covid, and he is forced to nurse her before she has to be hospitalized.

This is a romantic comedy made with a cast of two (and one or two others who occasionally pop up on video messenger programs). The story has an arc you can predict from the opening scenes — of two opposites who are forced together by circumstances but come to eventually have feelings for one another. Despite which, the film surprises you, and by the time that Geraldine is hospitalized, you feel an affection for the characters and hold your breath that she will pull through.

The Bubble (2022) was a film from Judd Apatow, who emerged as a writer out of several 1990s/2000s TV series — *The Larry Sanders Show, Freaks and Geeks* — to direct a series of comedy hits with the likes of *The 40 Year Old Virgin* (2005) and *Knocked Up* (2007), and to produce/write the likes of *Superbad* (2007) and *Pineapple Express* (2008).

The Bubble is based on *Jurassic World: Dominion* (2022) and the shutdown that occurred on set for several weeks due to a Covid outbreak. The film takes place on the shooting of the fictional sequel *Cliff Beasts* 6. Apatow charts the various actors and key personnel involved in a series of amiable, occasionally funny caricatures that take aim at things like Tik-Tok popularity and the making of a major studio tentpole production.

Iris Apatow, Pedro Pascal, and Leslie Mann on the film set in *The Bubble* (2022).

Apatow's work during the 2000s changed the face of comedy and brought to prominence names like Seth Rogen, Steve Carell, Christopher Mintz-Plasse, Michael Cena, and Paul Rudd. *The Bubble*, on the other hand, feels like a film that takes aim at relatively easy targets without ever pushing the comedy towards something uncomfortable or uproarious. The Covid lockdown is part of the film but not given any especial prominence.

THE BIZARRE

5G: The Reckoning (aka *Ascension*) (2023) is a film from Canadian director Micheal Bafaro who usually specialises in low-budget horror films. This concerns a group of university students who have elected to remain behind at their halls of residence as lockdown goes into effect. They see strange lights in the sky, while a mysterious fog surrounds the area. People disappear and return emitting light from their mouth and eyes, whereupon they are driven to attack the others.

For much of the film, there is never any clue as to why things are happening — like what the lights in the sky or mysterious fog are, why there are weird temporal dislocations, and why people suddenly erupt with light glowing out of their eyes and mouth. "None of this makes any sense," says Colm Hill at one point, and he could be voicing exactly what the audience feels.

To his credit, Bafaro does offer an eventual explanation. This takes a deep dive into conspiracy theory territory and the belief that was prevalent for a time that Covid was caused by 5G cell phone networks. However, the film takes this far further than any of the conspiracy theorists ever did, making the claim at one point that there is no virus: "I'm saying the virus has only ever been online." The film rather hilariously suggests that the entire lockdown has been instituted so that authorities can roll out of the 5G network, but that this has somehow gone wrong and the network has become alive.

The two strangest films about the Covid pandemic are *Coronavirus Conspiracy: Safer at Home* (2021) (which is discussed in Chapter 14) and the Japanese-made *The 12 Day Tale of the Monster That Dies in 8* (2020). The latter comes with such a deadpan approach that I am not sure how to classify it, and place it here in comedy treatments.

As with a number of other pandemic-shot films, this takes place entirely as a series of vlogs and video messenger conversations. These centre around Takumi Saitoh as an actor rendered unemployed by the lockdown. He amuses himself by deciding to raise capsule monsters, which he has ordered online.

Capsule monsters, or what the Japanese call *gachapon,* are toys dispensed from vending machines, a phenomenon that has been around since the 1970s. Many of the toys have become collectible items. The Pokémon phenomenon evolved out of this — Pokémon's creators originally wanted to call their creatures Capsule Monsters but found it easier to copyright the term Pocket Monsters.

The capsule monsters we get are immobile oddities that look like crudely formed plaster casts of fossils and only about the size of a thumbnail. Takumi talks about how he wants to raise them to fight Covid. One later forms itself into a tiny mask and attaches itself to his nose, and he theorizes that cloth Covid masks are actually the creatures trying to protect humanity.

Interspersed throughout are scenes with dancers wearing masks that resemble the capsule monsters. Another girl talks about the creatures on a YouTube video channel that she broadcasts from her bathtub. Takumi's friend (Non) says that she prefers aliens, and raises an alien that is invisible (its image apparently doesn't turn up on the video monitor). She makes a decision to leave Earth with it, but then changes her mind because her parents disapprove. The alien departs leaving behind a vaccine against Covid.

CHAPTER 13
TALES FROM COVID LOCKDOWN

Mitesh Patel, an Indian-born director living in the US, has the distinction of having made *two* Covid films during the pandemic. The first of these was *Anti-Coronavirus* (2020), which came out in September 2020. This features Keith Lopez as a middle-aged man who returns to his Arizona home after a trip to Europe. As he begins coughing, he shrugs off any suggestion of it being the coronavirus that is being mentioned in the news and spreads it around, including fatally infecting his elderly father. As he is hospitalized, his wife, daughter, and grandchildren try to come to terms with the possibility he will not pull through.

Patel was clearly shooting soon into the pandemic — early enough where people can make references to toilet paper shortages that were a brief concern during the first few weeks. Keith Lopez is also the first person in town to be affected and this becomes of fascination to the local TV news who harass his wife wanting a story — one's suspicion is that the virus spread so quickly in reality that there wouldn't have been time for the fascination with one infected individual — while fearful locals spray paint the word 'Corona' on the side of their house. We do see people masking up but more often they don't — including the doctor who makes Keith's initial diagnosis.

Anti-Coronavirus is never much more than a film about a man who gets sick and how everyone around him worries — it could be a standard Disease of the Week TV movie. The performances are okay, but it is a straightforward story with no real dramatic complications. This is such a traditionally minded film that it ends with Keith Lopez standing up in church and thanking God and his family for helping him survive (and for some reason paying tribute to the joys of feeding ducks).

Mitesh Patel's other film was *House of Quarantine* (2020), which came out three months later in December 2020. This takes place somewhere in unidentified suburban USA (in actuality Patel's preferred location of Arizona), where a film crew of nine are shooting in their producer's house as lockdown comes into effect. One of their number is infected and they enforce isolation by locking him into the basement suite. With food supplies running low and one person who is constantly eating everything, tensions mount among the group over various matters, including who is in charge. A gun is found, and everybody is made prisoner by the stress-eater.

The lockdown here appears to be more extreme than any of the ones that went into effect in the USA in reality. Outside of China, I am not aware of any lockdowns where people were forced to stay inside and not go out for *any* reason — here the group are not even permitted to go out and obtain basic food supplies, meaning that their diet is reduced to crackers with peanut butter. Also, the response of authorities seems extreme — at one point, a diabetic without his insulin staggers outdoors in an incoherent state and is promptly shot by police for breaking curfew and the body left on the sidewalk covered with a sheet.

This is a resourceful film made on a low budget (and a much better one than *Anti-Coronavirus*). It develops reasonable tension amongst the group in a confined situation, concerning the jostling and bickering for power and debate over who is in control and who doesn't want to go along with the program.

The Finnish-made *Gracious Night* (2020) takes place at a Helsinki bar that has been forced to close due to the pandemic. People are celebrating May Day (which should date the film as occurring on April 30-May 1 of 2020, fairly soon into the pandemic). Three middle-aged men gather over the course of an evening. As with *Corona* (discussed in Chapter 12), they sit and talk, where the confined location becomes a soul-baring confessional. One man, a social worker, tells how he stood up to a client's violent ex-husband and had to flee after accidentally killing the other man; a doctor confesses that he is in a dead marriage; while the bar's owner has decided to burn the premises down that night because, having built his dream bar, he cannot bear closing it.

This is a reasonable drama wherein three men simply sit and open up about their problems. There is nothing much more to the film beyond that. Certainly, the pandemic is of little relevance to the story — it is merely the reason why the bar is closed. Nobody masks up or seems concerned about transmission, and the pandemic does not appear to have affected their lives on any wider scale.

The Covid Killer (2021) takes place in New York City in the early days of the pandemic. It follows police detective Mike Benz as he investigates a serial killer who is nicknamed The Covid Killer because he wears a disposable surgical mask. Benz is suspended from the force after his DNA is found on the body of a victim with whom he had earlier had sex. He nevertheless determines to continue on his own and apprehend the killer.

Despite making reference to the pandemic in the title, this is not a film *about* the pandemic as opposed to one that merely takes place during it. There are assorted TV news clips of Donald Trump and Dr Anthony Fauci discussing the pandemic in the background. We get various scenes where the police captain (Melanie Maldonado) calls people in to insist on masking mandates — hero Mike Benz bitches about this and makes a half-hearted effort to remember to put a mask on. However, in almost

every scene, Benz and everyone else never bother to wear one, or else wear their masks below the nose. In fact, the only person throughout who maintains proper masking procedure would seem to be the titular killer.

Mostly, *The Covid Killer* is a really badly made police procedural. The film follows incredibly lazily employed tropes like the cop on the trail of the serial killer, their suspension, and subsequent personal vendetta. Hero Mike Benz looks more like a wannabe pimp than he does a detective, driving about in an open-top sports car with bling and hair in a net or pork pie hat. This is not quite as bad as when he is introduced to two other detectives — one who wears a police cap at a rakish angle, the other looking like some Che Guevara wannabe in khakis and bandolier.

A better variant on the Covid psycho plot was Last the Night (aka Pacerville) (2022). Brian Austin Green plays a recently divorced history teacher in Sacramento during lockdown. While teaching his class over Zoom, he overhears his students talking about him, calling him weird and a creep due to the way he shows favouritism to one girl student. He also overhears that they are planning to hold a paintball game in the closed school and joins the game, only to turn the tables and begin hunting them with firearms.

Brian Austin Green plays a variant on the Downtrodden Man Who Snaps as per Robert De Niro in *Taxi Driver* (1976), Michael Douglas in *Falling Down* (1993), and Joaquin Phoenix in *Joker* (2019). As with most of these other characters, the petty frustrations of life — a divorce, years toiling in thankless jobs, the taunts of his students, frustrations with lockdown — pile up and result in a rampage.

Green, stuck in too many B action roles post-*Beverly Hills 90210* (1990–2000), is good in the part and the film develops a reasonable tension when he begins messing with the teens and hunting them. As Teacher Snaps and Goes Psycho plots go, one's preference still goes out to the British-made *The Lesson* (2015), but this is a decent entry.

The Era of the
COVID-19 PANDEMIC

I was surprised by *Scenes from an Empty Church* (2021) from director Onur Tukel. The film is set in a Catholic church in New York City at some point during the early days of the lockdown. The story focuses on two priests (Kevin Corrigan and Thomas Jay Ryan) coping in the aftermath of the death of the church's head priest from Covid: they make a decision to deal with this by reopening the church and offering succour to the flock.

On screen, Catholicism has been defined by long-standing clichés of priests losing their faith, and in more recent years in terms of its controversies. By contrast, this feels like one of the few down to earth portrayals of Catholic priests as ordinary human beings.

The film has no real plot — it is just the two priests and others talking about how they feel and expressing their doubts with often haunting poignancy. The biggest drama in the film is about the two priests insisting on maintaining masking mandates and restrictions on numbers as they tend to the parish. (That said, the dutiful pro-masker in me notes that in almost every single scene where they insist on people following said guidelines, they end up abandoning them.) Nevertheless, it is a strangely hopeful film about finding something positive in the midst of catastrophe.

Another worthwhile effort was *Shelter in Place* (2021) from newcomer directors Christopher Beyrooty and Connor Martin. The film features Brendan Hines and Tatjana Marjanovic as a newlywed couple on their honeymoon. He has made his money in finance portfolios, while she is an online model. However, California has just gone into lockdown, and they have been forced to remain in their hotel. The only others present are the hotel's manager/barman Kevin Daniels and the Dutch maid/cook Ola Kaminska. The boredom of staying there with nothing to do causes cracks to emerge in the newlyweds' relationship. At the same time, they believe that something sinister is going on in the hotel.

The film has a fantastic location — the real-life Roosevelt Hotel in Los Angeles, which is on Hollywood Boulevard right across from the famous Grauman's Theater. In some miraculous arrangement, Beyrooty and Martin appear to have gotten the freedom of the empty hotel, and make magnificent use of it — the hallways head off into dim perspective with seemingly haunted effect. We see the bored newlyweds amusing themselves in the bowling alley and bar, or racing around on luggage trolleys in an empty parking garage.

The film captures a great sense of what lockdown was — a period when time and the stuff of the normal world was suddenly suspended; of people bored with their everyday routine having been disrupted and looking for some way to while away the time. In a recurrent theme that appears in several other lockdown-shot films, this suspension of normality and confinement indoors in close quarters serves to bring out the tensions and previously unseen fractures within the couple's relationship.

Shelter in Place is a horror film. It compares favourably to other haunted hotel

Anne Hathaway and Chiwetel Ejiofor in *Locked Down* (2021).

films such as *The Shining* (1980), *1408* (2007), and *The Night* (2020). Beyrooty and Martin create some undeniably spooky scenes — bodies crawling across the hallway unnoticed in the background; or a scene where Tatjana Marjanovic ventures down the stairs to the basement using her phone to light the way and the sweep of the light seems to momentarily illuminate a figure standing against the wall.

One of the best among these shot-during-lockdown films was Locked Down (2021) from director Doug Liman. Liman has maintained a strong presence, working between the US indie scene and mainstream filmmaking since the 1990s with works like *Swingers* (1996), *Go* (1999), *The Bourne Identity* (2002), *Mr. & Mrs. Smith* (2005), and *Edge of Tomorrow* (2014). The film comes with a script from Steven Knight, the British screenwriter of *Dirty Pretty Things* (2002) and *Eastern Promises* (2007) and creator of TV's *Peaky Blinders* (2013–22).

The film is set in London early during lockdown — a news report in the background features the announcement of British Prime Minister Boris Johnson contracting Covid, which would date things to around March 27, 2020, when such was officially announced (although the film itself was shot later, around October 2020).

Chiwetel Ejiofor and Anne Hathaway play a couple on the verge of splitting up. He works as a van driver, though has been frustrated in advancing anywhere beyond that because of a criminal conviction for an assault several years earlier. She is the CEO of the London branch of an American company. After being required to fire a bunch of employees via a Zoom call, her distaste for the job spills over. At the same time, Chiwetel's employer (Ben Kingsley) offers him the job of transporting valuables from department stores as they are closed for the lockdown. Due to a shortage of drivers, Chiwetel is given a fake identity for the job — however, a supervisor who doesn't like him has issued his ID card in the name of Edgar Allan Poe. Anne has been ordered to facilitate the transfer of a $3 million dollar diamond to New York after it is sold to an international despot who is guilty of war crimes. Things coincide when one of Chiwetel's assignments happens to be transporting the diamond from Harrods department store. The two of them make the decision to substitute a duplicate and steal the original, during the course of which they reignite their relationship.

Liman does a fine job of depicting what lockdown was — queues to get into stores with people forced to line up to maintain social distance and the weekly banging of pots and pans to celebrate the work done by health professionals. To this, Liman adds a few unique touches of his own such as Ejiofor standing in the middle of the street to read D.H. Lawrence poems to the neighbourhood. In another scene, Anne Hathaway takes Chiwetel through Harrods and gets him to take whatever he wants from the food selection, including meats with a retail value of £3000, to make a picnic before everything is donated to food banks as the store is closed down. There is also a rather funny scene where Chiwetel confronts two intruders in the garden and finds they are drug users searching for something to get high from because the lockdown has forced all the dealers off the streets.

There are all the requisite conversations by Facetime and Zoom — indeed, a number of well-known actors, including Ben Kingsley, Ben Stiller, Mindy Kaling, Mark Gatiss, and Stephen Merchant, deliver their entire performances by such means (with the latter two turning up in person right near the end). Ben Stiller has a side-splitting scene where he conducts a business call with Anne Hathaway via Zoom from Vermont while in the background his son is taping up handwritten signs saying, 'Fuck Vermont' and 'Vermont Sucks Ass'.

What the film gets well is the sense of a couple who have reached a point where they don't like each other and should have parted ways some time ago but are staying together because the circumstances of lockdown have forced them to do so. The dialogue in many of the early scenes comes with an excoriating bite and is delivered with the grandiloquent theatricality of an Edward Albee play.

The heist is a relatively low-key affair without too many complications — it involves no more than Chiwetel reaching his hand into a fish tank. Part of this is due to restrictions forced by the actual lockdown — most of the people in the background are real Harrods employees because Doug Liman was unable to hire extras during lockdown. On the other hand, you feel that this is less to do with the circumstances of shooting than the fact this is not primarily a heist film so much as it is about the reconnection of a couple, at which the film arrives at its ending with a satisfying uplift.

James McAvoy and Sharon Horgan in *Together* (2021).

Another of the best films about the Covid pandemic was *Together* (2021), which aired on the BBC. This comes from Stephen Daldry, a celebrated director known for films like *Billy Elliott* (1999), *The Hours* (2000), *The Reader* (2008), and *Extremely Loud & Incredibly Close* (2011), and as producer of the TV series *The Crown* (2016–23). Daldry has earned three Academy Award nominations as director and has another career as a stage director.

Together is essentially a filmed stage play with only two characters, played by James McAvoy and Sharon Horgan who, as you quickly gather, are another couple who should have parted ways some time ago but have been forced to stay together because of the lockdown. The film begins in the first days of the pandemic in the UK then jumps forward several months at a time over the next year, taking in the announcement of Boris Johnson's infection and the implementation of the vaccination program, quoting statistics each time.

The film takes place as a series of scenes where, in between conversing with one another, McAvoy and Horgan's characters are often breaking the fourth wall to directly address the camera (often in long monologues). The directness of their dialogue is jolting — the opening scene has the two of them calling the other a cancer and tossing off lines like "You've got the same level of charm as diarrhoea in a pint glass". The way in which the two characters — who are given no names beyond He and She — are peeled apart, and how we see them change over the course of events, contains some astonishingly personal writing and acting.

There are times that this holds considerable emotional impact — in particular, a long single scene monologue where Sharon Horgan talks about going to visit her mother dying in hospital with Covid and of the male nurse who promised to be with her mother at the end, but had to abandon her to die alone while he tended another patient.

Like *Help* (2021), discussed in Chapter 12, the film digs into the actions of the UK's National Health Service, forcing infected Covid patients into retirement homes, leading to mass infections — both films quote the figure of how this led to forty-four percent of the deaths in UK during the period March–June 2020. Sharon Horgan details what was done in a powerful monologue, decrying the management of such as "organised murder".

Quarantine Girl (2021) was a low-budget US-made film co-directed and written by its star Nicole D'Angelo. She has just returned to her California home from a business trip as lockdown restrictions come into effect. As her sanity frays while isolated on her own, she believes someone is stalking her and has surveillance cameras installed in her house.

Like a number of other pandemic films, this gives the appearance of having been shot in somebody's home using those in the director's isolation bubble as cast and crew. When it comes to depicting the isolation and Nicole's fraying sanity, you feel that the film only dips its feet in the water. The scenes with Nicole losing her marbles — running about with a Nerf gun, conducting imaginary cooking shows, and having dinner with cardboard cut-outs of lions and Fabio as her guests — hold nothing on the disturbingly subjective portraits of women going mad we get in films like *Repulsion* (1965) and *Saint Maud* (2019), or the *It's Inside* episode of *Isolation* (2021) (discussed below).

The film, which runs just over one hour in length, comes to a somewhat unsettling ending. Nicole's ex, Shane Ryan, confesses to being her stalker, and to having broken into her house and installing the surveillance cameras. Rather than rushing to call the police and get a restraining order, she sees this as a sincere declaration of love and the two walk off hand-in-hand. You are left with the troubling suspicion that if she ever did try to leave him, she would end up buried in landfill somewhere.

In a very similar vein was the Canadian-made *Into Schrodinger's Box* (2022). Ada Shkalia plays a pianist who returns to her home in Toronto after her concert in Washington, D.C. has been cancelled due to the pandemic, only to find her husband (Geoff Mays) collapsed, having been infected with Covid. He is rushed to hospital, while she remains at home in quarantine. Isolated on her own, she becomes certain there is an intruder in the house. Another woman (Lee Lawson) enters the house and Ada imprisons her in the bathroom. This turns out to be her husband's mistress; the two befriend and then become involved with one another.

This aligns itself with far superior works, such as Roman Polanski's *Repulsion* (1965), in its story of a woman isolated whose mental health starts to blur reality. In the end twist, all of this is revealed to be a contrived gaslighting scheme masterminded by her husband to cheat her out of her money and/or kill her (his plans are not entirely clear).

There was also the British-made *Cam Girls* (2021), which is also available as *Lockdowners* (2021), a sixty-two minutes cut that removes some of the more explicit content. This features three girlfriends who chat by video messenger and discuss their sexual fantasies. Barbara Dabson's fiancé, who is away overseas, admits to a cuckold fantasy and wants to see her with another man and so she proceeds to seduce the postman. Abi Casson Thompson's husband, who is also away, admits to fantasies of being dominated and so they explore some BDSM scenarios. In order to make ends meet, Sara Langley decides to start stripping on a cam girl site, where she is taken by one attentive fan who says he wants to meet her.

It seems a stretch to label this as a work of erotica, although it is not quite clear what the film is trying to be. It essentially consists of three girls who spend most of their time in their lingerie, sitting and chatting on video messenger conversations. Their fantasies are the ones that you tend to get in adult films — they are always gloriously liberating and come free of any real-world complications. That said, the cam girl story does end in a letdown after Sara Langley meets her fan but walks away from him when he proves to be a middle-aged man who has misrepresented himself online.

What is notable is how these fantasies seem to take place almost entirely detached from the anxieties that marked the real world lockdown: about safety, fear of infection, and economic stress. It is mentioned that Sara Langley takes up camming because she needs extra income, while Barbara Dabson rationalizes letting the postman in in terms of being allowed to have one person from another household come to visit. However, that is the most that concerns about the real world pandemic ever enter the film's bubble of fantasy.

In direct contrast to the bubbly fantasy of *Cam Girls/Lockdowners* was the Polish-made *Love, Sex & Pandemic (Milosc, Seks & Pandemia)* (2022) from director Patryk Vega. Vega sets out to take a snapshot of modern relationships through the eyes of three women and one man.

Zofia Zborowska is a lawyer, who describes herself as a feminist and is fiercely against Islamic men because of the way they treat women, only to be romanced and swept off her feet by a Middle Eastern poet. Malgorzata Rozenek-Majdan is a photographer, who starts seeing one of her male models and impedes his career for her own selfish purposes. Anna Mucha is a journalist, who decides to teach a pick-up coach a lesson by rejecting him and then humiliating him in print. Sebastian Dela comes from a Jehovah's Witness family, but finds a career as a male stripper where he indulges himself among the plentiful women who throw themselves at him.

The arrival of Covid-19 puts abrupt brakes on their respective lifestyles. The four meet in a church where Malgorzata disparages the self-absorbed hedonism of their lives. All of them decide to change direction — Malgorzata becomes seriously involved with her model and starts promoting his career; Zofia kicks her husband out and moves the Middle Eastern poet in; Sebastian devotes himself to charity work for an orphanage and becomes involved with a girl he meets there.

This is a film that wants to make a point about modern sexuality and relationships — although you reach the end unclear what it is trying to say. One moment it seems to opt for a conservative point-of-view with the characters decrying their hedonistic lifestyles; later in the film, it choreographs erotically charged seduction scenes.

The film takes the characters on a journey but leaves all of them in a very messed-up place — Malgorzata promotes her model's career only to leave him after he cheats with other women to gain advancement. Sebastian leaves his girlfriend after he finds she has a career as a porn actress. A lonely Anna invites the pick-up artist over, only to prosecute him for rape after he forces himself onto her, resulting in him being convicted and hanging himself in jail — before the ending reveals that Anna fabricated all the evidence against him.

Particularly uncomfortable are the scenes watching the self-described feminist Zofia settling in with her Islamic poet who treats her in a demeaning way, including slapping her around for defying him and tossing his cigarettes from a balcony, demanding she go down and pick them up, then throwing them down again. She seems on the verge of going back to her husband, but decides she likes the drama instead.

Never Better (2022) is a US-made film from director Julianne Fox with Sofia Bryant as a woman in her early twenties suffering from cystic fibrosis. Because of her condition, she is more fearful than usual about potential exposure to Covid. Her fears are not taken as seriously by her roommate (Sarah Kane) whom she proceeds to drive crazy with her strict insistence on hand-sanitizing and masking up. At one point, she even drives a guy Sarah brings home on a hook-up out of the house.

Much of the film is relayed with sometimes comedic effect via Sofia Bryant's internal monologue, which covers everything from her fears about potential exposure, her attraction to the cute guy next door, and her panic when she appears to show symptoms, before these are anticlimactically revealed to be just a common cold. This is a likeable if lightweight effort.

The Falls (Pu Bu) (2021) was a Taiwanese-made film that follows a divorced mother (Alyssa Chia) in Taipei, whose teenage daughter (Gingle Wang) is sent home from school for mandatory isolation after a classmate becomes infected with Covid. What starts as a film about the tension between the two of them under quarantine gradually takes on another dimension. Because of the daughter's quarantine, the mother is sent home from work (and her job later terminated). This causes her mental health to dramatically deteriorate, culminating in her setting a fire in the apartment.

As opposed to some of the other films here where isolation serves to dramatically amplify the tensions within relationships, this is a gentle and affecting film, following two people who strengthen their bond through adverse circumstances. Rather than the dramatics of films like *Locked Down* or *Together*, this is a film of measured silences where both actresses give fine performances. Through its investment in the characters, the film eventually arrives at a reiteration of the "better together" mantra that comes out more heartfelt than many of the other entries here.

De Openbaring (2022) is a Dutch film, whose title translates as 'The Revelation'. Victor Low plays Jacob, a middle-aged loner with possible mental health issues, who moves back in with his aging mother (Leny Breederveld) as The Netherlands goes into lockdown. There he proceeds to drive everyone else away and make her life a misery with his insistence on maintaining strict quarantine. At the same time, he begins to converse with a conspiracy vlogger and evolve a series of alarmist theories about the pandemic.

This is the only full-length film to delve into Covid conspiracy theory. The oddity about this is that it takes a position that is entirely contrary to all the other conspiracy theories that were circulating during the pandemic. These were centred around things like the belief that the virus was manufactured, that it was created by 5G phone networks, that vaccination was a form of government control, or that vaccines contained microchips masterminded by Bill Gates.

Victor Low's character is someone who is merely germophobic. In fact, some of his practices — being insistent that family members do not visit during quarantine, getting angry at people for not masking up in public spaces, not going outdoors — were ones that actual governments were promoting as safe practices during lockdown. Whether such was the case in reality or not, the film gives the impression that nobody in The Netherlands regarded the pandemic as much of a threat, as few of the other people we see throughout seem to adopt basic precautions about masking and staying at home.

Certainly, the film holds some disturbing effect, watching Low go down a rabbit hole of germophobic paranoia and into nonsensical theories, before the film arrives at an apocalyptically surreal ending.

The Era of the

COVID-19 PANDEMIC

The US-made Sick (2022) is set in April 2020. It concerns university student Gideon Adlon and her best friend Beth Million, who head to Gideon's father's luxury cabin to quarantine. However, masked figures in black enter and pursue them through the house trying to kill them.

Sick comes from director John Hyams with a script by Kevin Williamson, the creator of *Scream* (1996). Early in the pandemic, Hyams had a success with *Alone* (2020) in which a woman was forced to run for her life through the woods pursued by Marc Menchaca (who plays a not dissimilar role as one of the masked attackers here).

Alone was shot before the pandemic but became a hit after being released during it. By contrast, *Sick* was actually shot during the pandemic but has a fairly similar plot — rather than one girl fleeing for her life pursued by a stranger, it features two girls experiencing a home invasion in which they are pursued by two masked strangers. This is an okay entry where Hyams puts the two girls at the centre of the action and gives them (and his camera people) a vigorous workout as they flee through the house and fight for their lives.

The film takes place during lockdown, which leads to a twist where we find that the attackers are seeking revenge because Gideon was Covid positive and attended a campus party where she was responsible for infecting and killing their son. The film also offers a rather amusing scene with the students watching the news where they turn mention of Dr Anthony Fauci into a drinking game.

Isolation (2021) is an anthology film — a film that tells multiple stories within a standard running time. In this case, eleven filmmakers tell nine primarily horror stories set during the pandemic. The opening states that the film depicts how people around the world reacted to the pandemic. To this extent, each episode opens with a title card identifying it by the city where it takes place — although it should be noted that of the nine episodes only two take place outside the US.

Most of the episodes give the impression they were shot with the filmmakers at home under lockdown using their families as cast and production crew. To this extent, the episodes often fall into identical themes. Four of the nine episodes, for instance, are about someone isolated all on their own, which has a tendency to make the stories seem repetitive.

Among these, there is the odd inventive treatment. *Pacific Northwest* comes from director Bobbie Roe, whose own children play two young kids left alone in a house after their parents have died where they then have to deal with masked intruders.

Meat Hands, from directors Adam Brown and Kyle I. Kelley, offers an amusing take on the shot-at-home story. Brown plays the person isolated and living on their own. The episode opens with the perverse image of Brown warming a plastic glove filled with meat and holding it against his face just to have the sensation of human companionship. He then sees a body fallen on the front lawn outside his window and debates whether the person is dead or alive. In the sardonic end coda, he curls up under a blanket on the lawn with the corpse.

It's Inside comes from British duo Alix Austin and Keir Siewert and is the standout episode of the anthology. Austin plays the role of a Covid conspiracy theorist who believes the government is spying on everything she does. Austin sinks her teeth into the role and the film enters an admirably paranoid state of mind with grim images where she starts tearing her own teeth out with pliers and slits open her arm and begins pulling imaginary implants out of her veins.

The episode *5G* from director Andrew Kasch also digs into conspiracy theorists. Graham Denman plays a man on home detention who short circuits his ankle bracelet after jamming it in a toilet bowl. The bracelet then starts talking to him, spouting conspiracy theory nonsense and urging him to destroy a 5G cellphone tower (which was posited as the cause of Covid-19 in some conspiracy theories).

One of the best films about pandemic isolation was The Harbinger (2022), even if it is not a film about the pandemic as such, more one of the films in which the pandemic occurs in the background. The film was shot by Andy Mitton, who had previously co-directed the impressive mass insanity film *YellowBrickRoad* (2010). Mitton shot the film in Binghamton, New York in February 2021, a point when lockdowns and masking mandates were in full force.

Gabby Beans receives a call from old college friend Emily Davis asking for help and goes to her despite the concerns of her family. Emily has been suffering from terrifying dreams and nightmares in which a demon stalks her and from which she is unable to wake up. Gabby then begins to have the same dreams. A demonologist tells them they are haunted by a Harbinger, a demon that wears a person down through their dreams, before erasing all memory of their existence from other people's lives.

Mitton shoots in a low-key manner. A good part of the film takes place in a mostly empty apartment. Because of pandemic restrictions, the most we ever get is two, occasionally three people in a scene. It is a bare and austere film. While it is ostensibly a film about a demonic force, it is hard not to draw analogies between people secluded in isolation suffering loneliness and the characters affected by The Harbinger causing them to fade away from people's memories.

The blur of reality and illusion that Mitton draws us into comes with a series of startling dream sequences that jolt you out of your seat. However, the most chilling effects come as we see people's memories being erased — such as when Emily Davis picks up a photo commenting on how it seems to indicate that she had a relationship with another guy but that she has no memory of who he is. That is, before Gabby Beans abruptly wakes up in an empty apartment and we realize that Emily Davis has now disappeared, along with all her belongings, before she faces an annoyed landlord who turfs her out as a squatter.

CHAPTER 14
THE WORLD IN THE AFTERMATH OF A PANDEMIC, PART II: COVID EDITION

In the previous two chapters, we discussed films made during and about the Covid-19 pandemic. Most of these concern themselves with people at home in isolation and are often small-scale works made with family and friends in the filmmaker's isolation bubble. There are also a lesser number of films about infectees and frontline workers. You can say that these are films *about* the pandemic and its effect on people.

There is another whole body of films in which it is imagined that the Covid pandemic extends into the future. In these films, it is almost always assumed that this will be a nightmare world — one where society has collapsed, vast numbers of the population have been killed, or quarantine procedures have resulted in a totalitarian nightmare. Most of these are variations of the films discussed in Chapter 4 about the world in the aftermath of a pandemic.

The first post-pandemic film to be released during the Covid-19 pandemic was Anthropocene (2020), a micro-budgeted US film from director Emir Skalonja. This apparently started shooting before the outbreak of Covid-19, then halted production and underwent substantial changes to the script to take the pandemic into consideration. In fact, you can almost pinpoint the scenes where this occurred — from about the point where central character Michelina Houlihan suddenly starts wearing a face mask as she wanders about the countryside.

The setting is a world in the aftermath of a pandemic, although one that is far more extreme in its effects than what occurred in reality. Here the pandemic has killed seventeen million people in the US and supplies of food and drinking water have run out, leaving society in a state of near collapse and anarchy. (The term 'anthropocene' incidentally refers to a proposed addition by scientists to the classifications of geological age of the earth — pliocene, holocene, miocene, etc. —

and is so named for humanity's ability to change the environment.)

The film is mostly shot on deserted country roads and in the woods. After marauders kill Houlihan's partner, we follow her as she wanders through the ruins, scavenging for supplies, occasionally encountering survivors. There are crazed infectees and cannibals who are attacking others and the film climaxes with Michelina facing off against one such attacker.

The film suffers from a lack of any real plot — there is hardly any dialogue apart from a handful of scenes. It is not even really a film about the pandemic — more one about people struggling to survive in the aftermath of social collapse and mass starvation. It is one of several of the Covid bandwagon films (discussed below) where you feel you could remove all mention of Covid without making any difference.

The first major studio release to concern itself with the Covid-19 pandemic was Songbird (2020) from Platinum Dunes, the production company of Michael Bay, director of the *Transformers* films, who were also behind *The Last Ship* (2014–18) (discussed in Chapter 4).

The film is set in Los Angeles not far into the future, where the virus has mutated into an even more lethal variant Covid 23. The government has set up walled internment camps for the infected and issued a strict mandate that everybody stays indoors. The story follows a crosscut of characters, in particular K.J. Apa who works as a bicycle courier and is allowed to travel freely because he has a natural immunity. K.J. maintains a relationship with Sofia Carson, a girl locked in her apartment with her grandmother, although K.J. and Sofia have never met in the flesh.

While most of the other films shot during lockdown were quick efforts made with small crews and casts due to restrictions, *Songbird* has been afforded a decent budget and has a reasonable name cast (including Demi Moore, Craig Robinson, Peter Stormare, and Alexandra Daddario). It is a very nicely photographed film — when you see the shots of the deserted city during the opening montage, you know for certain that it is director Adam Mason and his camera crew having gone out to shoot in the empty L.A. streets.

I won't get too hung up on comparing the film's scenario to the reality of Covid for the simple reason that Adam Mason and crew were shooting soon into the outbreak (July–August of 2020), when scientists worldwide were still trying to get a grasp on what type of threat they were facing and official pronouncements, particularly in the US, were rife with misinformation.

That said, the solution where people stay permanently indoors seems a little far-fetched — how does normal society deal with things like the need to obtain food and supplies or go to work when everybody is forced to stay inside with no apparent exceptions? (Although as I am finishing editing this chapter in April 2022, this is something that has been implemented as policy in Shanghai by the Chinese government.) The film does predict a black market in immunization passports, even if the immunization talked about here and the one that subsequently occurred in real-life are completely the opposite — the film talks about a natural immunity in some individuals, whereas the immunity in real-life came from a vaccine created in laboratories.

There are only occasional moments where the scenario is presented with some imagination. One of these is the intriguingly provocative scene where Bradley Whitford sneaks out of his home and pays a visit to cam girl Alexandra Daddario who comes and gives him a lap dance while wearing a full-face shield.

The film's latter sections focus on Apa's efforts to find a blackmarket immunity passport for his girlfriend and get away to freedom with her. The film arrives at an absurdly optimistic ending that has them defiant of the system and ends on the belief that true love will win out against an authoritarian regime. As with the two lovers left on the runway at the end of *The Carrier* (2015) (discussed in Chapter 5), this is a happy upbeat ending that only leaves you wondering where it would be possible for the two of them to go where infection would not continue to be an issue.

Breakdown (2020) — not to be confused with the Kurt Russell-starring thriller *Breakdown* (1997) — was another micro-budgeted film. It was a film from US director/writer/actor Thomas Haley, who has racked up quite a number of credits as an actor since 2010, and has even hosted his own cooking show.

In the film's scenario, the world has been struck by a pandemic (although this is never specified as being Covid) and millions are dead. The social situation depicted is far more extreme and authoritarian than things ever were in the US during the Covid pandemic. As in *Songbird*, the authorities have forcibly rounded up the infected and placed them in quarantine zones. (This is said to be conducted by the CDC who have apparently gone from a group of scientists who deal with infectious threats to a militarized force.) Besides directing, Haley also plays an infected scientist who takes refuge in an office as he tries to perfect a potential cure.

All of the film takes place in the single locale of what looks like the office building of a small company consisting of maybe three to four rooms. Nothing much happens as we watch Haley looking through a microscope, talking to his lab mouse, and scrabbling through the cupboards for supplies — at one point, he is reduced to drinking water out of a fish tank. The most ridiculous scenes are the ones where a mannequin in the office comes to life and converses with Haley.

A better budgeted film would have pumped up the dramatic elements that occur — marauders breaking in, Haley aiding a young teen refugee (played by Haley's own daughter Brooklyn) who is searching for her brother. Instead, the action looks cramped due to the small offices that are being used to shoot, which fail to give the dramatics any room to open up. As a result, things occur without much incident and then it is back to more scenes with Haley wandering around the office before a frustratingly irresolute ending.

Covid 19: Invasion (aka *Lockdown)* (2021) comes from Texas-based filmmaker Micah Lyons. The film takes place in the year 2035 where the Covid pandemic has reduced the world population to thirty-nine million. David Ford is a former soldier who is approached by a militia group to join a vigilante operation to go into an abandoned school in order to wipe out the homeless living there and eliminate the source of infection they present. He refuses but then realizes he must go in to rescue his sister, an addict living in the school, which involves taking on the militia group.

I am not sure if I can buy the film's premise of a world that has been reduced to a population of thirty-nine million and whether modern society would still be able to function. The last time the world had a population that small was 2000 B.C. — humanity had just tamed the horse and the major cultures were centred around Egypt and the Indus Valley. Given that the US has four percent of the world's population, and assuming an even distribution of survivors around in the world, this would leave the US with a population of around 1.56 million, slightly larger than the present day city of Philadelphia. Such a drastic depopulation never seems to trouble anybody in the film, however. We see the school abandoned but the postal service seems to be still operating. David Ford and wife Brooke Lyons seem to live a placid untroubled existence — he is seen growing food in his garden, but they have no wider survival concerns beyond that.

In actuality, this is not a film about the pandemic so much as a standard post-apocalyptic film that has, like several other works in 2020–22, simply claimed a pandemic-related title as a selling point. Take either of the titles away and all that would be left would be a film about a man trying to rescue his sister in a socially collapsed future world.

The film reads like another of the numerous B-budget copies of *Mad Max* 2 (1981). The film is clearly made on a low budget. (The bulk of it seems to have been shot in an abandoned school — which would appear to be Marshall High School in Texas given that we see the football team's jerseys and banners around the school). Micah Lyons seems unable to afford any of the usual revved-up car chases of the *Mad Max* genre and so has the marauders running about on foot.

The one amusing thing here, and in several other of these post-pandemic films, is seeing how the ragged leather chic patented by the *Mad Max* films has now been replaced by the full-face respirator mask as the default wear for post-apocalyptic marauders.

2025: The World Enslaved by a Virus (2021) comes from German brothers Joshua and Simon Wesely who direct, write, and produce the film, while Joshua also plays the lead character. There doesn't seem to be much information about the Weselys available online. They run a YouTube channel that has uploaded a good

Joshua Wesely in *2025: The World Enslaved by a Virus* (2021).

deal of Christian content — unfortunately, all of this is in German so I can't tell any more about them than that (although the film here does come with its dialogue in English).

The film places itself fairly and squarely in anti-masker/Covid conspiracy theory territory. The setting is the year 2025. The opening title cards tell us: "The world as we have known in 2020 does not exist anymore. The virus changed the world. Communism is all over the place. A global state developed, meetings are illegal, travelling is illegal, and Christianity is illegal." Unhappy with how things are, Joshua Wesely and his sister (Antonia Speer) begin a protest movement. This attracts others to the cause, where they organize an online movement to get videos and messages of Christian hope out to the world.

First of all, your mind has difficulty parsing the connections being made here. Debate as much as you want whether lockdown and social distancing restrictions and stay-at-home orders imposed by various governments have been authoritarian — in my opinion, they are no different from road traffic rules or the health regulations that food service industries are required to follow for the overall safety of the public. In some areas, church services were placed on the prohibited gatherings lists (which most churches dealt with by holding services online) — but there is no government in the world that used this as an opportunity to ban Christianity outright.

The Weselys seem to have difficulty distinguishing between authoritarianism, totalitarianism, and communism. Authoritarianism occurs when a government suspends civil liberties and rules by decree or force. Totalitarianism occurs when a government demands its citizenry follow their authoritarian decrees with absolute obedience and no dissent. By contrast, communism is an ideology that dispenses with traditional business owner and worker relationships, where the state owns all the capital and everybody is paid equally. Most communist states are authoritarian if not totalitarian but there is no dictate in *The Communist Manifesto* (1848) that states this has to be so. However, a government requiring stay-at-home mandates, social distancing and the suspension of social gatherings is most certainly not a communist state — by definition, communism requires a redistribution of capital and the worker/business owner relationship.

Most of *2025: The World Enslaved by a Virus* consists of rather dull scenes where Joshua Wesely and followers sit around their apartment and make plans. They defy the banning of Christianity by spray-painting the ichthys (the Christian fish symbol) everywhere they go. Somehow, this sparks a movement, and others join them. One of these is a girl (Laura Wieder) with magical hacking abilities who organizes distribution of their videos and CDs, while making all traces of them disappear from the government's computers. At one point, they hold a church service from the couch in their living room and livestream it to the world. As a revolution against an authoritarian (or for that matter a communist) system, this seems to die a death of insipid dullness.

The Survivalist (2021) was a US-made film from director Jon Keeyes, who has made a number of low-to-medium budget horror and action films and thrillers. The film is set at some point in the future where civilization has collapsed with the spread of Covid 19 Delta. The uninfected were placed in camps before one infected person managed to get into the last remaining camp, killing 20,000 people. Ruby Modine flees from the Land Pirates, marauders that roam the socially collapsed landscape. The Pirates are led by John Malkovich, who is certain that Ruby has an immunity and that he has been ordained by God to produce children with her. She takes refuge at the farmhouse of former FBI agent Jonathan Rhys Meyers, which turns into an armed siege as Malkovich and his followers determine to break in and claim her.

Here we have another film that speculates that the virus has extended into the future. Indeed, the film is canny enough that it can predict a variant called Delta — the film was shot in December 2020 while the real-life Delta Variant was not reported until several months later in May 2021, although the film sees its effects as far more extreme, causing the almost complete collapse of civilization.

If you took away the mention of Covid Delta at the start and Ruby Modine's explanations of why the Land Pirates are hunting her, this could be a standard post-apocalyptic action film. Indeed, the scenes where the Land Pirates lay siege to

The Land Pirates in *The Survivalist* (2021) with John Malkovich.

Jonathan Rhys Meyers' farm are essentially a rerun of the scenes in *Mad Max 2* where the wasteland crazies surround the small community that is hoarding a supply of gasoline and Mel Gibson's loner hero Max comes to their defence.

Jon Keeyes does a solid job of containing the action around the single locale of a farmhouse. Just as much as its fight sequences and shootouts, the film often takes place in taut conversational confrontations between Rhys Meyers and Malkovich, who gives a particularly captivating performance in the role of the lead wasteland crazy.

Safer at Home (2021) is included here solely because it is a Covid pandemic film that takes place in a future setting — the film was released in February 2021 but a caption on the opening news broadcast identifies the date as December 2022. It is said that the Covid pandemic has killed over thirty-one million in the US — while other films like *Anthropocene*, *Breakdown*, *Covid-19: Invasion*, and *The Survivalist* see such a drastic death toll as having led to the collapse of society, it does not seem to have affected society here in any way.

The film takes place in Los Angeles among a group of four friends and their assorted partners as they meet up to hold an online party via a video conferencing program in lieu of a planned trip to Las Vegas. Things take a turn for the uglier when one of the couples has an altercation during the course of which the woman

(Jocelyn Hudson) falls and slams her head on the floor and is apparently killed. The man (Dan J. Johnson) then flees as the authorities come looking for him.

This resembles *Host* (2020) (discussed in Chapter 12), which took place entirely as a Zoom video conference and before that *Unfriended* (2014) — in both cases, the computer screen becomes the film screen for the duration. This also tries to mimic the long-take films — shot in a single take or multiple unbroken, unedited takes — which seem to have become a default mode for several works shot during the pandemic (see also *Corona* [2020] and *Help* [2021], both discussed in Chapter 12). The film takes place as a real-time video conference, although a number of cuts have clearly been made throughout.

The film starts with a good hook where we watch a group of friends consuming edibles and joking around, before things take a twist with the unexpected death of Jocelyn Hudson. This is a strong and effective set-up for a thriller but not one that director Will Werneck does a particularly good job developing. Thereafter, the show is simply about following Dan J. Johnson as he drives from place to place in a panicked state, which takes place across livestream as the others watch. (This comes with the improbability of scenes where Johnson and others are driving while also looking at what is happening on a computer screen on the passenger seat beside them and somehow not managing to crash.)

The film stretches plausibility — despite there being a nurse present on the video conference, Johnson flees the scene assuming he has killed his wife without even bothering to check whether she still has a pulse. Or the idea that police would pursue someone for murder solely on the report of a neighbour saying they heard an argument, including tracing the fugitive's known associates and conducting a search of said associate's home, all without even entering the apartment to see if there actually is a dead body in the first place.

COVID BANDWAGON FILMS

There are also a number of films that can be counted here more by their desire to use pandemic-related titles or employ pandemic-related marketing campaigns than that they necessarily have anything to do with the Covid pandemic. In other words, if they had been made at any other time you suspect they would have made nary a mention of any pandemic or virus.

One of these was the Spanish-made *Covid-21: Lethal Virus* (2021), which is set after global warming has released a prehistoric and far more virulent version of Covid from beneath the Antarctic ice. This has swept across the world with deadly effect, transforming the infected into maddened zombies. The film follows Loretta Hope as a scientist with a potential cure who becomes stranded when the zombies overrun the military convoy that is escorting her. Her only hope is to trust in lone survivalist Christian Stamm, who reluctantly agrees to escort her to safety through the zombie-overrun wasteland.

The zombie apocalypse and its deployment of pandemic themes is discussed in Chapter 8. This is a standard zombie film by another name that has simply been slapped with the Covid buzzword as a selling point. As another among this vast shuffling horde of zombie films, *Covid-21* proves unremarkable.

A very similar example was the Argentinean-made Virus: 32 (2022). This concerns a mother (Paula Silva) who is left to care for her daughter due to a custody scheduling conflict. She takes the daughter with her as she heads to work as a security guard on the night shift at a rec centre. This abruptly turns into a life-or-death struggle as zombies overrun the building.

This is an undeniably effective zombie film that frequently pushes the material into grim and uncomfortable places — at one point, Silva is forced by a man to help deliver his pregnant zombified wife's baby.

On the other hand, the title is of no relevance to the film. Take this away and there is no mention of any viruses or pandemics anywhere in the film. In fact, there is no explanation at all given for the zombie outbreak.

Exactly the same can be said of Lockdown 2025 (2021), which the promotion advertises as taking place during a global pandemic. The film follows Glenn Plummer and his family in San Pedro, California, as martial law is declared around the country and a countdown appears on TV screens. The film takes place inside the family home as mysterious lights appear in the sky outside and the city becomes a war zone.

Things go sideways in an ending where a local cop bursts into the house and decides that the collapse of society is a perfect time to announce that he fathered Glenn's son, before this ends in a shootout that kills everybody present. At the end, Glenn wakes up and everything is revealed to be a dream, before he opens the door and invites in two Jehovah's Witnesses, deciding it is time to start re-examining his life.

The film toys with a number of explanations about what is going on — an alien invasion, the activities of a revolutionary group — but clarifies none of them. Certainly, the one thing the film is *not* about is a pandemic as, despite the publicity announcing that it takes place during one, there is no mention made of any pandemic anywhere throughout the film.

Virus Shark (2021) is an effort from Mark Polonia who, along with his twin brother John, has been making some of the cheapest horror films ever made since the 1980s. John died in 2008 and since then Mark has continued as a solo director with over ninety films to his credit at current count.

Virus Shark falls into the fad for Gonzo Killer Shark Films that emerged in the late 2000s before going stellar with the cult bad movie hit of *Sharknado* (2013).

This period gave us an entire industry of cheap but sometimes entertainingly ridiculous shark films based around absurd title puns or wacky conceptual mashups. A sampling of titles includes *Jurassic Shark* (2012), *2-Headed Shark Attack* (2012), *Avalanche Sharks* (2013), *Raiders of the Lost Shark* (2015), *Roboshark* (2015), *Shark Exorcist* (2015), *Zombie Shark* (2015), *House Shark* (2017), *Post Apocalyptic Commando Shark* (2018), *Santa Jaws* (2018), *Sharks of the Corn* (2021) and *Shark Side of the Moon* (2022). In this niche genre alone, Mark Polonia has also made *Sharkenstein* (2016), *Land Shark* (2017), *Shark Encounters of the Third Kind* (2020), *Noah's Shark* (2021), and *Sharkula* (2022).

The film takes place after the world has been struck by SHVID-1, a pandemic that originated from a shark bite, and millions have been killed. The action is located at an underwater research laboratory as scientists work to perfect a cure for the virus.

As with any Polonia film, *Virus Shark* gives the impression that it was made on a budget of about $1.98. The underwater laboratory looks as though the characters are running through the hallways of some educational facility. At several points, we also see that this supposed sub-oceanic facility has been built with cinder block walls. There are some really crappy shark effects. At the end, Jamie Morgan returns to the surface to find it is now inhabited by infected survivalists along with fish-headed and green-skinned mutants.

The Deal (2022) was a Serbian-made film from director Orsi Nagypal. It was produced by Dean Devlin, a former Roland Emmerich associate who was writer/ producer on films such as *Stargate* (1994), *Independence Day* (1996), and *Godzilla* (1998).

The film takes place in a dystopian world after civilization has been devastated by a pandemic. The survivors are gathered in an enclave where the scarce resources are managed by the autocratic The Bureau. People can take The Deal, which grants them access to decent accommodation and food supplies, but at the end of twenty years they must agree to be euthanized. Sumalee Montano (who also writes the script) has taken The Deal and is nearing the end of her twenty-year term in four days. However, her daughter (Emma Fischer) has just discovered that she needs a kidney transplant. The Bureau has scheduled Emma's operation six months away but refuses to delay Sumalee's euthanizing to allow for a transplant, effectively sentencing Emma to death. The only hope is joining the mythical railroad that smuggles people out of the city, although this may not exist.

The opening title card states that the film is set after a pandemic, although no mention of any pandemic features after that — you suspect this was thrown in to give the film a contemporary relevance. The film is otherwise a standard post-apocalyptic dystopia. The scenario draws much from *Logan's Run* (1976), which was set in a future world where people accept compulsory euthanasia at the age of thirty. Both *Logan's Run* and *The Deal* have very similar plots where two characters defy the system and go on a quest to find an underground railroad that will take them to a sanctuary outside the walls of the city where they can live freely.

Montano and Fischer give performances that carry the story more than the fairly generic dystopian scenario does. The major failing of the story is its dependency on some bad plotting to create a frankly unbelievable happy ending.

One of the strangest among these Covid bandwagon films was Coronavirus Conspiracy: Safer at Home (2021), which sounds like it should be the title for an anti-vaxxer documentary but is actually far stranger than that. It was the first fiction film from director James Sunshine who the rest of the time works as a producer on reality TV series such as *Big Brother* (2000–), *Project Runway* (2004–) and *Hell's Kitchen* (2005–). Sunshine can be briefly seen on screen as one half of the couple that walks across the street at various points.

John Lehr plays a man who wakes up to find he is held prisoner in his own home by a crazy person (Joseph D. Reitman) who insists on calling him The Zookeeper and refers to himself as The Economist; he claims to be a professional creator of internet memes. After finding he is unable to leave, The Zookeeper realizes that this is actually a replica of his house, and that the world has been destroyed and uploaded as a computer simulation by the ape overlords. The Economist holds The Zookeeper responsible for the state of the world, due to his shooting of the gorilla Harambe. The Zookeeper realizes that The Economist's computer can reboot the system and the two of them proceed to try out a variety of alternate scenarios where they change aspects of history, only for each of these changes to make things worse.

The film feels like a mad piece of improv theatre shot in someone's home with two actors making up their dialogue as they go along. Reitman, who spends the entire film wearing a dressing gown open to the waist, launches in with a series of monologues about creating memes. We then discover that Lehr was the zookeeper who shot Harambe — the gorilla that had to be put down after attacking a person in a real-life incident at the Cincinnati Zoo in 1999, where the humorous online reaction to such is believed to have started the phenomenon of the internet meme.

The film then gets into some way-out territory with Reitman's claim that the monkey overlords have uploaded the entire Earth into a computer simulation where they run a series of experiments to see how horrible they can make things. Here, the film launches into the realm of simulation theory that has become prevalent in the last few years, inspired by *The Matrix* (1999), specifically the idea that we might all be living in a computer simulation of the real world.

The latter half of the film has Lehr and Reitman using the computer (which runs on Windows XP!) to create a mind-bending array of alternate history scenarios — everything from where Hillary Clinton wins the presidency in 2016 to where Dr Phil and Oprah Winfrey become the President, to where there is no Jesus Christ and the dinosaurs were not wiped out. In keeping with the film's low-budget approach, these changes are only denoted by a series of newspaper headlines and always end in disaster.

The disappointment of the film is that, contrary to the title sounding otherwise, this is not a film about the coronavirus at all. It certainly is mentioned but as the film's storyline becomes apparent, Corona is merely one of a series of scenarios that are being tested on humanity by the monkey overlords. At the very least, this makes the title misleading.

CHAPTER 15
WORKS ABOUT OTHER PANDEMICS

We will end discussion with several works that were made during the pandemic but which are not works about Covid but refer instead to different types of outbreak. Not included here are three other works shot during the Covid pandemic — *Y: The Last Man* (2021) and *Creamerie* (2021–), both depicting a world where a pandemic has wiped out all men — which are covered in the discussion on pandemics that wipe out one or other gender in Chapter 11, and *The Sadness* (2022), discussed among the mass insanity outbreaks in Chapter 10.

The TV series Sweet Tooth (2021–) is based on a comicbook created by Jeff Lemire and published by Vertigo between 2009 and 2013. This is set after a pandemic known as The Sick has caused civilization to collapse. In the aftermath, a series of human-animal hybrids have emerged, which have been brutally hunted down by the authorities. The series concerns Gus (Christian Convery), a young boy born with antlers, who is raised in seclusion and emerges into the outside world after his human father dies. He is reluctantly taken under the wing of a world-weary mercenary Jepperd (Nonso Anozie), who keeps it a secret that he used to hunt hybrids, as they set out on a quest to find Gus's mother.

This series has a charm and sweetness that wins you over. The relationship between the innocent, unworldly Gus and the grumpy, recalcitrant Jepperd is the backbone of the series and is endearing. Their journey is interspersed with flashbacks to Adeel Akthar as a doctor trying to find a cure for the pandemic.

One work conceived before the pandemic and shot during it was Station Eleven (2021-22). Based on an award-winning 2014 novel by Canadian author Emily St. John Mandel, this TV miniseries aired on HBO Max in ten episodes of around forty-five minutes each between December 2021 and January 2022. The series opens in present-day Chicago as Jeevan Chaudhary (Himesh Patel) attends a performance of Shakespeare's *King Lear* starring the film actor Arthur Leander (Gael Garcia Bernal). When Leander starts to falter and then collapse on stage, Jeevan rushes to aid him. He is left tending to the young child performer Kristen

Raymonde (Matilda Lawler) as medics arrive. While news of a pandemic sweeps across the country, Jeevan takes Kristen to his brother's apartment to seek refuge. Twenty years later, the adult Kristen (Mackenzie Davis) is part of The Travelling Symphony that journeys around the post-apocalyptic communities putting on Shakespeare plays. Arthur once gave Kirsten a copy of *Station Eleven*, a comicbook written by his ex-wife (Danielle Deadwyler), and Kirsten has held onto it over the years, finding philosophical meaning in its story. She now has to deal with The Prophet (Daniel Zovatto), a mysterious stranger who has knowledge of *Station Eleven*, and who has been wooing away members of The Travelling Symphony and their children. As she discovers, many aspects of what is happening have connections that lead back to Arthur.

My initial expectation was that this would be no more than a standard post-apocalyptic series exploiting the topicality of the Covid-19 pandemic. That topicality certainly seems pertinent but there is nothing standard or in any way predictable about *Station Eleven*. What strikes most is its non-linear story, constantly moving back and forward between different characters at various points over the space of twenty years. The scripts for the series feel less like linear storylines than a vast board of Post-it notes with different coloured threads mapping onto characters and places from one point to another. Every major character seems to tie back to Arthur Leander in some way, people connecting again and then reappearing in often unexpected ways. It is a story that comes with surprises hiding around every corner. And connecting everything is the mysterious importance of the *Station Eleven* comicbook and a good many allegories to Shakespeare.

This is also a depiction of the post-apocalyptic world unlike anything seen before. There is the appealingly oddball eccentricity of a travelling troupe of players that travels in a caravan of old cars drawn by horses, putting on Shakespeare plays in various communities, using scavenged clothing as costumes. It is a far more optimistic and eccentric depiction of a post-apocalyptic future than you usually get on screen — the kinetic action movie sensibilities of *Mad Max 2* and copies, or the relentless grimness and harsh survivalism of TV's *The Walking Dead* (2010-22) (see Chapter 8) being a perfect counterpoint.

The miniseries is often a study in the ways that spaces not intended for specific purposes are transformed into something else altogether — a swanky golf club turned into a children's home with the course booby-trapped with mines; a department store becomes a hospital; a hotel conference venue becomes a tomb — and especially in the ways we see an airport terminal turned into a home by a group of stranded survivors and then returned to years later where it has been entirely transformed. There are so many pieces of great writing and multilevel allegory throughout that this is a show that lends itself to multiple viewings.

In a somewhat similar vein was the South African-made <u>*Glasshouse*</u> (2021). We are told that this takes place in the aftermath of Covid and a variety of other plagues, in particular The Shred, which erases people's memories. The film is set inside the titular glasshouse where a matriarch known only as Mother (Adrienne Pearce), three younger women and one young man, all live together. Things are disrupted when one of the girls shoots an intruder (Hilton Pelser). As the victim is taken in and makes a recovery, he claims to be one of Mother's children, although he may well be making this up.

I was initially intrigued by the world director Kelsey Egan creates: a large glasshouse with everyone dressed in bloomers, like some kind of dreamy Victorian schoolgirl fantasy — I was reminded of *Picnic at Hanging Rock* (1975) — all contrasted with the girls venturing out to tend the garden wearing gas masks while using the bodies of intruders as fertilizer and hanging bones from the trees.

Not dissimilar to *Anazapta* (2002) in Chapter 2, this becomes a work about a mysterious stranger who enters an enclosed social environment and has a disruptive influence as he proceeds to seduce and kill people, while much ambiguity exists about who he claims to be. Beyond an initially intriguing set-up, I struggled with *Glasshouse* — it was a film with a great set-up that never seemed clear where it was going.

<u>After the Pandemic</u> (2022) is a low-budget film that takes place in the environs of Salt Lake City. An unspecified pandemic has wiped out 5.3 billion people around the world. (Infectees all turn scarlet red.) The only survivors are those who sheltered in underground bunkers and a handful of young people who have natural immunity. The people from the bunkers prowl the ruins in contamination suits seeking to capture survivors, using sound detecting equipment as they search for any evidence of human activity. One teen survivor (Eve James) encounters and is aided by another girl (Kannon Smith), a loner survivalist. A friendship grows as they seek to avoid capture.

Among the low and micro-budgeted post-apocalyptic films discussed throughout this book, this is more likeable than most. The relationship between the two girls — reluctant friendship with a hint of attraction — is conducted with sincerity and even tenderness.

On the other hand, this is a film that seems to want to be a copy of *A Quiet Place* (2018), the surprise hit (also produced by Michael Bay's Platinum Dunes company) that featured a family who must live in complete silence following an invasion by alien monsters that will kill anything that makes the slightest sound. *A Quiet Place* developed considerable fascination in seeing the ways the family had adjusted to living their lives without making any noise. In the place of alien creatures, *After the Pandemic* substitutes figures in white contamination suits and transit vans hunting the teens with sound detecting equipment, but otherwise the scenario is almost identical in both films.

THANK YOUS

This book would not have been possible without the support and encouragement of a number of people.

First and foremost, thank you to M, whose tireless support, supply of to-*mar*-to sandwiches (as opposed to to-*may*-to sandwiches, which are poisonous to people not from the North American continent), and whose faith in the author even on his days of greatest self-doubt, have been an inestimable pillar of support in getting this volume out.

A huge thanks to Shade Rupe for inspiration and encouragement in turning what started as a quickie eBook into something more substantial and in making the essential connections to get this to a publisher.

And an enormous thank you to my publisher David Kerekes and Headpress in getting this from manuscript to print.

A huge thank you also to Peter Friend for an exemplary line edit of the manuscript and in the process being able to make me more aware of some of my shortcomings and failings as a writer.

A thank you to all throughout the course of this project who have offered inspiration and support, including Christina Boyce, Rex and Elaine Gredig, Ian Rosen, Brett Garten, and Zach A.D.

And to all the Facebook friends and contacts who reached out and had video conversations during the lockdown. It was a pleasure catching up with many of you after all these years and an equal pleasure making contact with those I had never met. For those I didn't get around to, I'm always happy to talk when you have a moment—a lockdown need not be the occasion to say hi.

INDEX

A VIEWING GUIDE TO THE PANDEMIC

Depictions of Plague and Pandemic on Film and TV

A VIEWING GUIDE TO THE PANDEMIC

Depictions of Plague and Pandemic on Film and TV